ANCIENT WISDOMS FOR MODERN CRISES

道

ANCIENT WISDOMS FOR MODERN CRISES

LEARNING FROM LAOZI'S "DAODEJING"

STEVE HALLETT

PURDUE UNIVERSITY PRESS
WEST LAFAYETTE, INDIANA

Cataloging-in-Publication Data on file at the Library Congress.
978-1-62671-295-9 (paperback)
978-1-62671-297-3 (epdf)
978-1-62671-296-6 (epub)

Cover images: White background of watercolor paper: xamtiw/iStock via Getty Images Plus.
Three Ensoes painting created by the author.

To all my family.

CONTENTS

ACKNOWLEDGMENTS

The most important thanks go to my wife, Shelley, who endures my strangeness with heroic patience. Thanks go to lots of people, particularly family, who have helped me work through some of these ideas in my mind: Shelley, Dan, Pat, Sami, and Chris. Huge thanks to my colleagues Yiwei Huang and Andrew Flachs for thoughtful critiques and valuable editorial comments. Great thanks to the wonderful people at Purdue University Press, particularly Neal Novak.

PROLOGUE: WISE ANCIENTS?

An unbroken thread of nameless things from now back to the chaos before the first. Call it the formless form; the imageless image; the unthought thought. (v. 14)

WHAT A FASCINATING TIME TO BE ALIVE—"May you live in interesting times," they say—more curse than blessing. The first half of the twenty-first century is certainly turning out to be interesting: vibrant, rich, and comfortable for some, impoverished and difficult for others, and so terribly precarious for us all. And more than just a little bit strange.

Are we entering an era of crises? Yes, I think we are, but it's worth reflecting on the fact that the world always seems dangerous. We worry about the coming apocalypse every generation, despite the relative infrequency of apocalypses. Are our so-called modern crises real? Are they actually modern? It would be nice to know which of our problems are novel rather than recast so that we could appraise them in the light of experience. If history repeats itself, ancient wisdoms should be essential tools for responding to modern crises.

"History repeats itself" is a well-used truism, but like most truisms it's sometimes right, sometimes wrong, and therefore useless. (The truism "there are plenty of fish in the sea" has succumbed to our sushi-eating heroics; the truism "some things never change" has been subject to mission creep.) Mark Twain's comment that "history doesn't repeat itself, but it often rhymes" might be more accurate, and it's cute, but it's also useless. Others have claimed that history is cyclic. It isn't. Meanwhile, George Santayana observed that "those who cannot remember the past are condemned to repeat it." This too is unfounded. We shouldn't accept advice just because it has the resonance of wisdom.

Part of the reason we always seem so gloomy about the future is that we have an innate negativity bias: we evolved gloomy as a survival strategy. Our brains are wired to make us cautious. If you mistake the rustling of the wind for a snake you might get a little fright, but if you mistake a snake for the wind you might get a lethal bite.

Sights and sounds (and other sensory inputs) transmitted to the brain are first vetted by the thalamus. If the thalamus decides that a rapid response might be required, it fires a signal to the amygdala, right below it, near the brain stem, and if the amygdala detects something troubling, it triggers a rapid response. All of this happens deep in your "unconscious brain" before your "conscious brain" even knows about it. Your brain detects a snake, you jump back, your heart pounds, and your senses go onto high alert. The "conscious brain" then "thinks" about what just happened: "No, you idiot: just wind rustling the grass."

Erring on the side of caution is tried and tested. Combine negativity bias with confirmation bias, anchoring bias, conservatism bias, and availability heuristics—and any number of other cognitive fails—and it's a miracle that we get anything right and no surprise at all that we might be gloomy about the future.

So, focusing on the negative is hard-baked into our nature, and the modern world gives us violent and cynical TV shows, books, movies, websites, and social media. No wonder we think the world is rife with never-before-seen serial killers, terrorists, rogue states, and pedophiles. Human negativity bias evolved in a world with real but infrequent dangers and is not well suited to a world with artificial but annoyingly constant dangers. You may encounter very few actual snakes, but metaphorical ones are hiding under every bush.

But what we're feeling today isn't just negativity bias. There's data, lots of it, and it shows that we are living in dangerous times when a range of environmental, social, and economic crises are on a collision course. Everyone seems to feel the looming danger, but there's very little consensus on either causes or solutions.

I started looking at ancient wisdoms when I became disenfranchised with our modern ones. Most modern proposals for "saving the world," whatever that means, are delusional. Brilliant, often, but misguided and hubristic. Nuclear fusion? Biodegradable plastic that turns out to be not so biodegradable? e-scooters? Organic hydroponic microgreens? Bigger, better, electric trucks? Sulfur particles blasted into the atmosphere to cool the planet? Madness. I think we're wasting a lot of time and effort looking for solutions in the wrong places, and most of our so-called solutions are actually making bad situations worse. We insist that we must join together in common cause, but how—and whose cause? I doubt we will act collectively to solve our looming crises. We are not being honest with ourselves about the true nature of our crises. This should not come as a surprise: we are not being honest with ourselves about the true nature of our selves.

Most of our problems are, at base, perennial. Climate change is new, at least at its current rate, but our failure to protect the environment is not. Social problems—inequality, exploitation, instability—are old no matter how new social media make them seem. And the suffering of humans from our own follies and mental machinations—that's ancient.

The ancients taught us a lot about how to live on Earth, and their wisdoms are worth another look. And where better to look than into the magical text that is the *Daodejing*? But we must be careful. I'm leery of so-called ancient wisdoms, and you should be too. Many people cherish exactly one collection of ancient wisdoms—the Quran, the Upanishads, the Bible—and see truths that simply aren't there. What could we possibly learn from people who believed in krakens and unicorns? What could people who had no electricity or plastics and for whom top speed was horse speed teach us about the modern world? They had no experience of democracy. They fought with spears, for Ra's sake!

"Why even bother with these relics of a savage time?," writes Roy Scranton in *Learning to Die in the Anthropocene*.[1] "What do Homer and Aeschylus have to do with ISIS or global warming? . . . [T]hese ancient Greeks grow to seem strange, even barbaric." But the ancients were still people, like us, with the same pains and pleasures, hopes and dreams. Scranton continues: "They are us; not only historically, but genetically; technologically." Perhaps our modern crises have less to do with the wonders and horrors of modern technology than with human nature[2] and humankind's relationship to nature. Perhaps a crisis is a crisis no matter the epoch. If so, perhaps the ancients have a good deal to say about living sustainably on Earth.

A quick parenthetical is required regarding the term "ancient wisdom." Religion, spirituality, and philosophy all fall under the broad umbrella of "ancient wisdoms," but they are not the same thing. Religions demand deep skepticism because their animating stories are so obviously imagined. Jesus of Nazareth was not born of a virgin. Moḥammad didn't split the moon in two. You are not reborn as some species determined by your karma. Shiva does not create and destroy worlds. There is no Hell, and so there is no reason to live in constant fear of it. Nor is there a Heaven. The cosmos had no you for billions of years and has a you now, for this brief moment, and will have no you again soon and will be just fine with that.

Taken literally, religious teachings are naive and hubristic, but let's not throw the baby out with the bathwater. Religions also contain great myths and have been the repositories of the grand ideas of ancient cultures. Our oldest-surviving philosophies are embedded in religion. In the same way that human memory functions best when it embeds information inside stories, perhaps religion is best viewed as a carriere—a philosophical solvent, if you will—that has protected ancient wisdoms through millennia of human history. If we discount the specifics and historicity of religion, we can treat its stories as metaphors: as important myths. We should respect religions as carriers of philosophy.

Myths, however, can present us with difficulties. The messages embedded inside ancient stories are often opaque, their meanings unclear and therefore contested. There are a number of very old carved stones along the coast of Japan that say things like, "after earthquake, beware tsunami." That's pretty clear. If only it were always so.

There can be philosophical gems embedded in ancient mythologies, but there can also be monstrosities. Jesus of Nazareth was carried forward to be used by Woody Guthrie in the service of humanitarianism and by Joel Osteen in the service of capitalism. The Bible has lots of wonderful advice on compassion and humility but also has atrocious advice on the owning of people and the appropriate roles of women.

The ancient Hindu classic the Mahabharata is another case in point. It's a huge document, regarded as the longest epic poem in history, and it's not an easy read. It has multiple parts, including the famous Great War in which Krishna speaks to Arjuna. Broadly speaking, the Pandavas fight the Kauravas, and we receive aspects of their ideology in mythological form. Kamesh Aiyer speculates that ecological responses to environmental crises were embedded in the Mahabharata, such as course changes in the major rivers of the Ganges Plain.[3] The Mahabharata contains many stories that may indicate environmental or social policy proposals. Some of these are now prohibited, such as infanticide and polyandry, while others are challenged, such as the caste system, and others persist, notably the sacredness of cows. We can learn from mythologies but must be careful. Aiyer suggests that the caste system was exploited by the British to gain control of the subcontinent during the expansion of their empire. India would have been better off doing away with that social monstrosity long ago. That it persists in ancient writings makes it ancient but not wisdom.

Ancient Wisdoms for Modern Crises will discuss the wisdoms of many people from diverse times and places, but our central focus will be on the *Daodejing* of Laozi. The *Daodejing* is a very real text. The oldest surviving versions of it, written on bamboo slips excavated from a tomb in Guodian village, Hubei, were carbon dated to before 300 BCE. The oldest fully intact versions, written on silk, from Mawangdui, Hunan, were dated to 168 BCE. The *Daodejing* is a document of approximately five thousand Chinese characters first laid down in a now obsolete script called seal script. It was originally written as a single, unbroken document but has since been divided into eighty-one verses.

I present a new translation and interpretation of the *Daodejing* in this book along with an explanation of my process.

The *Daodejing* is a very real document, but its authorship, usually attributed to a man called Laozi, is much more speculative. It's much more likely that the *Daodejing* is a compilation of the sayings and writings of various people, possibly from various times and schools of philosophy. The name Laozi means "Old Master" or "Old Child" and is as good a way as any of representing the first Daoist philosopher, whoever that may have been.

So, is the *Daodejing* a philosophical test or a religious text? Well, it's both, of course, depending on who's reading which interpretation. My interpretation of the *Daodejing* is strictly philosophical. I have very little interest in the religious schools of Daoism that have branched off through the centuries and attributed supernatural qualities to Daoism and Laozi.

Part of the beauty of the *Daodejing* is that it seldom makes wild pseudoscientific claims, and it tends to veer away from the dogmatic. It also has a fascinating eco-centric orientation that is found in few other ancient texts. The Bible and the Quran, for example, are distinctly anthropocentric: "And God said, Let us make men in our image, after our likeness: and let them have dominion over the fish of the sea, and over the fowl of the air, and over the cattle, and over all the earth, and over every creeping thing that creepeth on the earth" (Genesis 1:26). "It is He Who hath created for you all that is on the earth" (Sura al-Baqarah, 29). Yikes. Is it any surprise that we behave as if we own the place? The emphasis of the *Daodejing* is different. Its focus is on promoting a sense of harmony with nature, the cultivation of inner peace, and guidance in building peaceful communities. The book is not without its issues. Laozi had an innate acceptance of hierarchy and authoritarianism that I sometimes find frustrating, but its avoidance of didactic religiosity is refreshing.

The philosophy of the *Daodejing* is radically gentle and gently radical. Here are some of its key concepts.

First is the concept of Dao itself, which translates directly as "way" or "path" and is a simple word used in Chinese to mean a road or a street, but it has many deeper meanings. In addition to a physical way or path there are also mental and metaphorical ways and paths: the ways of the mind, the ways of nature. The key tenet of this philosophy, then, is to reveal the physical, mental, social, spiritual, and natural ways to live in the world:

> *The Path that can be trodden is not the Eternal Path. The name that can be named is not the eternal name.* (v. 1)
>
> *The Path maintains eternal nonaction and yet leaves nothing undone.* (v. 37)

De is the second key concept of the *Dao-De-Jing,* and despite being an unassuming little two-letter word in its romanized form, it's freighted with many meanings—and it's devilishly difficult to translate. I usually translate "De" as "virtue" but not without unease. We're not talking about virtuous maidens here or the virtues of table manners. We're talking about all the various personality traits—empathy, compassion, patience, humility, equanimity—that guide us along the path, the way, to the Dao:

True virtue is higher than virtue; unassuming, and therefore virtuous. Fake virtue is simply for display and therefore not virtuous at all. The most virtuous observe nonaction and are unselfish. The less virtuous make sure they are seen to act. (v. 38)
To big or small, to many or few, speak to vice with virtue. (v. 63)

The third key concept of the *Daodejing* is the balancing of complementary opposites. Yin and yang feature frequently in the *Daodejing* and represent the dark versus light, masculine versus feminine, fast versus slow, forceful versus gentle, and up versus down polarities of life and the cosmos. But in the Dao, yin and yang are not considered to be in opposition but instead are essential poles of a whole. Neither is better or worse. They are guides to the Middle Path, toward balance. In the *taiji* symbol, swirls of black and white "chase" each other around a circle constantly devouring and creating each other. Each swirl carries an "eye" of its opposite phase representing the nucleus of repeated exchange of yin with yang. *Existence and nonexistence arise together* (v. 2). Although the Dao seeks balance between yin and yang, it often does so by emphasizing yin, the softer, gentler pole, in order to balance out the sometimes overaggressive yang. *Thirty spokes join at the hub but the axle turns in its empty space. . . . What is present makes a thing valuable. What is absent makes it work* (v. 11).

The fourth pervasive lesson of the *Daodejing* is *wuwei*, which means "not doing." Often presented as *wei wuwei*, it suggests doing not-doing. This can require a little mental gymnastics, but the idea is to think of doing nothing as a positive choice. The idea of purposeful not-doing, or making the choice of deliberate inaction, is a common theme in the *Daodejing*. *Wuwei* asks us to slow down and do less. The idea is to reduce our impacts on the world, our demands on others, and the stresses and strains on our own bodies and minds. *Wuwei* has the additional meaning of effortless or unforced action. It is the perfected action of the fully trained professional:

Who by nothing but stillness can render muddy water clear? (v. 15)
Do without doing. Act without acting. . . . Tackle the difficult in its simplest form. Tackle big problems while they are small. (v. 63)

Pu and *ziran* are lovely concepts that convey the environmental ethics of the *Daodejing*. *Pu* represents the uncarved block, which is a metaphor for untapped potential. Carve the block carefully by taking away extraneous material and you can reveal the beauty within. People are not made more beautiful by accumulating material wealth but by judicious carving. Nature is most beautiful when left uncarved. *Be simple; like undyed silk; like the uncarved block* (v. 19). *Ziran* means "nature," "natural," or, more literally, "self-so." The *Daodejing* repeatedly advises us to be like nature, and one of its most frequently employed objects of metaphor is water.

Be like water: *The highest good is like water. . . . It settles in the lowest places. This is how it shows us the Path* (v. 8).

The goal of *Ancient Wisdoms for Modern Crises: Learning from Laozi's "Daodejing"* is to take a step back and examine our modern crises in the light of ancient wisdoms, particularly those found in the *Daodejing*. If our modern crises are truly modern, we are unlikely to find much help in a 2,500-year-old book. If they are older, however, and especially if they have their origins in perennial human failings, perhaps we'll find some good advice. Perhaps we'll find a bit of both and can take the difference.

We will contemplate three particular crises. First, we will consider the climate crisis and the broader environmental crisis of which it is a part. This crisis is new and beyond the scale of anything the ancients imagined, and yet we will find eloquent and essential treatises on humankind's place in nature.

Second, we will consider the threat of societal breakdown from intensifying inequalities, social polarization, the rise of authoritarianism, and the undermining of democracies. Coping with these crises and shaping a new world beyond them will require all the wisdom, ancient and modern, we can muster.

Third, we will consider the ever-present crisis of human suffering. How humans suffer is largely unchanged since antiquity. We all suffer: rich and poor, East and West, young and old. On this subject, Laozi writes as if he were writing yesterday.

We will also contemplate solutions. Where the environment is concerned—the climate crisis; the biodiversity crisis—we will be attentive to the concepts of Dao and *wuwei*, which will admonish us to learn from the rhythms of nature, to be cautious in our interventions, and to relinquish control.

Where human societies are concerned, we will be particularly attentive to De and yin-yang. A good portion of the *Daodejing* was written as direct advice to leaders in troubled times: the Warring States period of Zhou dynasty China. The key virtues, De, are humility, modesty, compassion, and selflessness. The imagery based around yin-yang polarities promote restraint in conflict, asking us to resist the urge to conquer, control, and dominate.

This is a lot to expect, probably too much. Does it make sense to keep asking for miracles that may never come? Is there any point in asking our growth-hungry global economy to slow down? Is it simply naive to ask people to come together and form restrained, sustainable, just, supportive, and compassionate societies? It might be, yes, and the hardest part may be yet to come.

The *Daodejing* perhaps offers its most valuable wisdoms on human nature. Here, we will be attentive to the ways in which this great ancient text urges us to temper our control over nature and each other and how, if we are to accomplish this, we must first know our own minds and relinquish control over our selves.

I

THE WAYS OF NATURE

The Dao is eternally nameless: the uncarved block. Minuscule, and yet beyond the scope of heaven and earth. (v. 32)

The great whole seems incomplete, but can be used forever. The completely full seems empty, but can never be drained. (v. 45)

OUR UNDERSTANDING OF NATURE HAS IMPROVED DRAMATICALLY SINCE the *Daodejing* was written, and yet the scale of our impacts on nature has increased even more. Shouldn't science, especially ecology, have made things better? We have been unable to prioritize the natural environment over the human-made environment despite knowing that the one is built upon and within the other. Our understanding of nature continues to improve even as we watch it disappear. We are on the cusp of a planetary environmental hiatus that will crush our societies. Neither technological innovation nor ecological negotiation can prevent this. Our impacts are now beyond our powers to solve. We can make the best of it or the worst of it, but our first intellectual and emotional problem is to understand it and to summon the courage to say it out loud.

If the sky loses its clarity it might shatter. If the earth loses its tranquility it might splinter. (v. 39)

Climate scientists have spent the last few decades trying to convince us to reduce greenhouse gas emissions using the logic that since climate change is human-caused it can also be human-cured. We have worked under the assumption that once we began to reverse our temporary insanity, nature will patch up the rest of our mess and bring the climate system back into equilibrium: photosynthesis will assimilate excess carbon dioxide, chemical cleavage will disintegrate chlorofluorocarbons, and hydroxylation will mop up excess methane. But the corrective forces of nature are being overwhelmed, and negative feedbacks are yielding to reinforcing cycles that are beginning to accelerate the warming. It's as if the planet has decided that a spate of accelerated warming might be just what's needed to be rid of us.[1]

Warming is melting Arctic ice, which is increasing the planet's albedo, which is causing more warming. Warming is thawing permafrost, which is releasing trapped methane, which is causing more warming. Warming is accelerating the hydrologic cycle, and since warmer air holds more water vapor, itself a greenhouse gas, warming begets water vapor, begets warming. Major global cycles have been tipped out of balance. Deforestation is reducing precipitation in the Amazon Basin, which is accelerating deforestation. A collapse of the Amazon rainforest biome is a realistic and terrifying possibility. Ocean circulations are being affected. The climate system is entering an era of nonlinear, unpredictable, erratic change that will affect everything.

Picture a snow globe taken down from a mantlepiece and shaken. The snow traces unpredictable spirals and eddies and swirls on even after you have put it back down. Planet Earth will take some time to settle even after our madness ends. We cannot predict how all the processes now set in motion will unfold, but some general trends are clear. Temperatures will continue to rise long after anthropogenic emissions end. Some parts of the planet will become too hot and humid for continued human settlement. Forest fires, floods, droughts, hurricanes, cyclones, tornadoes, dust storms, and heat waves are likely to change in frequency and severity: the specifics are unpredictable. Oceans will rise for a thousand years: large parts of all our existing coastal cities will drown.

When the perturbations caused by modern humans are long forgotten—when the snow globe of planet Earth has finally settled—human societies may be unrecognizable.

Nature, however, will remain largely familiar. Many extinctions will have occurred, but the broad patterns of life on Earth will rumble on. Give the planet about 20 million years, and its diversity and beauty will be fully restored in glorious new arrangements, but for humans these coming decades, probably centuries, are going to be bad. I'm fully aware that I'm supposed to tell you that all the bad climate impacts will occur *unless* . . .

. . . But there is no *unless*. This is more or less what's going to happen. There are two reasons we're not going to do much about it. First, much of what we are proposing, such as generating more solar and wind energy, will be ineffectual. Second, we won't muster the cooperative action required to do the thing that would be the most effective and should be the simplest but is paradoxically the hardest: to slow down and do less.

> *The massive tree first grows as a sapling. The tall tower is built from a pile of bricks. The journey of a thousand miles begins with a single step.* (v. 64)

Land-clearing for agriculture began to release carbon dioxide, and rice cultivation and domesticated cattle began to release methane millennia ago, which means that the first murmurs of anthropogenic climate change were uttered before the time of Laozi, although they could not possibly have been heard. The pace of greenhouse gas emissions accelerated when the pace of everything accelerated. After living our lives integrated with natural systems for tens of thousands of years and as agriculturists for thousands of years, we became industrialists in just a few short centuries. The agricultural revolution started the engine of global change, colonialism and capitalism set us on a path of efficiency and exploitation, the Industrial Revolution threw the machine into high gear, and the petroleum interval has put us into overdrive and overshoot.

One precipitating change was the advent of capitalism, a system of cheapening, commodifying, and cashing-in on nature. A second precipitating change was the first machine powered by a fossil fuel, coal, and as we made more and more efficient machines, and then graduated to oil and gas, the unimaginable became commonplace: boats carrying thousands of tons of freight, cars shuttling us from city to city, intercontinental flights, and new materials and inventions such as pharmaceuticals, polyester, iPhones, pesticides, paint pigments, and Play-Doh.

Fossil fuels changed the thermodynamics of civilization. No longer did we need to harness the energy of the sun as it arrived on the planet, in agriculture and forestry, we could now access the stored energy of millions of years of an ancient sun. Everything changed. Everything sped up. Our agricultural output soared. Our cities expanded. Our populations exploded. Pollution, freshwater depletion, soil degradation, greenhouse gas emissions—everything is linked.

What a remarkable time in which to be alive. What happens next?

What happens next is that the system collapses. A series of economic, social, and environmental failures will occur as our climate and environmental crises collide with the depletion of essential resources.

Let's pause for a moment and consider the scale of the human imprint on the world. Roughly 40 percent of the water that evaporates from the land into the atmosphere comes from cropland and pastures. Roughly half the nitrogen fixed on land is made by industry, in a factory rather than by biology, in an organism. The biomass of humans is now eight times that of all wild mammals, and the biomass of humans plus their livestock is now greater than the biomass of all other land vertebrates combined. Our population is over eight billion, nearly 60 percent urban. These are shocking numbers. What we have done, at a planetary level, is remove nature to make space for ourselves and our food.

These few short centuries of civilization will show up in the fossil record as the sixth extinction.[2] Future rock strata will exhibit the sudden extinguishing of vast numbers of species, and the archaeologists of the future will be greatly befuddled. Where did all these species go? And why is this strange, depauperate era shrink-wrapped in plastic?

The Holocene, our current geologic era, is over, and a new one, the Anthropocene—or Homogenocene, or Capitalocene[3]—has begun. Humans are a planetary-level force of nature, and our civilization cannot persist much longer in anything resembling its current state.

Stillness overcomes heat. Calmness keeps the world in order. (v. 45)

It is obvious that we are too many and our impacts are too great. We must do less—much less—but that's too hard, so we look to technology for fixes and try to negotiate with the environment.

Energy is central to the climate crisis, and since three-quarters of our energy comes from greenhouse gas–spewing fossil fuels, the solution seems obvious: we must use less energy from fossil fuels. But again, this would threaten our economies, and so we balk.

There appear to be two loopholes that make us think we can keep our fast-paced economies moving without destroying the environment. The first loophole is efficiency, and the second is substitution.

Energy efficiency is a trap.[4] We have known this since William Stanley Jevons's 1865 book, *The Coal Question*.[5] A new more efficient machine should be adopted, we are told, because it can do the same job as the old inefficient machine using less energy. But the new more efficient machine is used more to do more and is then modified to do new tasks. Efficiency increases step by step, but so does consumption. Our cars are many times more efficient than they used to be, but there are many more of them on many more roads. And they go farther and faster and carry more stuff. What we need is not more efficient cars but instead to slow down and go less far. In the words of Peter Drucker, "There is nothing so useless as doing efficiently that which should not be done at all."[6]

Ah, but cars are now substituting gasoline for electricity, you say, and this will surely reduce emissions, but energy substitution is just another false loophole. A slightly less impactful car seems better, but it's still made of steel, plastic, and rubber—and now lithium or nickel as well. It still runs on asphalt or concrete roads. And for now, at least, much of its electricity comes from coal. This is another way of pretending we can go far and fast without impact. It's another lazy negotiation, and it's not enough. Fossil fuels may symbolize the addictions of the modern world, but the true disease is the desire for more. We have to make some sacrifices. Sacrifice speed. Sacrifice productivity. Slow down. Do less.

Who, by nothing but stillness, can render muddy water clear? (v. 15)

Environmentalism, as we perceive it, was not a preoccupation of the ancients, but the relationship of humans to nature is a common theme in ancient texts. Two of our earliest documents, *Atrahasis* and *The Epic of Gilgamesh*, written on clay tablets in ancient Akkadia and Sumer, respectively, describe how the Gods used plagues, famines, and floods to control overpopulation. In *Atrahasis*, having failed to control human populations with various die-offs, the gods finally invented mortality. How disappointed they must be to find that even this hasn't worked.[7] The Buddha said, "Walk softly upon this earth giving what you can and taking only what you need."[8] Similar sayings come down to us from other times and places, such as from Indigenous Americans:

"We do not inherit the earth from our ancestors, we borrow it from our children" (Hopi saying).

"The earth does not belong to man; man belongs to the earth. Whatever we do to the earth we do to ourselves" (Chief Seattle).[9]

The *Daodejing* provides numerous invocations to care for the environment:

The way of heaven empties what is too full and fills what is too empty. (v. 77)

Conquer the world and change it? It can't be done. The world is sacred. It can't be controlled. Try to defeat it, you will lose it. (v. 29)

It's tempting to view ancient wisdoms about the environment in an uninquisitive romantic light, but the cautious words of the ancients do seem wiser with time, while our studied modern ideas seem more like hubris. We see ourselves as *apart from* nature, but we are *a part of* it. To defeat nature is to defeat ourselves.

EVERYTHING CHANGES

An unbroken thread of nameless things from now back to the chaos before the first. . . . To know the ancient beginnings is the essence of the Dao. (v. 14)

Quarks change within atoms; atoms change within molecules. The limestone mountain was once a living coral reef. The seam of coal was once a vibrant forest. A nebula births new stars that will implode or explode in their turn, feeling no pain and having no regrets.

Every cell in the human body is replaced in an ordinary lifetime. We are not a fixed thing but are a flow of things, not an object but a process. There are more bacterial cells than human cells in our bodies, each with a lifespan of mere days, and each human cell is home to organelles that are the descendants of ancient prokaryotes: we are a multitude. Nothing is permanent. Everything is change. *A flower grows, blooms, returns to the root. Though the self is ephemeral there is no fear* (v. 16).

Everything changes is one of the key teachings of the Dao and other ancient philosophies, notably Buddhism. Failure to accept change causes human suffering—the adolescent unsatisfied with the aching slowness of their maturation, the middle-aged man unsatisfied with the worrying advance of his senescence—and a key focus of mindfulness and meditation is to witness the ceaselessness of change. Indeed, it would be fair to translate Dao not just as *the Path* or *the Way* but also as *change*, or *the Way of change*. The Path does not only travel through space but also travels through time. *Knowing this is true wisdom. Not knowing this is disastrous* (v. 16).

But if everything changes, where does that leave us in our quest to counter environmental crises with sustainability? The dictionary definition of "sustainability," after all, is the ability to sustain, to maintain, to keep going for a long time, to keep things the same. To sustain something is to resist change.

The first clue that not everything is right with sustainability is the glibness with which the word is bandied about. You can buy sustainable paper towels and sustainably bottled water, in sustainable bottles no less, and for want of something random, let's choose a sustainable bamboo taco holder (sustainably yours from Amazon, next-day delivery, just $14.49). It's revealing that sustainability has become a growth industry.

The only things that can last are those that can change, and their change must come within the larger rhythms of the change occurring around them. We lament the horrible impacts we're having on the environment and on each other, but the fundamental problem with our attempts at sustainability is that we want to sustain our lifestyles. We know we need to change our ways, but we keep thinking, *if only we could get everything under better control.*

> *Gain the world by not-doing. Try to control the world and it will evade you.* (v. 48)
> *To raise without possessing, to nourish without spoiling, to guide without controlling. The is the Primal De.* (v. 51)
> *Use not-doing in dealing with the natural world.* (v. 57)

We need to relinquish control and accept change. This is one of the central concepts of the *Daodejing*, represented as *wuwei*. There will be no surprise that translating *wuwei* is fraught and that these two simple characters can mean a whole raft of different things. Literally, *wuwei* means "not do" and often comes in the phrase *wei wu wei* or *wei wuwei*, which makes it an instruction: do not-do, use not-doing, do not-acting. We might also translate *wuwei* as to not fuss with, to not interfere with, or to not force. *Wuwei* asks for a purposeful relinquishment and gives us the clearest possible instruction to stop trying to control nature. How should we go about protecting the natural world? *Wei wuwei*: use not-doing. Stop meddling. Leave it alone.

Consider the story of the Chicago River.

The first people to live on the swampy land where the Chicago River meets Lake Michigan named the place for a wild allium that thrives in wetlands. Yes, Chicago is built on a swamp. Not to worry. There's an engineering solution to every environmental problem, right? The swampiness of the land was tamed by raising buildings on pillars and pumping the water away.

So, a city emerged and grew. Chicago attracted massive slaughterhouses and meatpacking plants, so it developed a massive sewage problem.

So, a sewage system was laid above the swamp, and the roads and buildings were raised so Chicago's shit could flow into the Chicago River and out into Lake Michigan. So, this caused stinking messes in the lake, the city's freshwater supply—no longer so fresh.

So, Chicago developed one of the great engineering marvels of the nineteenth century. Remarkably—brilliantly?—Chicago reversed the flow of its river so that its shit would flow away to the west. This was done by cutting a canal to link the eastward-flowing Chicago River to the westward-flowing Des Plaines River.

So, the Great Lakes watershed, a huge catchment draining three hundred thousand square miles from Duluth, Minnesota, to Chicago, Illinois, to the Atlantic Ocean along the St. Lawrence Seaway was linked to the Mississippi watershed, an even huger catchment draining 440,000 square miles of central North America from Montana to Pennsylvania.

So, Chicago's shit, instead of flowing east into Lake Michigan now flowed west into the Des Plaines River, the Illinois River, and the Mississippi River and out into the Gulf of Mexico. Problem solved. Like I said: There's an engineering solution to every environmental problem.

So, invasive species. Silver carp, which had invaded the Mississippi River system, damaging its fisheries, now threatened to swim into the Great Lakes, damaging them.

So, the solution—an engineering solution, naturally—was to stop the carp swimming into Lake Michigan with massive electrified barriers (seriously powerful zap-everything electrified barriers!). It's comforting to think that the barriers will work. They won't, of course, but it's comforting to think it.

And anyway, when the barriers do fail, I'm sure there'll be an engineering solution for that.

Or consider the story of the Salton Sea.

The Colorado River has wended its way off the western shoulders of the Rocky Mountains for long millennia, and as the Colorado Plateau has gradually risen, the river has had to find new meanders and cut new paths—and grand canyons—to find its way to the Pacific Ocean. Close to the river's delta, at the north end of the Gulf of California, its erratic path has periodically veered westward, spilling over Imperial Valley to create a vast lake, and then veered back eastward, abandoning the lake to desiccation.

Enter the agriculturists and the engineers.

The agriculturists noticed that the river's many meanderings had left rich alluvial soils in Imperial Valley—a fertile patch amid the sand but no water—so they called the engineers. The engineers cut an eighty-two-mile trench, the All-American Canal, from the Colorado River to Imperial Valley. Another victory for engineering over the environment!

Disaster struck soon after construction in 1905 when spring floods broke a canal gate and water poured into the old lake north of Imperial Valley. Poured and poured for two years. The water formed a salty lake fifteen miles wide and thirty-five miles long on the salty old lake bed. Oops. Thus was formed the Salton Sea, a body of water in a salty depression that had been dry for centuries.

The irrigation of Imperial Valley proceeded apace. Farms sprung up, water flowed, fertilizers were poured, pesticides were sprayed, and a goopy mess of farm runoff was diverted, you guessed it, to the Salton Sea.

For a while in the middle of the twentieth century all seemed well. The farmers were happy, and the Salton Sea brought wildlife, including geese, pelicans, and skimmers. Vacationers came to sail boats, fly kites, and build castles in the sand. The real estate agents came. Holiday homes were built. A city grew up on the western shores of the Salton Sea: Salton City.

But the lake was drying up again, and the water flowing into it was contaminated with farm runoff from Imperial Valley, and as it dried its exposed salty bed spewed toxic dust. And it stank. You could smell it hundreds of miles away in Los Angeles—even through the stink of Los Angeles. The tourists left. Salton City crumbled.

It's a shame for California to be host to one of the most embarrassing environmental cock-ups in the world, but think of it this way: The United States stole—still steals—a river. It steals precious water from a poorer country along a ditch that runs just north of the border. The Colorado River rarely reaches the ocean these days. It dries and dies at the US-Mexico border, as do many Mexicans. The dry bed of the Colorado River is a lethal crossing point from Mexico to the United States.

Many who make it across the border and the All-American canal are exploited on the irrigated farms of Imperial Valley.

All-American, indeed. Just awful.

But we split the block and give the pieces names: to control, to govern. When the names multiply, it's time to stop. If you know when to stop, you are safe. (v. 32)

The highest good is like water. Water benefits everything without fuss. It settles in the lowest places. This is how it shows us the Path. (v. 8)

The stories of Chicago's and California's hydrologic engineering are not even the worst of our environmental hubris. Consider the Aral Sea, the Panama and Suez Canals, the

Dutch polders, the Three Gorges, Atchafalaya, and Aswan High dams, the wheat fields of Saudi Arabia, and the MOSE floodgates in Venice—to list only water-management projects. We see ourselves as masters over nature, as if we were in a quarrel with it, and we seem to think that we must keep arguing until we win—whatever winning means. That we think we can and should control nature is the most remarkable hubris. Perhaps Jean-Jacques Rousseau had it right when he said that "nature never deceived us; it was always we who deceived ourselves."

> *The wise manage without controlling, teach without telling, tend to everything without favoritism, raise without possessing, and claim no reward.* (v. 2)
> *Nature is ruthless. It has no special love for any creature.* (v. 5)

Some people have a strictly utilitarian view of nature. They consider the destruction of a forest undesirable because of lost usefulness. Future pharmaceuticals might be lost, for example, or board feet. Others have a love of nature that transcends its utility. The forest should be protected irrespective of its value to humans and should be viewed as having its own rights.

To the parts of nature that are inanimate, unthinking, and unfeeling, what happens to them or their surroundings matters not one whit. A star doesn't suffer when it explodes as a supernova. Rocks don't suffer when they are eroded by wind and rain.

Very few living things have the capacity to suffer. Microbes don't suffer. Plants and fungi don't suffer. Most animals—sea cucumbers, for example, and dung beetles—appear to live out their natures exchanging energy and elements without conscious awareness.

But what is consciousness? If it is merely the capacity to respond to the changing world, then all living things are conscious. A sunflower turns toward the sun. A seed waits for spring to germinate. A monarch butterfly migrates from Michigan to Mexico. Many animals endure at least pain, and many, including all the primates, cats and dogs, whales and dolphins, parrots and crows (and octopi, oddly, from the evolutionary distant Cephalopoda, in a weird and wonderful eight separate tentacles kinda way) appear to possess sophisticated consciousnesses. Our careless disregard of nature causes an abundance of pain: turtles choked by plastic bags, pigs raised in squalor for mass slaughter, mistreated pets, and polar bears calmed with Prozac to endure zoo enclosures. Their suffering is unlike ours. Humans are susceptible to quite remarkable mental suffering, but each of these animals also suffer.

I think that one of the most fascinating things about the pickle we're in is the recognition that it has been caused by an increase in neither human smarts nor human stupidity. We have always applied both smarts and stupidity to conditions as they have arisen, and our technologies have merely magnified them. Our genius for both brilliance and self-destruction stems from our big, brilliant, flawed, poorly understood brain. The same brain that interacts with other brains to create societies with art and music can also interact with other brains to create squalor and exploitation. The same brain can make us happy or miserable. The same brain, strangely stymied from protecting the planet, is an evolved product of the planet.

That we have become global agents of environmental destruction seems so terribly unfair, and it is. But does the rest of the planet care? What we see as desecration or destruction most of the planet experiences merely as change. An iron atom can move from Earth's mantle to a microbe to an oak tree without any awareness or suffering on the part of any of them. So, what matters? Well, the larger view of *everything changes* is that *everything exchanges*. The elements of a fish and some potatoes are incorporated into you, for a while, and then returned. You, the fish, and the potatoes are part of a whole, and since everything exchanges, everything is you. We are a part of nature, a part of a single, greater whole, so when any part suffers, we are all a part of the suffering.

If everything in nature changes, does it matter that humans have become agents of environmental change with global impact? Yes, a caring human will endure empathic suffering when the unconscious or inanimate is harmed, a form of suffering mediated by a sophisticated conscious mind. We know in our bones that what we have done to the planet is intolerable. The terrible irony is that our environmental destruction is also our self-destruction. We *are* the system we are destroying. We *are* the world, the cosmos. We are how the universe knows itself.

THE UNCARVED BLOCK

But more important is the foundation: Be simple, like undyed silk, like the uncarved block. (v. 19)

But we split the block and give the pieces names: to control, to govern. When the names multiply it's time to stop. If you know when to stop you are safe. (v. 32)

The Carrara quarries in Italy's Apuan Alps swarm with men driving cranes, trucks, and wielding monstrous diamond-tipped saws—as they have since they were driving oxen and wielding ropes and chisels in the glory days of Rome. The Apuan Alps boast the world's best marble, which is detached in huge blocks from a honeycombed mountainscape of quarries and mines. Sculptors stand at the foot of the mountains waiting to receive their uncarved blocks and itching to reveal the shapes that hide within.

Miners have mined for millennia, and sculptors have sculpted rock pulled from the mountains, shaped and distributed to the wealthy of the world. Emperor Augustus boasted that he had transformed Rome from a city of brick into a city of marble.

Later the marble accumulated in the Louvre and at Versailles and then in the apartments of wealthy New Yorkers and Los Angelenos, and now it flows out, in all its intricately carved and meticulously polished glory, to Beijing, Dubai, and all points of the global capital compass.

One way of thinking about art imagines a process of adding-to: paint to a blank canvas, for example. Another way of thinking about art—the sculptor's way—imagines a process of taking-from: marble from a block, for example. Other than Laozi, Michelangelo might have said it best: "The sculpture is already complete within the marble block before I start my work. It is already there; I just have to chisel away the superfluous material." This is the first interpretation of the uncarved block, *pu*, which garners numerous mentions in the *Daodejing*, although in the time of Laozi the uncarved block would more likely have been jade rather than marble.

And so it is with people. Self-improvement is a process not of adding-to but rather taking-from. We are improved not by the accumulation of things but instead by the simplification of ourselves. One does not grow by taking; one grows by giving.

And the metaphor of the uncarved block encapsulates much more. Imagine a block of wood rather than a block of marble or jade—or imagine the uncarved block as anything in its natural, untampered state: an organism, an ecosystem, a person, a human mind. The uncarved block represents infinite possibility. The carved block has only one form. Great beauty may have been revealed, but all the other possible expressions of beauty have been sacrificed.

Great beauty can be revealed by an artistic process that simplifies, removes the superfluous, unveils the splendor entombed within, yes, but an even greater beauty is retained by doing nothing: by leaving the block uncarved. The mountain left unmined. The tree left standing, silent, in the forest. *Know your honor but cleave to your humility . . . your virtue will be inexhaustible, and you become like the uncarved block. The uncarved block can be worked and shaped into useful things. The wise are turned into leaders without any carving* (v. 28). Or, as Aldo Leopold said in his seminal work *A Sand County Almanac*, "A thing is right when it tends to preserve the integrity, stability, and beauty of the biotic community. It is wrong when it tends otherwise."[10]

Trained as a scientist, it has taken me a long time to understand how science represents the carving of the uncarved block and how this can be a problem. Scientists figure things out by designing experiments with testable hypotheses, well-defined variables, and appropriate controls that will generate unambiguous results. Robust science is performed in a strictly controlled way, and much of it is conducted with the goal of understanding the natural world. Much more of it, however, has the goal of controlling the natural world. Beautiful science unravels marvels of form and function, and great science can be high art, but too often science is performed for the generation of wealth and for providing short-term comforts through control.

All scientific inquiry is underwritten by a human craving for knowledge. This is seen as a universal good but is a double-edged sword. We need to be humbler and more equanimous in the presence of mystery. Inquisitiveness is healthy. Craving knowledge gets us into trouble.

The Dao is an empty vessel that cannot be drained. It is bottomless. (v. 4)

Jean Baptiste Van Helmont was investigated by the Spanish Inquisition in 1634 for demonstrating that plants don't eat soil. He put two hundred pounds of dried soil in an earthenware pot, watered it with rainwater, planted a willow sapling, and then watched the tree grow for the next five years. At the end of the five years the willow had grown to a weight of 169 pounds, and the soil (after redrying) had decreased in weight by only three ounces. Heresy!

We learn two things from Van Helmont. First, religious fundamentalists are dangerous when you show them up. Second, nature is insanely efficient. Laozi seemed to have some inkling of the nature of things when he wrote

The space between heaven and earth is a bellows: empty and yet inexhaustible. The more it is pumped the more it produces. (v. 5)

The great whole seems incomplete but can be used forever. The completely full seems empty but can never be drained. (v. 43)

Trees, it turns out, are made mostly of air and water, and the process of converting air and water into tree is powered by a star ninety-three million miles away. Nature does really useful things effortlessly, silently, and for free. You'd think we'd be able to stay within its broad limits.

We struggle so hard to make things sustainable. We even struggle to define sustainability, and yet it is obvious what makes systems sustainable, and it was obvious to the ancients. The solutions to our sustainability problems are all around us. We have lived in sustainable systems since before we were human, and yet we still seem unable to see what makes them continue on. This is what Laozi was trying to get at in the verse 40 title "Everything Is Cyclic . . . Except Everything": *The motion of the Path is circular. The method of the Path is yielding. Everything is born of being except being, which is born of nothing*" (v. 40). There are only two rules of sustainability. They are simple but absolute, and it's time we learned them:

1. If it is to be sustained, all parts of a system must be perpetually recycled.
2. If it is to be sustained, a system must receive a reliable input of energy.

The fundamental problem of human societies is our insistence on progress. We seem to be comfortable only when we are busy, producing, and moving forward. We glorify hard work; we honor busyness. This constant drive for more, more of everything, is central to our failure to live sustainably on the planet. But how to prevent this?

At first blush, economics would seem to have some solutions. The words "*eco*nomics" and "*eco*logy" have the same root after all, *ecos*, which means "home," and the core business of both free market economics and natural selection is competition. Competition among suppliers of goods and services will naturally select the optimum price. Competition among variants within a gene pool drives evolution by natural selection. Adam Smith appears to make sense in his 1776 magnum opus *The Wealth of Nations*,[11] when he says

> It is not from the benevolence of the butcher, the brewer, or the baker that we expect our dinner, but from their regard to their own self interest. We . . . never talk to them of our necessities, but of their advantages. (Vol. 4)
>
> Every individual . . . [,] by directing that industry in such a manner as its produce may be of the greatest value[,] . . . intends his own gain, and he is . . . led by an invisible hand to promote an end which was no part of his intention. (Vol. 1)

So, shouldn't free markets, left in a state of nature-mimicking competition, keep systems in check? Unfortunately, while their responsiveness to prices is agile, their responsiveness to shortages is sluggish, and their responsiveness to the environment is virtually nonexistent. Indeed, markets can't respond to environmental degradation or depletion until they are severe enough to cause feedbacks that affect them—in other words, until after it's too late. And the comparison with evolution in terms of competition is also too simplified. Evolution is driven by not only competition but also cooperation.[12]

Ecological systems appear to be boundless, and they do have very broad limits, but those limits are strict. Economic systems appear to be bounded but actually spill outside their boundaries and cause what are called *externalities*. Extinctions are externalities. A dried-up lake is an externality. A removed mountaintop is an externality. Pollution is an externality. Extinctions, resource depletion, and pollution should cause massive damage to economic systems but are pushed outside it—made external to it—so that their effect on prices is removed. Thus, the economic system is spared at the expense of the ecological system within which it exists.

So, an impasse. To be sustained, an ecological system must not grow, but an economic system—so we are told—must always grow. The unbounded economic system is driven by productivity, and so productivity is viewed as progress. We are stuck in a double bind.

Great means always flowing. Always flowing leads to reaching far. Reaching far results in returning to the root. (v. 25)

Since ecological systems are bounded and cannot increase in size or productivity, an economist might consider them stagnant—stale, static—but there is nothing stale or static about ecological systems. They grow in ways economists discount. Bounded by a limited source of energy—by the laws of thermodynamics and the electromagnetic output of the sun—and by a finite supply of resources within a circumscribed geography, an ecological system cannot grow in either size or productivity, but this does not prevent it from being a vibrant system that seethes with competition, cooperation, and every other possible form of interaction. All the organisms in a bounded ecosystem are constantly challenged by natural selection to perfect their competitive, parasitic, and cooperative abilities. They evolve. They specialize. They differentiate into new species occupying new niches. The system diversifies. It becomes more complex, more stable, and more beautiful. Will we ever learn how to mimic this in economic systems? I doubt it. I suspect that we will always push our economies beyond their ecological boundaries, suffer their repeated booms and busts, and sacrifice the beauty of nature to grim, efficient progress.

THE ECOLOGY OF EVERYTHING

Existence and nonexistence arise together. (v. 2)
The Path maintains eternal nonaction and yet leaves nothing undone. (v. 37)

Jason W. Moore's book *Capitalism in the Web of Life* helped me fit a significant piece into the jigsaw puzzle of my worldview.[13] Moore's key insight is that ecological and economic systems are not separate things but instead are parts of a complex whole. Moore sees capitalism as a force of nature that stores pools of wealth much the same way that trees store pools of carbon and lakes store pools of water.

All systems—biochemical pathways, organisms, ecosystems, economies—have pools and flows. How materials flow from pool to pool depends on the availability of those materials, the availability of energy, and how each system links to other systems. Capital is simply a pool of wealth. It can be stored or can flow into other pools.

More fundamental than capital, therefore, are the materials from which it is created. Jason Moore describes pools of capital as islands of commodification amid oceans of *cheap*, and in *A History of the World in Seven Cheap Things* he and coauthor Raj Patel show how pools of capital flow from cheap nature, cheap work, cheap energy, cheap food, cheap care, cheap money, and cheap lives. Thus, capitalism is a process that draws down ecological and social pools, stores their value in pools of capital, and gives whoever controls that capital the power to redistribute it as they see fit.

Seeing capitalism as a force of nature enables us to define its origins. Moore and Patel showed me that I had made a mistake in my first book, *Life without Oil*, in which I argued that the first use of fossil fuels represented the critical transition into the age of accelerations that is the modern world: "No longer would it be necessary to harness energy as it was delivered by the sun, flowed on the wind and water, or needed to be grown before it could be collected. Now, it was possible to delve into a source of energy that had been prepared millions of years before and stored underground awaiting the civilization that could tap it. Nobody at the time could have had any inkling, but a new era in the history of civilization had begun."[14] Fossil fuels changed the thermodynamics of civilization. What could be a more fundamental turning point than that?

Well, Jason W. Moore gave me the answer in *Capitalism in the Web of Life*:

> To locate the origins of the modern world with the steam engine and the coal pit is to prioritize shutting down the steam engines and the coal pits (and their twenty-first-century incarnations). To locate the origins of the modern world with the rise of capitalist civilization after 1450, with its audacious strategies of global conquest, endless commodification, and relentless rationalization, is to prioritize the relations of power, capital, and nature that rendered fossil capitalism so deadly in the first place. Shut down a coal plant, and you can slow global warming for a day; shut down the relations that made the coal plant and you can stop it for good.[15]

To correct the errors of humankind demands much more than simply exchanging one technology for another or this economic model for that one. It demands that we change our relationship with the natural world.

A number of people and groups have tumbled to the same recognition of the deep connectedness of systems. Norwegian philosopher Arne Naess is generally credited with originating the concept of deep ecology with his 1973 lecture to the World Future Research Conference in Bucharest, "The Shallow and Deep, Long-Range Ecology Movement: A Summary."[16] His principles of deep ecology "reject the man-in-environment image in favor of the relational, total-field image" of nature. His philosophy explicitly acknowledges the rights of all sentient organisms and the principles of evolved diversity and complexity as superior to controlled sustainability and promotes anticlassism, local autonomy, and decentralization.

Many of these modern conceptions of a holistic ecology encompassing economic, biotic, and abiotic systems resonate with ancient conceptions of humans in nature, including the Dao. The *Daodejing* repeatedly asks us to consider the ways in which things are linked and draws us to a deeper understanding of our oneness with the living world:

> *Nature is ruthless.* (v. 5)
> *The great Way is wide, in flood, flowing left, flowing right. Everything depends on it for life.* (v. 34)
> *The Way of Heaven is like a stretched bow . . . [and] empties what is too full and fills what is too empty. The way of people is not so. It take from those who already have little and gives to those who already have much.* (v. 77)
> *All living things arise in unison, and their arising is a return. A flower grows, blooms, returns to the root.* (v. 16)

Earth systems are linked in surprising ways. I'm not sure why I continue to be surprised, but new ways to amaze keep cropping up. I watched the Will Smith–narrated Netflix series *Welcome to Earth* the other day and was captivated by a piece on salmon migration.[17] Salmon make their way hundreds of miles along a convoluted path from ocean to river to tributary to stream to find very specific, distant spawning grounds. They do this in part by smelling the water.

Each patch of forest emits a unique cocktail of complex chemicals. Roots leak sugars and drop leaves, animals poop and die, and microbes decompose organic matter into humus. Rain washes some of this musty concoction through the soil into rills, gullies, streams, and rivers. So, it's not so much that the salmon smell the water but that they smell the land. It's almost as if the land is beckoning them home—and perhaps it is. The salmon represent a huge source of nutrients. Bears catch them by the thousands and poop them through the forest, drawing the resources of the ocean onto land.

So much is linked in this dramatic migration. A large spawning in the upper reaches of the Snake and Columbia Rivers results in a large salmon population in the Pacific Ocean, so trees on the western slopes of the Rocky Mountains are linked in a vast nutrient cycle that feeds roving pods of orcas in the Pacific.

Understanding the ways in which different parts of Earth's system are linked sometimes requires us to get really close to things or really far away. Sometimes it requires us to spot things that flash past, and sometimes it requires us to observe things that move slower than a lifetime.

Camille Dungy has a wonderful poem, "Trophic Cascade,"[18] in which she links the reintroduction of gray wolves to Yellowstone National Park with ecosystem change, both biotic and abiotic. A cascade of events links wolf to elk to beaver to the meandering of the river.

How does the Amazon Basin remain so insanely productive? It turns out that the region is fertilized by dust blown across the Atlantic Ocean from the Sahara.

Be astonished, again and again, that the white marble of a massive mountain in the Apuan Alps is made from seashells. A seabed pushed up into a mountain range. A mountain range that will be washed back onto the sea where coral polyps will sculpt it into reefs infinitely grander than the statue of David.

Did you ever notice that the east coasts of the Americas are shaped mysteriously as though they might fit snugly against the west coasts of Europe and Africa? They once did, and on the volcanic Mid-Atlantic Ridge where the gap between Africa and America continues to unzip, thousands of feet beneath the Atlantic Ocean, live strange microbes, mussels, and eyeless shrimps. How in Horus's name did they get down there? Well, they evolved their way down there as the ocean deepened—over tens of millions of years—adapting to survive at greater and greater depths. The shrimp lost the function of their eyes on their multigenerational journey. It's just the same thing, really, as a diver avoiding the bends. Divers must descend and rise slowly through deep water to avoid deadly bubbles forming in their blood. They ascend and descend slowly because the human body needs time to adapt to the change in pressure. The adaptation of those crazy eyeless shrimp takes thousands of generations is all. They may well come back to the surface and look at the sky again with new eyes. It will take a while, for sure, but what's the rush?

Life is not so much a collection of scattered beings as momentary snapshots of emerging, merging, dissembling processes, a collection of whirlpools of energy. Indulge me by coming on a little journey. This serves as a great meditation, by the way.

Imagine yourself in orbit above Earth looking down. Look at the patterns of clouds: layers, wisps, and swirls. It turns out that your spaceship is also a time machine: go ahead and push the fast-forward lever. Gently, at first. Watch the clouds speed up. The layers thicken, thin, and dissipate. The wisps form into trails, coalesce, and then scatter. The swirls speed up, concentrate, dance across an ocean, and then break up over a continent. Everything moves, gathers, and divides. Breaks up. Re-forms. It might seem random, but watch long enough and patterns and principles will emerge. Fronts move west to east here, following the spin of Earth, but east to west there. Storms spin out of the oceans and gather into great galactic spirals as they push west against the flow and then weaken and curve away. Clouds pop up here when the sun rises and dissipate there or pop up here and there as the sun sets. The atmosphere dances.

Get closer. Move your spaceship–time machine into the atmosphere and beneath the clouds. Hover above a forest, in New England, say, where the fall colors glow like a sunset. Instead of fast-forward, put your time machine into reverse. Gently, at first. Watch the green trees return to bud, to black and brown branches divested of leaves, to gnarly fingers and knuckles above a pristine white snowy ground. Now the ground is brown with fallen leaves, now the leaves have been miracled back into the trees: brown, now crimson, orange, yellow, now green again. Faster reverse. The forest flashes: green, white, brown, red, green, white, brown, red. The forest is suddenly gone in a flash of light and a whiff of smoke—and is suddenly back. The colors are changing. The crimsons, oranges, and yellows have gone. Now there is only green and white, green and white. You pause to take a closer look: the deciduous forest is now boreal: conifers! Continue the time lapse. Green, white, green, white, and then eventually all white. An Ice Age. The forest dances.

Earth is all one thing, and it seethes with activity.

Go back four billion years and watch the whole thing on fast-forward. A dead planet springs to life. A billion years as a slime ball: life splurged everywhere, but all of it microbial. The planet suddenly greens as vast forests spring up. Dinosaurs spring from the earth. Boom!—gone. Eventually the planet peoples—it peoples in the way an apple tree apples.[19] Oh, look! There you are. I see you zipping around—how wonderful! And now you're gone. Sorry: a nanosecond was all that could be spared.

Earth is a single system with whirlpools of cloud and water and whirlpools of life spinning and dancing on its surface. Energy and elements are passed from one part to another, sometimes among the living, sometimes between the living and the nonliving. All things are temporary patterns, momentary shapes, constantly shifting, constantly exchanging: people in a city, clouds in the sky, a whirlpool, the flame of a candle—a thing as real as any other but made of nothing more than the light from burning gases flowing through.

And is the manner in which a candle combusts hydrocarbons all that different than the way a human body combusts carbohydrates?

And what is life but the flame of one candle perpetuated by touching it to the next candle?

Meditate on this. Gradually comes not just an intellectual understanding of the connectedness of things but also a sense of it. A oneness with it. A deepening felt connection to the world.

So, back to this so-called modern crisis of sustainability. What of it? Earth will be sustained until it is swallowed by the sun. In the meantime, Earth will distribute the energy of the sun through swarms and spirals of living and nonliving things on the land, in the waters, and in the air. Some of those things are us. Others will follow us. We are a temporary glitch that, in the greater scheme of things, matters not one whit.

In the shorter scheme of things, however, in the here and now it is our hubris that is causing great suffering to our selves and our greater self. Can we do better, or is this as good as it gets?

2

EMERGENCE

Nameless, it is the origins of the universe. Named, it is the mother of the ten thousand things. (v. 1)

Something came to end the chaos before the formation of heaven and earth. Silent. Empty. Standing alone, unchanged. Everywhere. Always. Call it the mother of everything under heaven. (v. 25)

We return to the Dao. The Dao is the way, the path, the recognition that everything changes, is impermanent, flows one thing into another, one process into the next. It is the Great Path of the cosmos, the flow of things from the Big Bang to whatever is at the end: the Big Crunch? The Dao is the ecology of everything, the physics of everything. The Dao is also *our* path, best illuminated and trodden with equanimity and abnegation of the self.

Our impermanence is obvious, but we seldom confront it. Our death is inevitable, and yet we somehow don't believe it. The full acceptance of impermanence and death comes from a deep-felt sense of the phrase "earth to earth, ashes to ashes, dust to dust" by awakening to life as a process, a flow rather than a thing, and by discarding the clinging, self-deceiving idea of the immortal soul. (We'll get back to that.)

What also should be obvious is our imperfection, but many people appear to think of humanity as an evolutionary end point, as if evolution was directed toward us as its culmination. This apparent perfection is most imagined (by our amazing minds) to be represented by our amazing minds. We do have the most sophisticated minds of any species on Earth, but much of what seems sophisticated is very much an evolutionary work in progress—and still quite glitchy. This idea of human perfection is evident in religious doctrine. "And God said, Let us make man in our image, after our likeness: and let them have dominion over the fish of the sea, and over the fowl of the air, and over the cattle, and over all the earth, and over every creeping thing that creepeth on the earth. So God created man in his own image, in the image of God created he him; male and female created he them" (Genesis 1:26–27). "Verily, Allah created Adam in His image"

(Sahih Muslim, 2612). Humans *seem* to be the best species, but we're not. We're not the best at flying, climbing trees, living in boiling mud pots, or digesting wood in the guts of termites. Nor are we likely to be the most persistent. Species emerge, their form and function gradually coming into focus, and then they fade away, their form and function morphing into something else. We cannot buck this trend anymore than any one of us can cheat death.

All life on Earth is doomed to extinction. The Earth will burn up and be consumed by an expanding sun. The sun will end. The energy and matter (and antimatter, whatever that is) of our solar system will be redistributed in the cosmos and will create new forms as it continues to change. Our galaxy, the Milky Way, will crash through (not into) the Andromeda galaxy in about four billion years, and the two galaxies will dance and swirl together and coalesce into a new galaxy twice the size.

This is all best seen as a flow, a transfer from process to process, from whirlpool to whirlpool, but we can also visualize it in steps. If steps are to be our image, however, we should not imagine discrete steps, like a staircase, but rather steps walked along a level path. "Strides" might a better word. When we walk, we neither roll smoothly, like a ball, nor step in clearly defined jerks. We sort of roll like an end-on-end egg, repeatedly tumbling forward and catching ourselves. It's not entirely clear where one stride ends and the next one begins.

TEN STEPS ON THE COSMIC PATH

The idea of "ten evolutionary steps" comes from Nick Lane's *Life Ascending: The Ten Great Inventions of Evolution*,[1] although he describes ten slightly different steps: the origin of life, DNA, photosynthesis, the complex cell, sex, movement, sight, hot blood, consciousness, and death.

An unbroken thread of nameless things from now back to the chaos before the first. . . .
To know the ancient beginnings is the essence of the Dao. (v. 14)
Dao gives birth to them. De raises them. Matter forms them. Energy animates them. (v. 51)

1. The Big Bang

The Dao . . . I do not know whose child it is. It seems like the ancestor of god. (v. 4)
Everything is born of being except being, which is born of nothing. (v. 40)

From the Big Bang to big brains, all it takes is hydrogen, gravity, and time.

Physicists describe a Big Bang cosmology beginning with a tiny hot speck of everything for which the laws of physics didn't yet apply and for which the concept of time had no meaning, suddenly going "whump!"[2] The hot speck exploded (expanded), and physics invented itself. A lot happened in the first picosecond. The gravitational and electromagnetic forces were formed, and the matter, antimatter, and energy of the speck were flung out into (making) space.

By the end of the first second, we were getting subatomic particles: protons and neutrons, which began to form the first simple atoms, hydrogen and helium. This first stage was mad, full of very stressed, busy, subatomic overachievers, but after about 20 minutes the universe had expanded enough to cool down. Nuclear fusion stopped, and bazillions of hydrogen and helium atoms splurged out into the void (which was no longer void) in nebulous clouds. It went dark. We then had to wait half a billion years or so before anything else interesting happened, which must have been a bit disappointing after those exciting first few seconds . . .

. . . But then those nebulous clouds of hydrogens and heliums did eventually begin their own dance.

Gravity is a weak force that draws objects with mass together. Objects in close proximity with a big mass gravitate together dramatically. Picture a person falling off a roof elevated less than a trillionth of a light year from the surface of an earth-like planet. Far-distant objects with tiny mass, such as atoms of hydrogen in a cloud, share an almost negligible gravitational force, but even they are eventually pulled together, swarm and swirl, accelerate, and "whump!" Stars, explosions, implosions, collisions, planets, moons, nebulas, and black holes.

One of the products of cosmic coming-togethers and tearing-aparts was our solar system: a medium-sized star orbited by planets, some of which are orbited by moons. We're preoccupied with the third planet from the sun, because although it's probably not particularly special, it's home. Our sun is one of a few billion trillion stars, and our planet is one of Krishna knows how many similar planets. Earth was formed out of a great big mass of swirling space stuff. The planet seethed with fire and brimstone, was crashed into, lost a hot chunk that became the moon, and then cooled and solidified.

And then it came alive.

2. The Replicators

Dao birthed one. One birthed two. The two birthed a third. The three birthed the ten thousand things. (v. 42)

Defining life is curiously challenging. It seems obvious what's alive and what's not alive until you start thinking about it, but what is clear is that the fundament of life on earth is DNA.[3] All terrestrial biology is coded and transmitted between organisms as DNA. A planet teeming with life is therefore a planet teeming with DNA. Problem: the machinery for copying and maintaining DNA is complicated. It couldn't have popped out of nowhere.

Richard Dawkins describes a process that he calls "survival of the stable," as a precursor to Darwin's "survival of the fittest," in his groundbreaking book *The Selfish Gene*.[4] If the Big Bang was a physics experiment that set us on the path to evolving life, which is a biology experiment, we first had to pass through the chemistry labs.

First step: What chemistry is available? If materials A, B, and C are available, there is some chance that the compounds ABC, BBC, and ABBA can be made. Second step: energy. If the reactions forming ABC and ABBA require less energy, we're likely to end up with more of them in the mix. Third step: stability. If ABBA is more stable than ABC, we're likely to lose ABCs and accumulate ABBAs. So, survival of the stable imagines a chemical soup in which ABBAs accumulate more successfully than any chemical-else.

Stanley Miller was a brilliant (and apparently quite cantankerous) graduate student at the University of Chicago when he designed the now-famous Miller-Urey experiment. He made concoctions of gases hypothesized to comprise the atmosphere of the early Earth (mainly methane, water, ammonia, and hydrogen) and zapped them with energy. Nothing crawled out of the jar speaking Sumerian, but a wide range of organic compounds associated with life were produced, amino acids (the building blocks of proteins) and nucleic acids (the building blocks of DNA) among them. So, a primeval concoction of gases could, by sheer dumb luck, sort out some useful stable chemistry.

Next step: replicators. A key step from chemistry to biology is a compound that gathers up its chemical building blocks to make more of itself: a molecule that copies itself. A voracious, stable, replicating ABC will mop up all the As, Bs, and Cs in the primordial soup until it is outcompeted by a more voracious, more stable ABBC, which will dominate until the even more successful ACCABAD comes along. Things will get very interesting when ABACADABA dominates by eating ABBAs, CABs, and DADs.

So, when does chemical competition become chemical evolution, and when does chemical evolution become biological evolution? No lines can be drawn. Life is a flow that flowed from nonlife more than three billion years ago. The victorious replicator was DNA, which lives on in organic machines that now blanket the planet. It is now these organic machines, organisms, who must find new ways to commandeer the resources of the planet to continue its maintenance and replication. And DNA is voracious: it consumes the building blocks it needs in many forms: sugar, flour, or gazelle. And it's incredibly stable: it has stuck around for billions of years. Most importantly, DNA evolves.

DNA writes the language of life not in As, Bs, and Cs but instead in As (Adenine), Gs (Guanine), Cs (Cytosine), and Ts (Thymine). All of life is written in this code and has been for billions of years. If somewhere on the billion-letter genomic code a mutation of A for T or C for G makes its organic machine more effective, it will adopt that new, improved code.[5] It will evolve. And new forms will emerge.

Perhaps we can define life quite easily after all. Life is a code that replicates itself from the resources of its environment and persists because its code adapts as the environment changes.

Earth is alive in the form of DNA, which swirls through life formations like water droplets swirl through cloud formations. DNA spins through whirlpools of life like a river spins out whirlpools of water in a rapids. DNA's formations and whirlpools are distinctive. They have clear structure and definite form. We, who are one of them, call these forms organisms, but perhaps that's just another of our muddled ideas. From a broader perspective, we can see that DNA is the only living thing on Earth. DNA is Earth come to life.

3. Cells and Membranes

> *Doors and windows are cut to make a house, creating the voids that allow you to enter and live.* (v. 11)

The chemical road from the Miller-Urey experiment to the complex machinery of DNA replication, epigenetics, and protein synthesis is long and winding, but its outlines are clear. Nonliving self-replicating chemicals duked it out in the primordial soup for millions of years, and the eventual winner was DNA. But the machinery of DNA replication is complicated, and so for DNA to emerge its ancestor replicators must have already evolved a decent home.

The term "primordial soup" conjures an image of chemicals reacting with each other while gently sloshing around in some soupy ocean, but there are two problems with this image. First, chemistry requires energy, and a soup won't provide energy just by sloshing. The energy part will get complicated here if we're not careful. It involves an awful lot of shuffling electrons and protons to synthesize high-energy molecules, such as adenosine triphosphate (ATP), and high reducing-power (hydrogen-adding) molecules, such as nicotinamide adenine dinucleotide. The energy-consuming reactions most likely emerged in places such as thermal vents where energetic and highly reducing chemicals such as hydrogen sulfide spew from Earth's mantle.

Second, chemistry reacts slowly in three dimensions because it takes too long for chemicals to bump into each other. Fast chemistry, especially biochemistry, won't happen in soup; it needs surfaces. Deep ocean vents may also solve part of this riddle because they are honeycombed with protective nooks and crannies that may have served as the first work surfaces, but DNA is no longer trapped in hydrogen sulfide–spewing deep ocean vents. How did it escape?

The replicators built themselves mobile workshops: membranes. Membranes have become complicated over the eons but are, at heart, very humble structures. They have had billions of years to incorporate polysaccharides, proteins, ion channels, proton pumps, receptacles, and receptors, but membranes are still basically self-organizing bubbles of fat. They come in double layers with a hydrophobic (water-repelling) core and a hydrophilic (water-attracting) skin, and their most basic function is to hold water. Make a bilayer of lipid into a sphere and you have a cell: a home; a workshop for replicators. It's a fixer-upper, for sure, but with stunning potential.

4. Photosynthesis

The space between heaven and earth is a bellows. Empty and yet inexhaustible. (v. 5)

So, life probably emerged from nonlife when evolving replicators began using the energy and reducing power bubbling out of the earth to replicate themselves. Life made a massive leap when it figured out how to graduate from these sulfurous crevices to the rest of the planet.

Skeptics of evolution struggle to visualize the evolution of things like humans and eyes. It takes a reasonably nimble mind to visualize such momentous changes. It's tricky at first to see that humans and chimps, such different animals, have a common ancestor or that something as complex as the eye could evolve by natural selection. ("What's the use of half an eye?" is a common refrain.) Compared to the evolution of photosynthesis, however, these are trivial ideas. The eye evolved from crude photoreceptors into something pretty functional in only a few hundred million years. The divergence of chimps and humans from a common ancestor occurred only a few million years ago. Photosynthesis is much more remarkable. It harnesses the radiation reaching Earth from its nearby star.

Photosynthesis happens on membranes, which perform a sequence of insanely cool, linked reactions. Photosynthesis takes carbon dioxide (CO_2), the most boring, stable, unreactive compound, and converts it into biochemical rocket fuel by sticking a bunch of hydrogens onto it to make glucose ($C_6H_{12}O_6$). Once you have abundant glucose you can do almost anything, but making it requires lots of energy and reducing power. Life had spent millions of years grubbing around in sulfurous volcanic crevices until the first photosynthesizers figured this out.

The hydrogens that are stuck onto carbon dioxide in photosynthesis come from water, another remarkably stable chemical. Photosynthesis splits the hydrogen and oxygen from water (H_2O) unleashing gobs of energy. Consider this: gasoline is too wimpy to power rockets; they are powered by liquid oxygen and liquid hydrogen, which are superexplosive. Consider this: plants make and use hydrogen fuel every day in the arctic tundra and the Sonoran desert, silently and without fuss. And photosynthesis doesn't just strip hydrogen from H_2O; it also splits the oxygen into protons and electrons: star stuff!

The machinery of photosynthesis is mind-bogglingly complex and involves large pigment molecules, notably chlorophyll, embedded in membranes. A photon of the right wavelength of light excites chlorophyll, which pulverizes water molecules. Protons flow *across* the membrane to generate energy (ATP), and electrons flow *along* the membrane, a bit like electricity, to generate reducing power nicotinamide adenine dinucleotide phosphate (NADPH). The energy of ATP and the reducing power of NADPH are then consumed to glue hydrogen onto CO_2 in a multistep process that makes glucose. Light energy has been converted to stable, versatile biochemical energy, and oxygen is the by-product:

$$6CO_2 + 6H_2O \rightarrow C_6H_{12}O_6 + 6O_2$$

Photosynthesis is quite a trick, and its emergence on Earth transformed the planet in many ways. First, photosynthesis brought life out of the shadows and into the light and scattered it across the planet. Second, photosynthesis spewed oxygen into the atmosphere. Once devoid of oxygen, our atmosphere is now around 21 percent oxygen. That's some impressive global change (pollution, frankly). Third, photosynthesis brought a reliable flow of energy from space to Earth and formed the thermodynamic basis of the biosphere. With a flow of energy ensured from its local star, the biosphere could now start to evolve in some really interesting ways.

I'd guess that photosynthetic life is common in the universe. The specific anatomy and biochemistry is likely to be vastly different in each case, but replicators probably capture the materials of many planets by harnessing the energy of their nearby stars. I imagine arrays of living solar collectors on many planets with suitably positioned stars. Life may be an emergent property of any chemically suitable planet, and photosynthesis may be an emergent property of any planet suitably located in its solar system.

Billions of planets may be alive.

I suppose some of them may be green, whatever that means.

5. Complex Cells

Some who yield conquer. Some who yield are conquered. . . . Both can have their way. It is fitting to yield and merge. (v. 61)

Imagine Earth a billion or so years ago. The replicators have been scrapping over its resources, capturing its light, replicating, and evolving for two billion years or so. The planet is seething with life, but every living thing is a tiny single cell. (So not seething, then, I guess.) This is Slimeball Earth, but the replicators are working on their next big breakthrough.

There are four basic ways of making a living: producer, predator, parasite, and cooperator. Life began with the producers that scooped up the energy of the sun and raw materials of the environment to build their bodies. The producers became food for consumers, and evolution started to get really interesting when organisms began to kill and parasitize each other and to form alliances. This was still Slimeball Earth without claws, teeth, or paragnaths, but something strange started happening to the earthlings.

Lynn Margulis came up with a bizarre theory that her colleagues thought was nuts. The cells of bacteria and archaea (prokaryotes) are tiny and unadorned. The cells of multicellular organisms, meanwhile, such as plants and animals (eukaryotes), are much bigger and more complex. They are full of structures called organelles, including mitochondria, which make energy, chloroplasts, which photosynthesize, and nuclei, which house the kingly replicators. It dawned on Margulis that the organelles of eukaryotic cells looked awfully prokaryote-ish, and she proposed serial endosymbiosis theory. She was laughed off the stage in the 1960s and then cheered back onto it in the 1980s.

Serial endosymbiosis theory goes like this. Cell 1 swallows Cell 2 but fails to digest it. This would normally be a fail for Cell 1, but in this case it ends up suiting both cells because Cell 2 is a photosynthesizer. This means that Cell 1 now hosts a lean, green, sugar-making machine and that Cell 2 has a home. Let's say that Cell 1+2 now engulfs Cell 3, a motile spirochete. The Cell 1+2+3 combo is now an eating, photosynthesizing swimmer. And on it goes. Cells combine again, again, and again to form complexes of cells. Eventually the internalized cells, comfortable in their new homes, shed the clutter of their former free-living selves and become dependent organelles.

Lynn Margulis nailed it long before the decisive evidence came along. It turns out that many organelles still carry a small complement of their ancestral DNA, and when you sequence that DNA you find some gloriously strange relationships across the tree of life. The DNA of a mitochondrion from an animal (or plant) is not remotely animal (or plant). It maps to a billion-years-old ancestor of the purple sulfur bacteria. When you sequence the DNA of a chloroplast from a green alga, a fern, or an oak tree, it maps to a billion-years-old ancestor of the cyanobacteria.

The complex cell sent life into a new flow. Life moved out of its dorm room into a house with a kitchen, a living room, and a workshop. The complex cell could perform more tasks more efficiently, and an explosion of diversity evolved new structures and forms. DNA's homes became modular as cells formed colonies and colonies morphed into multicellular organisms. The organisms got bigger, faster, and more complex. They started to chase each other with legs, flippers, and wings and found ways to hide from each other with camouflage, poison each other, and tear each other apart.

DNA, meanwhile, sat at the middle of it all, a copy in nearly every cell, quietly adapting to each change, quietly tweaking each organic machine.

Let's take a small detour to tidy up some misappropriation of evolutionary biology, which has been used to promote sociopolitical ideologies. The term "Darwinism" is one of those words. If you're an evolutionary biologist you're on safe ground, but if you're a social scientist, the word reeks of eugenics. Evolution is often considered to be all about "nature red in tooth and claw," as Alfred Tennyson called it.[6] Nature is violent, competitive. The toughest, fastest, smartest, and fittest survive, while the meek get pushed aside, trampled: eaten. Heady stuff if you want to apply evolutionary thinking to people and their societies. But as serial endosymbiosis shows, evolution is just as much about cooperation as competition. Stephen Jay Gould wrote hundreds of wonderful essays on evolution in evocative and clear language,[7] and one of his more fun articles was titled "Kropotkin Was No Crackpot,"[8] supporting the great anarchist's perspectives on the power of mutual aid and cooperation in the development of functional equitable societies.

6 and 7. Sex and Death

The nameless uncarved block tempers desire. With desire managed all is quiet. The world settles into peace. (v. 37)

A flower grows, blooms, returns to the root. Returning to the root is peaceful; a return to one's original nature; to the immutable.... Though the self is ephemeral there is no fear. (v. 16)

Early in life, much human suffering comes from seeking, securing, and coveting sexual partners. Later in life, much suffering can come from contemplating and confronting death.

Sex and death were both inherited from ancient common ancestors of the plants, animals, and fungi and have stuck around ever since. Why? Sex is ridiculous. It's risky, cumbersome, and a huge waste of energy. Consider the peacock, a tasty woodland treat for many carnivores who struts around in iridescent plumage looking to get laid. Consider the leatherback turtle, who swims ten thousand miles from the arctic to haul her cumbersome backside onto a tropical beach to lay eggs. Consider elephant sex. You're picturing that now, right? Why did life evolve sex? And what about death? Death seems so depressingly terminal. Why did life evolve death?

Well, when the replicators moved into their long-lived multicellular homes, they risked stanching the flow of evolution. Sex and death both mitigate the problem of living a long time in a world still dominated by short-lived microbes.

Evolution requires DNA to be copied with near-perfect but not actually perfect fidelity. Too many copying mistakes, and your offspring are likely to be defunct. Too few, and you don't generate enough variation for natural selection to select from. No mutations, no evolution.

DNA replication makes a mistake about once every one million to ten million copies, so variability is introduced into prokaryote genomes by the simple act of multiplying. Large multicellular organisms face a paradox. If they experience too many mutations during a lifetime, they become sick—cancerous, basically—but if they experience too few mutations between lifetimes, they lack the capacity to evolve defenses against fast-evolving pathogens and parasites.

The multicellular solution is to separate body (somatic) cells from specialized germ line (sex) cells. Most of the body can go about the business of protecting itself from change, while the sex cells can specialize in change by enhancing DNA-mixing between generations.

But what's to say the multicellular organisms won't get too lazy for risky, cumbersome, energy-wasting sex? Evolution has ensured that large multicellular organisms will reproduce by embedding genetically determined imperatives such as *cravings* and *desires* into their operating systems. (More about cravings and desires later.)

And death is not a mistake either. Death is selected. Why do mice live only about a year, dogs a decade or so, and bristlecone pines thousands of years? Why do mayflies live only one day? Why do humans live three score years and ten?[9] Each species lives the lifespan that's optimum for its replicators. These replicators really are ruthless bastards. They don't give a damn about you. Death is a breakpoint at which DNA ditches decrepit machines and upgrades them. But honestly, the machine shouldn't get too wound up about it. It's just a machine...

Evolution doesn't care what happens to you once you pass reproductive age. Your somatic cells lose their evolutionary relevance without viable germ line cells to protect. There is no natural selection against diseases that strike late in life as with cancer and Alzheimer's. Death is conditioned on sexual potential, and once your sexually viable years are done the countdown to death by old age begins. The body is relevant to the flow and process of life for only as long as it serves its replicator.[10] When it lives on beyond that role it receives fewer and fewer protections. Somatic cells die so that germ line cells can live forever.

8. Nerves and Brains

Stephen Jay Gould, whom we met in section 5, was most famous for his concept of *punctuated equilibrium*. Evolution moves slowly much of the time (in equilibrium) but has occasional periods (punctuations) of rapid change. South American finches puttered along in mundane finchiness for many generations until a flock was blown onto the Galapagos Archipelago, whereupon the birds rapidly evolved into the myriad species of "Darwin's finches." Little tree shrews skittered warily beneath the giant feet of clomping dinosaurs until the Chixulub asteroid extincted the dinosaurs, whereupon the skitterers rapidly evolved into the new clompers.

The inspiration for punctuated equilibrium came from Gould's studies of fossils from a formation in the Canadian Rockies known as the Burgess Shale. The formation dates to about five hundred million years ago when there was a sudden radiation of multicellular life, including the animals. Earth was full of life but devoid of animals for billions of years, and then millions of animals evolved in a sudden explosion of evolutionary change that has been called the Cambrian Explosion.

In truth, this explosion of life has less to do with the actual rate of change than with the rate of change of things that are obvious to us. A microscopic bacterium and a microscopic alga seem very similar, but they are separated by massive evolutionary distances. A bat, an elephant, and a whale seem vastly different, but their biology is very similar. One is small, one is big, and one is monstrous, one swims, one flies, and one is covered in flies (my bad), but they all have warm blood, large brains, and four limbs[11] with identical bone arrangements—likewise a mouse and a moose, a chicken and a chachalaca.

Some things appear vastly different, but their differences are only skin deep. The exoskeleton of insects represents a big evolutionary step, but different shapes and colors of exoskeleton are mere tweaks. We recognize millions of species of insect, but they're all the same basic thing. The exoskeleton was an evolutionary breakthrough that enabled the insects and their relatives to morph into myriad forms.

And so it goes with nerves and brains. The nerve cell represents a huge evolutionary breakthrough. It gives an organism the capacity to send rapid signals through a body along electrical circuits. Nerves enable the body to differentiate into parts that serve as senders or receivers of signals and eventually also signal processors. Once the basic system is in place, a modest tweak here or there can deliver a vast difference in function.

The nerve cell is old and is found in most extant animals. Sponges lack nerve cells but communicate with electrical impulses generated by calcium channels. Jellyfish lack a central nervous system but have diffuse nerve nets. The true innovators were the first bilaterians: worms with two sides, an "up" and a "down," or a front and a back. They're just tubes, really, with a mouth at the front and an anus at the back (so much has changed), but their bilateral asymmetry enables a nervous system running the length of the body that gives the tube directions: where to go to find food, for example, and to escape danger.

Distant relatives on the tree of life, you may think, and nothing like us, but the Californian sea slug, although it possesses only the skimpiest of nervous systems, shows us that the simplest of animals were already learning to think like us hundreds of millions of years ago.[12]

It is from these humble beginnings that the massive flourishing of the quick-moving, quick-reacting mobile heterotrophs—the animals—emerged. Once you can send a rapid signal from sensor to motivator, the possibilities are vast: nose and taste bud to salivary gland, eye to hand, cold skin to sweater closet. But what's really remarkable about nerve cells is their mysterious capacity to embody consciousness. How does *that* work?

9. Intelligence and Consciousness

> *Regard mental anguish as physical pain. . . . The mind devises its own suffering, but without a physical self how can it be conscious of suffering?* (v. 13)

Intelligence is relatively easy to conceptualize (if you have a modicum of it). It's similar to computing power. Nerve nets and ganglia evolved into nervous systems and simple brains and then more sophisticated brains with more channels and faster processing speeds. Nervous systems evolved to transmit more messages more quickly, more complex organisms evolved more complex nervous systems, and nervous systems eventually became very good at decoding and responding to their environments. We consider their organisms to be intelligent. Jump away from the snake: smart. Avoid the bush that conceals snakes: smarter.

Consciousness is less easy to conceptualize, and the ancients pondered this, just as we do. The fascinating early chapters of Genesis contemplate the origins of life and the origins of humans and then immediately turn to the problem of consciousness:

> "Then the Lord God commanded the man, 'You may freely eat fruit from every tree of the orchard, but you must not eat from the tree of knowledge of good and evil.'" (Genesis 2:15)
>
> "The serpent said to the woman, '. . . when you eat from it your eyes will open and you will be like divine beings who know good and evil.' . . . She took some of its fruit and ate it. She also gave some of it to her husband who was with her, and he ate it. Then the eyes of both of them opened." (Genesis 3:4)

The so-called hard problem of consciousness was described in the 1990s by David Chalmers,[13] who asked how the subjective experiences of consciousness could be generated by physical matter. How does the three-pound fatty blob in your head become conscious? How are feelings and abstractions such as the sense of self manifested by a biological brain that obeys the laws of physics in the real world?

What is consciousness? is a question for philosophy, but *what makes consciousness possible?* is a question for neuroscience. Max Bennett offers a summary of how the application and reapplication of the logic of the nervous system led from the humble bilaterians to intelligence and consciousness in five evolutionary breakthroughs in the complex, multifunctional brains of humans.[14]

The first breakthrough was *steering*, which enabled a tube to navigate toward food and away from predators, as we saw in the last section. After *steering*, the second breakthrough was *reinforcing*, which enabled basic learning such as "Jump away from snake: smart." This seems like very simple learning, but it requires significant computing power in both memory and processing speed. Reinforcing enabled the third breakthrough, *simulating*, and this is when nervous systems start to do some very interesting things. In order to simulate the world, the brain must house a mental map, and the map must contain recognizable objects that are "good" and "bad" as well as "here" and "there," upon which simulations can be run. Simulation builds the capacity to predict snakes rather than just react to them, and this is likely where the foundations of human consciousness lie.

The capacity to simulate the world inside the mind was solidified in the primates and further refined in humans in the fourth breakthrough: *mentalizing*. Mentalizing brought depth and breadth to our simulations of the world, gave them texture and vibrancy, and moved them onto a whole new plane of analytical possibility. Mentalizing generates a much more vibrant mind-world composed of a mental map that is not only geographic but also emotional and behavioral. It makes possible a sense of self, a mental map of the behaviors and intentions of other beings, and many other mental heuristics.

In the mentalizing species, the world is no longer a thing "out there" that is observed and responded to but instead is a thing "in here" that is based on the real world but is distinct from it. You can and do run simulations with your eyes closed, and you run them (in a weird untethered way) in your sleep. *Nothing is good or evil but thinking makes it so*. The fifth evolutionary breakthrough was *speech*, which emerged during the evolution of the now fully conscious primates.

Anil Seth, professor of neuroscience at the University of Sussex in the United Kingdom, in a viral 2017 TED talk and his wonderful book *Being You* explains that we navigate the world via "controlled hallucinations,"[15] and I think this is a brilliant description of simulating and mentalizing. The mind isn't just a computer that provides answers to difficult questions but is also a simulator that maintains an entire operational virtual world that it constantly tests to solve problems and updates with new data. The simulator is always running in the background. It runs when you think, drive, run, meditate, work, run away from a pack of mutant rabid dogs, and sleep. It only stops under general anesthetic and when you die.

And yet we still don't know how consciousness *works*. It seems obvious that it must be generated by the brain, but how? Consciousness is a mysterious emergence that arises from a community of neurons. What might be a good analog? Consider a community (a murmuration: great word!) of starlings. A flock of thousands of birds flies in complex patterns in the sky. The algorithm determining these complex flight pattens is surprisingly simple and based on each bird reacting to the birds around it but gives the impression of group consciousness. Is the flock conscious, and if so, how?

What about an ant colony? Thousands of not-very-bright critters follow simple behavioral rules so that the colony can forage, farm, and defend itself in ways that seem decidedly conscious.

Slime molds in the genus *Dictyostelium* associate into "fruiting bodies" and then dissociate into autonomous foraging "amoebas." A group of Japanese scientists did the coolest ever experiment with this organism.[16] They placed little blobs of its favorite food on the main subway stops on a map of the Tokyo subway system and watched it forage. The slime mold quickly "learned" the most efficient way to commute around "Tokyo" in search of food. The network of stations and lines "designed" by the slime mold was remarkably similar to the one that had been designed by some of the world's finest minds. So, a conscious and intelligent slime mold? No, but still.

Groups of humans give the impression of having a single group consciousness: fifty thousand Liverpool fans singing, a hundred thousand Nazis saluting, and so on.

Intelligence and consciousness enable the evolved replicator preserving and reproducing organic machine we call *Homo sapiens* to do all sorts of crazy things. All the replicators "want" is to convert energy and matter into more replicators. Intelligence and consciousness have expanded their access. Humans have used their intelligence to organize themselves into groups and manipulate their environment.

When we look at the great saga of evolution on Earth we see a path of emergence from nonlife to life, from simplicity to complexity, and a tendency, between each extinction event, for the flourishing of diversity. There is also a trend toward consciousness and intelligence. In our hubris, we have tended to think of ourselves as the culmination of evolution as if we were evolution's (God's?) plan. It makes no sense to think this way. Every living thing perceives itself as the center of the universe, because from its vantage point, it is. But by assuming that we were evolution's goal we have overlooked the fact that intelligence and consciousness are evolving all over the place. They might be fairly natural emergences of complex beings. Ants building fungus-farming colonies, geese flying in formation, murmurations of starlings roosting, termites building cathedrals, and shoals of sardines have fascinating emergent properties, as do the brains of all the vertebrates from armadillos to zebras. The octopus and the chimpanzee have fascinating intelligences and yet to be understood consciousnesses.

These properties are emerging everywhere, so here's a fascinating proposition, from Ishmael, the telepathic gorilla in Daniel Quinn's masterpiece of the same name:

> ISHMAEL: There is a sort of tendency in evolution, wouldn't you say? If you start with those ultrasimple critters in the ancient seas and move up step by step everything we see here now—and beyond—then you have to observe a tendency toward . . . self-awareness and intelligence. Wouldn't you agree?
>
> STUDENT: Yes.
>
> ISHMAEL: "That is, all sorts of creatures on this planet appear to be on the verge of attaining that self-awareness and intelligence. . . . We were never meant to be the only players on this stage. Apparently the gods intend this planet to be a garden filled with creatures that are self-aware and intelligent.
>
> STUDENT: So it would appear. And if this is so, then man's destiny would seem to be plain.
>
> ISHMAEL: Yes. Amazingly enough, it is plain—because man is the first of these. He's the trailblazer, the pathfinder. His destiny is to be the first to learn that creatures like man have a choice: They can try to thwart the gods and perish in the attempt—or they can stand aside and make some room for the rest. . . . His destiny is to be the father of them all. . . .
>
> STUDENT: How so?
>
> ISHMAEL: Just think. In a billion years, whatever is around then, whoever is around then, says, "Man? Oh yes, man! . . . He showed us all how it had to be done. . . . Man was the role model for us all!"[17]

Ishmael's contemplations on the emergence of a burgeoning diversity of intelligences and consciousnesses on Earth is reminiscent of the Buddhist conception of *bodhicitta*, which in the words of Dalai Lama Tenzin Gyatso is "the aspiration to bring about the welfare of all sentient beings and to attain Buddhahood for their sake. It's the distilled essence—the squeeze juice—of all the Buddha's teachings, because ultimately, the Buddha's intention is to lead all sentient beings to perfect enlightenment."[18] There's no reason to assume that humans are the end point of evolution, and that includes the end point in the evolution of intelligence and consciousness. The future is long.

10. Culture and Technology

> *The world is sacred, it can't be controlled. Try to defeat it, you will lose it.* (v. 29)
>
> *When the world is on the path fine stallions leave their manure in the fields. When the world loses its way mares are bred for warhorses.* (v. 46)

We have used the concept of the selfish gene as our centerpiece for biological evolution, but we are not quite done with Richard Dawkins. He advances two other brilliant evolutionary concepts that are useful here: the *extended phenotype* and the *meme*.[19]

The vast majority of the instructions encoded in our selfish genes pertain to building and maintaining our bodies, but their reach is wider than that. Behaviors performed at the behest of our selfish genes affect the broader environment, which means that environmental change can be subject to natural selection. Consider birds' nests. Storks, wrens, bald eagles, and Montezuma oropendolas each build nests distinctive to their species. The nest is a nonliving thing, a part of the abiotic environment, and yet its blueprint is encoded in the DNA of a bird.

Consider the beaver's lake. What is a beaver thinking when she builds a dam? Is she conscious of what she is doing as she gnaws down a tree and collapses it across a river? Does she know that certain trees in certain locations will create dams of a particular structure and that those dams will create lakes of certain sizes and depths? The phenotype of the beaver often extends miles outside its body. In replicating the selfish genes of the beaver, evolution shapes not only long, sharp, powerful teeth but also ecosystems.

Consider termite nests, Caddis fly houses, and manakin leks.

Consider the zombie fungus *Cordyceps unilateralis*,[20] a pathogen of ants and possibly the world's creepiest parasite. *Cordyceps* infects an ant from spores on the forest floor, grows into the body of the ant, develops a small mycelial mass beside the ant's brain, and secretes metabolites that turn the ant into a zombie. The ant climbs a tree and clamps and locks its jaws onto a leaf, and then the fungus eats it from the inside. *Cordyceps* mushroom caps erupt from the ant's dead body and release spores from the perfect height in the tree canopy. The zombified ant is therefore part of the extended phenotype of the fungus.

So, the hummingbird is part of the extended phenotype of the orchid.

So, the orchid is part of the extended phenotype of the hummingbird.

Humans have extended their phenotype in incredible ways. In the human body itself, we use a vast array of prosthetics: replacement limbs, joints, stents, pacemakers, eyeglasses, contact lenses, and hearing aids. We use them in our immediate habitat: our homes, places of work, and the vehicles we use to move among them. We use them in the way we acquire our food—atlatls and factory farms—and in the way we consume our food. Where does the human being end and the environment begin? It has become very difficult to say.

Another quasi-genetic phenomenon at work in human-environment interactions is Dawkins's *meme*. The word "meme" has been perverted of late, which is a shame.[21] It is now just any sticky idea, but Dawkins's meme is an evolving sticky idea.

The virgin birth is an illustrative example. The virgin birth is a convenient story that emphasizes the heavenly lineage of Jesus but is decidedly inconvenient from a biological point of view. Fascinatingly, the original Hebrew word *almah*, which simply means "young woman," appears to have been translated into Greek as *parthenos*, which also means "young woman" but can imply "virgin," and then *parthenos* becomes "virgin," a much more definitive word. Mary's image was gradually cleaned up by the selection of a mutable meme, and then the Council of Nicaea selected the Virgin Mary as church doctrine. A virgin giving birth is far more interesting than a young woman giving birth and happens to link the birth of Jesus back to an old prophesy from Isaiah 7:14, which means that Jesus can now be claimed as the long-promised messiah with more authority. Once the story had mutated, the new version replicated more efficiently and replaced the old. Who on earth (or in heaven?) was going to go back to the old version now? Natural selection had its way with poor Mary, and the dull young woman became a heroic virgin. The Bible evolved.

Actually, the whole nativity is a fine example of cultural evolution by meme. In Luke 1–2, we get the myth of the angel Gabriel and the three shepherds and no mention of three kings. In Matthew 1–2, we get the star of Bethlehem, three kings (Magi, if you prefer) with their gold, frankincense, and myrrh and no shepherds. On the lawn of the local church, we get the whole cavalcade: shepherds, magi, donkeys, cattle lowing, and the little Lord Jesus no crying he makes. And in the movie *Love Actually*,[22] we get three lobsters.

> "There was more than one lobster present at the birth of Jesus?"
> "Du-uh."

The nativity myth is demonstrably fictional and adapted, and yet it sits at the core of the Christian faith.

A meme, then, is a piece of cultural or technical information that is copied, and in copying, it mutates and can evolve. This way of thinking enables us to see culture and technology, like life, as emergences. Out of chemistry emerged life, out of life emerged consciousness and intelligence, and out of consciousness and intelligence emerged culture and technology.

Science is a form of culture tech and a process of meme evolution. One scientist advances an idea, others test and modify it, planes fly, rockets are launched, and Neil Armstrong steps onto the moon.

The culture and technology of our species are forces of global change. The planet's productive land is occupied by humans and their food. Its airwaves are full of signal. Its oceans are lined by wires and pipelines. The edge of its atmosphere is scattered with satellites. Just as life emerged from nonlife, culture and technology emerged from life.

And new forms of life may be emerging from culture and technology.

BEYOND HUMAN BEING

> *Following the Path leads to immortality. Though the self is ephemeral there is no fear.* (v. 16)

Life is a flow, a process. We designate its forms to domains, kingdoms, phyla, genera, and species, but life is a continuum. Lord Krishna told Arjuna, on the eve of battle in the Bhagavad Gita, "Know that through lucid knowledge one sees in all creatures a single unchanging existence, undivided." Form morphs into form. Life has existed on Earth since soon after the planet was formed, but no life form, no species, has ever lasted very long.[23] The Buddha advised us, "Whatever has the nature of arising, all of it has the nature of ceasing."[24] Is there any reason to believe that *Homo sapiens* will be more permanent than any other species?

Two interesting thought experiments are those of the antihumanists and the transhumanists. Antihumanists look at humanity's impacts on the planet and consider us a parasite—a virus on the planet, a scourge—better removed. They might have a point, but that's too bleak for me. The transhumanists see us as a template. We have great potential, they think, but could be improved. The transhumanists have some pretty interesting ideas, but what hubris! They're too creepy for me.

Creepy or not, the transhumanists, whether they are aware of the designation or not, are marching ahead. The extended phonotype of *Homo sapiens*, powered by both gene and meme, is moving into new territory. We became comfortable wearing eyeglasses, pacemakers, and replacement hips and with the ethics of amniocentesis for embryo selection. We have begun to attach ourselves to our computers, particularly our cellphones. We spend a lot of our time ignoring what's around us to live in our virtual worlds. The blending of the human and the artificial is well under way.

Two technologies are changing particularly rapidly and appear poised to have huge impacts on our future as a species. One is gene editing, and the other is artificial intelligence (AI).

Gene editing emerged from basic research on the forever war between viruses and bacteria. Viruses have assailed bacteria for billions of years, and bacteria have evolved weapons to repel them. One such weapon is CRISPR-Cas9, a small mobile DNA sequence armed with DNA-chopping enzymes that seeks and destroys virus code. And since DNA is DNA, whether it's in a bacterium, a sarcastic fringehead,[25] or a human, researchers can seek and chop it. CRISPR is cut-and-paste for DNA.

Scientists are making rapid advances in molecular biology using CRISPR and have their eyes on a number of applications. Among these are many efforts to combat diseases, including malaria, HIV, cancer, muscular dystrophy, and sickle cell anemia. CRISPR food products are already reaching the marketplace: lettuce lookalike mustard greens with their spiciness deleted and GABA-enhanced tomatoes are hitting the shelves in a supermarket near you. The technique is being used widely to accelerate drug development and was central to the rapid development of COVID-19 vaccines in 2020. The mRNA vaccines used in the COVID-19 response are now the state of the art in vaccine development and have delivered drastically improved pandemic response capabilities.

Meanwhile, infamous Chinese scientist He Jiankui blew the lid off gene editing by jumping straight in and performing the experiment everyone feared. He edited the genomes of three human embryos to give them HIV resistance. In how many ways is this insane? Never mind that HIV is a poor target for a first human experiment, and never mind that the editing infiltrated the genomes of the two embryos in unexpected ways, and never mind that we don't know whether it even worked. Now consider the three people those embryos have become. Lulu, Nana, and Amy are now seven years old (twins were Lulu and Nana born October in 2018, and was Amy born in 2019), "perfectly healthy," and living and "being monitored" somewhere in China.[26]

Oh, and He Jiankui just got out of jail and is trying to set up shop again as a gene editor in the Jiankui He Lab on the outskirts of Beijing.

To get a sense of the ways people are thinking, consider the titles of these recent articles:

"Toward a Bioethical Perspective for Posthuman Aesthetics," by B. Suwara, *World Literature Studies* 13 (2021): 81–96.

"Cognitive Enhancement through Genetic Editing: A New Frontier to Explore (and to Regulate)?," by A. Lavazza, *Journal of Cognitive Enhancement* 2 (2018): 388–96.

"Unconventional Settings and Uses of Human Enhancement Technologies: A Non-Systematic Review of Public and Experts' Views on Self-Enhancement and DIY Biology/Biohacking Risks.," by R. Gaspar et al., *Human Behavior and Emerging Technologies* 1 (2019): 295–305.

If you think that ethics and regulation will keep the lid on gene editing, bear in mind that CRISPR kits can be bought online and that gene editing can be done at home. You can order a kit from the-odin.com (yes, Odin) and make your own glow-in the dark bacteria. ODIN CEO Josiah Zayner injected himself with muscle-enhancing code in a livestream event in 2018.[27] It's unlikely that it did anything apart from make him notorious, but such behavior illustrates how gene editing has become the Wild West for biology. It needs to be regulated, yes, but the proverbial horse has already bolted, and CRISPR-Cas9 is just a stepping stone. Tomorrow's gene editing technologies will make today's seem cumbersome.

The critical dilemma for gene editing is the distinction between somatic cell modification and germ line cell modification. Modifying nerve, muscle, pancreatic, or photosynthetic cells to cure genetic diseases, enhance livestock growth, or modify crop tolerances is a complex enough ethical question, but these cells do not replicate. Codifying improvements permanently into genomes by modifying sex cells is much more far-reaching, and the temptation will surely overcome us. We can now direct the evolution of our species, and so it's reasonably safe to assume that we will and that it will eventually become normalized.

That AI was emerging rapidly became clear to me in 2023 when the quality of a short assignment submitted by one of my undergraduate classes mysteriously improved. I can confirm that ChatGPT, powered by GPT-4,[28] writes a strangely okay-ish college-level essay.

AI didn't emerge from smart humanoid robots, as has been the main preoccupation of science fiction; it came about due to the fast processing speeds of modern computers and the availability of big datasets in large networks. It wasn't a HAL, Daneel Olivaw, or Haley Joel Osment lookalike through which AI emerged but through the faceless interstices of the networked digital world. The first AI to become famous was Deep Blue, the supercomputer that beat Gary Kasparov at chess in 1997, but its power and range were trivial compared to those of the vast data-gathering, number-crunching networks of Google and Amazon. And now we have generative AI from Open AI, and everyone is trying to emulate them.

People seem to think that AI could never match the subtlety of the human brain, but I don't see why that would be. The subtlety of the human brain is magnificent, but it's not magic.

Consider intuition, one of our more remarkable faculties. We find it hard to imagine a computer having a sudden aha moment or a feeling that it has met someone before or getting the sense that the dude who just walked into the room is a creeper, because these thoughts and feelings seem natural, organic, and distinctly human, but they're just calculations made by electrochemical neural networks. And in any case, intuition is an approximation, a heuristic, and often a pretty poor one. Our brains make educated guesses, and they often get things wrong.

There's every reason to believe that AIs will do much better than human intuition. With faster processing speeds and massive memories, it seems logical to expect that AI will improve on human intelligence in every way. AI could be given better sensory inputs from high-speed cameras, microphones, chemical sensors, and vibration detectors. And why not add X-ray and infrared cameras, sonar, and GPS? AI might just do away with all those heuristics that make us uniquely human because they're basically glitches.

Other sticking points are consciousness and self-awareness, but again, although these mental faculties feel uniquely human and magical to the minds that conjure them, especially minds that fail to investigate themselves (their selves), consciousness is simply the mental backdrop onto which we project our mental maps of the world. I see no reason why other intelligences couldn't use the same, similar, or better methodologies. Self-awareness is a (flawed) mental model of ourselves with the practical application of helping us survive and reproduce. Consciousness and self-awareness are insanely cool, but they exist in the physical world, are not magic, and can therefore be emulated.

The human brain is an organic computer that uses electrical and chemical signals to interface with an organic body. AI is emerging from inorganic computers that use electrical signals to interface with machines. And we call it *artificial* intelligence, but what is it, exactly, that makes it artificial? And in what ways is our intelligence not artificial? Perhaps we need different terminology. Human intelligence versus nonhuman intelligence? That's too limited. It ignores mouse, moose, chicken, and chachalaca intelligences and the possibility that we may be on the cusp of seeing diverse forms of nonhuman intelligence. Perhaps the terms "biological intelligence" and "synthetic intelligence" work better. Perhaps the distinction is irrelevant.

The most fascinating emergences of gene editing and AI and their signaling of posthuman consciousnesses and intelligences may come from using them in combination. The possibilities are already hinted at by brain-computer interface (BCI) technologies.

The brain can adapt to signals planted in the cortex. Miguel Nicholelis, a professor of neuroscience at Duke University, has experimented with rhesus monkeys who can manipulate robotic levers with their minds.[29] In one of the earliest human applications, William Dobelle, an independent researcher and former director of the Division of Artificial Organs at the Columbia-Presbyterian Medical Center, implanted an electrode array into the brain of "patient Jerry," a blind man who temporarily recovered rudimentary vision. That was back in 1978.[30] Since then, progress has been made in vision restoration, the restoration of motor control, and communication using invasive, semi-invasive, and noninvasive brain-computer links.

The potential medical applications are spectacular and will enhance many lives. The darker horizons are equally vivid. The US military is interested in the use of BCI for instantaneous brain-to-internet-to-brain communication, which is basically mind reading. The toy maker Mattel has a game called MindFlex in which the operator uses brain waves to steer a ball through an obstacle course. Boy-man, father of roughly a dozen children (including X AE A-XII and Exa Dark Siderael), and self-declared transhumanist Elon Musk is the founder of a BCI development company called Neuralink. What could possibly go wrong?[31]

In 2005 Ray Kurzweil wrote *The Singularity Is Near*,[32] in which he predicted that the exponential acceleration of processing power in computers would eventually reach a point at which each increase became effectively instantaneous. To some extent this is an iteration of Moore's law, which predicted exponential increases in chip speed. Moore's law has begun to fail as inevitable physical and technical limits have been reached, but technocultural emergence might take unexpected sideways turns: unexpected zigs rather than zags into a sudden new emergence or a rupture rather than a steady accumulation. Maybe gene editing and AI herald an impending rupture, perhaps from their combination through BCI. Maybe a posthuman being will emerge by a gradual accumulation over many generations, arriving largely unheralded. Maybe the posthuman will emerge suddenly, disruptively, and in our lifetimes. Exactly what will emerge after humans is not knowable, but something will. Our species is as impermanent as any other.

What intrigues me the most about the possible emergence of life from human technology is that it need not be DNA-based.

Taking the long view of evolution, in which we consider life as singular—a flow, a process—rather than as multiple separate forms would mean that the single life form on earth, DNA, might soon be joined by a second life form.

HOW LONG IS THE PRESENT?

To know what endures is to be enlightened; majestic; heavenly; in accordance with the Eternal Path. (v. 16)

There is a charming and oft-cited story from the introduction to David Chadwick's biography of his longtime Zen teacher Shunryu Suzuki. At the end of a lecture, Suzuki had asked if anyone had a question, and Chadwick tells us about the naive question he asked, and the answer he received:

> "SUZUKI-ROSHI, I've been listening to your lectures for years," I said, "and I really love them. . . . But I must admit I just don't understand. . . . Could you please put it in a nutshell. Can you reduce Buddhism to ONE PHRASE?"
>
> Everyone laughed. He laughed. What a ludicrous question. I don't think any of us expected him to answer IT. . . .
>
> But Suzuki did answer. He said, "Everything CHANGES."[33]

Kurt Vonnegut's masterpiece *Slaughterhouse Five* depicts his experience of the firebombing of Dresden in February 1945.[34] Writing the book took him decades because it is about the central trauma of his life. It seems like a fantasy, which may be what makes it such a devastating and honest work of realism. Vonnegut created something strange and unsettling.

Billy Pilgrim has come "unstuck in time" and is hurtled on a disjointed odyssey through space and time, in and out of war, to his life before the war, after the war, and through a bizarre alien abduction in which he is displayed in a zoo on the planet Tralfamadore with a prostitute called Montana Wildhack. Pilgrim's scattered and fragmented life mirrors Vonnegut's journey through hell and his faltering recovery from PTSD. How to write about such real horrors? They can't be explained, only shown, and they can't be tackled head-on, which would be unbearable, and so we are drawn in sideways, out of sequence, and via Tralfamadore.

Slaughterhouse Five raises questions of all kinds. It forces us to confront the nature of humans in the face of the atrocities they commit. Billy Pilgrim bumbles through World War II, is faced with horrors, and survives by dumb luck. He is neither monstrous nor heroic but is infinitely human.

And what of those bizarre Tralfamadorians who display Billy Pilgrim in their zoo? Well, on Tralfamadore the four dimensions happen all at once, which means that Tralfamadorians witness the past, present, and future as one:

> Billy Pilgrim says that the universe does not look like a lot of little dots to the creatures from Tralfamadore. The creatures can see where each star has been and where it is going, so that the heavens are filled with rarefied, luminous spaghetti. And Tralfamadorians don't see humans as two-legged creatures, either. They see them as great millipedes—"with babies' legs at one end and old people's legs at the other," says Billy Pilgrim.[35]

Billy Pilgrim has no self. He is simply an embodied consciousness passing through time, and neither the length of time for which his mind and body will persist nor the sequence of his experiences is his to control.

Consider an exploding bomb. Picture the Alamogordo Bombing Range on the parched Jornada del Muerto Plains, two hundred miles South of Los Alamos, New Mexico. It is July 16, 1945, the first atom bomb detonation, code name "Trinity." Ralph Smith described the explosion:

> I was staring straight ahead with my open left eye covered by a welder's glass and my right eye remaining open and uncovered. Suddenly, my right eye was blinded by a light which appeared instantaneously all about without any build up of intensity. My left eye could see the ball of fire start up like a tremendous bubble or nob-like mushroom.... The light intensity fell rapidly.... It turned yellow, then red, and then

> beautiful purple. At first it had a translucent character but shortly turned to a tinted or colored white smoke appearance. The ball of fire seemed to rise in something of a toadstool effect. Later the column proceeded as a cylinder of white smoke; it seemed to move ponderously. A hole was punched through the clouds, but two fog rings appeared well above the white smoke column.[36]

There is a vast archive of photographs of the test. You've seen the photos or one like them showing the iconic mushroom cloud. The mushroom cloud is our image of the moment of the explosion, right?

Fourteen and a half billion years ago, a singularity exploded in the Big Bang that formed the universe, but a better way to think of the Big Bang is as an explosion than began fourteen and a half billion years ago—appearing instantaneously all about—in whose expanding mushroom cloud we now live as transient particles. Have you noticed how many galaxies have the shape of whirlpools?

3

THE WAYS OF PEOPLE

Lacking Dao, we fall back on De. Lacking De, we fall back on kindness. Lacking kindness, we fall back on morality. Lacking morals, we fall back on rituals and rules. (v. 38)

THE ENVIRONMENT WILL HAVE A LOT TO SAY ABOUT THE LIVES WE END up living in the coming decades and centuries. The climate will continue to change, fossil fuels will deplete, and biodiversity will continue to decline. With such dramatic global change coming so fast, our societies cannot remain as they are. Much will be out of our control, but not everything. There are many choices to make. What kind of societies can we build? What kind of societies will we build?

Visions of environmental collapse, advanced artificial intelligence, and tech-driven social control are offered by Isaac Asimov's *Foundation* series, Frank Herbert's *Dune* series, George Orwell's *1984*, and Cormac McCarthy's *The Road.* Or perhaps the future world will be more like Aldous Huxley's *Brave New World* in which we will live lives distracted by feelies and drugged into happiness by soma in a clonally propagated social hierarchy. Perhaps our clones will be slave replicants such as Yoona-939 and Sonmi-451 in the corporatocracy of David Mitchell's *Cloud Atlas.* Perhaps we will live our futures in the Matrix.[1] Perhaps we're already in a matrix . . .

Robert Costanza offers four possible futures in his article "Four Visions of the Century Ahead: Will It Be Star Trek, Big Government, Ecotopia, or Mad Max?"[2] He parses the future along the axes of scarcity and technology. A world of relative abundance and advanced technology might be like *Star Trek,* so advanced that many happy space-communists can boldly go wherever they want. A world of scarcity and failing technology might be like *Mad Max,* a world that insists on using internal combustion but has very little to combust. Mel Gibson–level chaos.

Peter Frase offers us *Four Futures* in an analysis that turns on the axes of scarcity abundance and equality hierarchy.[3] He posits communism, rentism, socialism, or exterminism, and his exterminism scenario is pretty grim.

Kim Stanley Robinson's *Three Californias* trilogy presents contrasting dystopian and utopian futures for Orange County, California, in *The Wild Shore*, *The Gold Coast*, and *Pacific Edge*.[4] Will California become an American Dune, Foundation, or Coruscant-Trantor? None, perhaps. There are many other possibilities.

What you expect future societies to look like will depend on your intuitive sense of what shapes them. An environmental determinist such as Jared Diamond will tend to put the environment in the driver's seat. Much is inevitable, Diamond would argue, as he did, retrospectively, in *Guns, Germs and Steel* and *Collapse*.[5] The environment that offers a, b, and c can support x and y societies but not z societies. As an ecologist, I have tended to favor this way of understanding the world, but I'm also swayed by the compelling, optimistic ideas of the possibilists. David Graeber, for example, will doggedly resist the notion that social repression of any kind must be baked in, natural, or predetermined in any way.[6] All societal structures can be challenged by organized people, and any society can be created, argues Graeber: anything is possible.

Much will hang on the state of the planet left behind in the wake of our current experiment in civilization. Much will hang on how we choose to interact as we pass through the coming era of unravelings. Both cooperation and conflict are integral to the ways of people.

ONE FIGHT

Why do we have things arranged the way we do? Why do we accept that some will be wealthy and others poor, that some will have medicines and doctors and others will suffer treatable pain and disease, that some will live in comfortable houses and have fast cars and others will live in the streets, in slums, in landfills and walk barefoot? Given the choice, each of us would change the status quo, but we find it very difficult to cooperate to find a reasonable shared path. It's actually not difficult to imagine a happy and peaceful society, and we have everything we need to build one. A truly intelligent species capable of cooperation, altruism, and complex forward planning would be able to build it. We must therefore be less capable than we think.

An honest appraisal reveals our species to be an omnivorous small-group mammal that has recently emerged as the first truly social animal on this planet. Having functional systems of socialization based on complex mental heuristics, we attempt to organize ourselves into large groups, but we find it difficult. We don't seem to quite possess the hardware required. We think we do, and perhaps it's the very failure to appraise ourselves honestly that makes it so frustrating. The brain spends time pulling us together and then pushing us apart. We are caring but defensive, kind but fearful. The rhetorical question "Why can't we all just get along?" is not rhetorical at all. It is important, needs to be asked with honesty, and demands answers.

The arrangement of societies seems so complicated. We have capitalism, socialism, libertarianism, communism, fascism, and conservatism. Lots of isms. But there has only ever been one consistent fight among people, and it has been between the wealthy and powerful few and the poor and oppressed masses. The wealthy and powerful seek to control the masses to maintain and expand their position. The masses seek their share. The wealthy and powerful must organize their wealth and power to oppress or placate the masses. The masses must unite. Or, as my colleague Rob Weiner put it, the constant fight is between organized money and organized people.

Our experiments with governance are ancient. The most influential political philosopher from the ancient East was probably Kongzi (Confucius), who advocated for a clear hierarchy guided by loyalty and meritocracy. The hierarchy of the government, in the Confucian view, should mirror that of the traditional patriarchal family. The *Daodejing* breaks from the political philosophy of Confucius but is heavily influenced by it.

The West has contributed richer ideas to political philosophy and has done so since the time of the ancient Greeks. Plato and Aristotle conceived democratic philosophies while Laozi and Kongzi were grappling within hierarchies. Some breakthroughs in the medieval period notwithstanding, most notably from Islamic philosophers, human political thought progressed little until the European Renaissance.

Or so Wikipedia and Britannica tell us. But we must pause a moment and check ourselves. Is that true? It's almost certainly not. The Dark Ages weren't dark everywhere.

The as yet uninvaded Americas were home to diverse cultures with diverse forms of political organization, but we seem strangely oblivious to them. To the victors go the spoils, they say, and the histories.

Americans have judiciously edited, polished, and curated a heroic narrative of the "discovery" of the Americas and of the American West. The mythology has been punctured again and again with a history that acknowledges past atrocities. Those who still embrace the "how the West was won" history are willfully ignorant. Those who have moved on feel enlightened, but even without the old prejudices we still maintain a deeply flawed understanding of North American history. We still embrace many myths.

One such myth involves the political origins of US democracy. It was the founding fathers, they say, inspired by the French Revolution, and it was their courage, foresight, and original thinking that brough the first glimpses of political freedoms to the world. They say. But there's something fishy about this narrative. The Europeans, recently arrived in North America, suddenly came up with a bunch of exciting new ideas, did they? And they did this while battling the troublesome, uncouth locals, did they? How did they find the time?

Maybe those locals weren't so uncouth as we have been led to believe. Maybe they were warm-blooded, complex, politically minded, intelligent people. You know, like people everywhere. And maybe they had a few ideas about how to arrange a society.

One of the most fascinating Americans is Kandiaronk (also known as Adario), of the Wendat (Huron), who lived from 1625 to 1701 in the Great Lakes region, mostly in the Makinac area between Lakes Superior, Huron, and Michigan.[7] Early in the colonization of North America by Europeans, generations before the Revolutionary War and the penning of the US Constitution, Kandiaronk was involved in complex negotiations with the French and the Haudenosaunee Confederation, initially maneuvering against his people's traditional enemies but then negotiating for a widespread peace. He was, by all accounts, a skilled orator who spent a lot of time arguing politics with the French. A fascinating account of Kandiaronk comes from Baron Louis Armand de Lom d'Arce de La Hontan (mercifully abbreviated to Lahontan), who served in the French army in New France in the 1680s, settled, explored the Great Lakes and the Missouri and Mississippi Rivers, and wrote about his adventures. His fascinating 1703 treatise *Supplement aux Voyages ou Dialogues avec the Sauvage Adario* (Supplement to Voyages or Conversations with Adario) is claimed to be based on the political views of Kandiaronk. In the book, Lahontan and Adario/Kandiaronk engage in long debates on ethics, spirituality, religion, and society:

> KANDIARONK: I have spent six years reflecting on the state of European society and I still can't think of a single way they act that's not inhuman.... [W]hat you call money is the devil of devils; the tyrant of the French, the source of all evils; the bane of souls and slaughterhouse of the living. To imagine one can live in the country of money and preserve one's soul is like imagining one could preserve one's life at the bottom of a lake. Money is the father of luxury, lasciviousness, intrigues, trickery, lies, betrayal, insincerity,—of all the world's worst behavior. Fathers sell their children, husbands their wives, wives betray their husbands, brothers kill each other, friends are false, and all because of money. In the light of all this, tell me that we Wendat are not right in refusing to touch, or so much as to look at silver?
>
> KANDIARONK: If you abandoned conceptions of mine and thine[,] ... distinctions between men would dissolve; a leveling equality would then take its place among you as it now does among the Wendat.... Over and over I have set forth the qualities that we Wendat believe ought to define humanity—wisdom, reason, equity, etc.—and demonstrated that the existence of separate

> material interests knocks all these on the head. A man interested by interest cannot be a man of reason.[8]

It's absurd—and xenophobic—to think that the invading Europeans learned nothing from the diverse cultures of the Americas they encountered over a period of centuries.

We get a further glimpse of this from the Haudenosaunee (Iroquois) Confederacy, which was formed of six nations occupying territory in the eastern Great Lakes region: the Mohawk, Oneida, Onondaga, Cayuga, Seneca, and Tuscarora nations. Their confederacy was founded through the Great Law of Peace, a constitution with 117 articles that was negotiated in the twelfth century. Many scholars note that its articles influenced Benjamin Franklin and others during the framing of the US Constitution.

Many tribes retain oral histories, rules, myths, and legends that point to social systems were designed to promote sustainable resource use. A wonderful chapter of Robin Wall Kimmerer's *Braiding Sweetgrass* titled "The Honorable Harvest" speaks to culturally embedded guidelines for the harvesting of wild foods from the forest.[9] Similar concepts appear in the writing of many Indigenous authors. Tyson Yunkaporta's *Sand Talk*[10] yarns at length about Indigenous Australian yarning and yarn-negotiated rules of bush harvest.

The cultures, systems of governance, and foodways of the Indigenous peoples of California were devastated by European colonization, but Kat Anderson's painstaking research paints a vivid picture of rich cultural diversity in *Tending the Wild*.[11] She shows that California's varied landscapes supported a diversity of human cultures matched almost nowhere else on the planet and that California was a mosaic of intensively and extensively managed landscapes.

Indigenous nations used councils of elders, systems of consensus building, and many other governmental arrangements long before the advent of representative democracy in the modern state. Much is known, but so much more must have been forgotten. If only we had a better appreciation of all the ways intact cultures long-settled and long-adapted to their landscapes managed their societies and their resources. There were many trials and tribulations, we know, and failures too—the fake glorification of cultures neither helps nor pays respect—but how much we could learn! All the cultures extant on the planet today are distorted by colonialism and globalization. We need to learn how to settle in place, become fully naturalized as an integral part of each environment in which we live, and develop social systems that honor each place. There are people still living in vibrant ancient communities on the planet who can serve as guides.

We pick Western political philosophy back up in the Kandiaronk et al.–inspired European Renaissance. Thomas Hobbes proposed a strong government—a

Leviathan—powerful enough to mediate any dispute as a neutral party.[12] John Locke wrote *Two Treatises on Government* that offered pathways to reject the divine right of kings.[13] The mind, according to Locke, was a tabula rasa, a clean slate, upon which could be written reason, tolerance, and a pathway to democratic self-governance. Jean-Jacques Rousseau outlined a social contract that paved the way to the construction of a legitimate social order—and the American and French Revolutions.[14]

Since Hobbes, Locke, and Rousseau we have learned from Burke, Smith, Jefferson, Hegel, Marx, Kropotkin, Lenin, Foucault, Chomsky, and Marjorie Taylor Greene (lol) and hundreds of others, such as the guy down the pub and your uncle (he's an expert).

There's a deep wellspring upon which to draw, and yet we take two steps backward and one step forward, one step backward two steps forward. Progress is made and then dashed. By some measures you could argue that there has been a gradual arc of progress over the last few centuries. Steven Pinker makes this argument in a series of compelling books.[15] The progress of some, however, has been made at the expense of others and at great cost to the environment. So, progress and regress. We stagger forward. We stagger backward. Again, perhaps we lack the capacity to solve the problems of society. Reasonable maps have been drawn, but we have been unable to follow them. Maybe we shouldn't feel too chagrined: no other species has even drawn maps. But still.

There are different ways of assessing our capabilities as a species. We are capable of great kindness and great cruelty, great attentiveness and an all-consuming torpor. What is it that guides our actions as individuals and groups?

Before we delve too deeply into the cognitive and emotional ways of people and ways of the mind, let's remember that we are, at base, a biological species. We evolved in an environment that selected us to secure resources, to compete, to fight, to hunt, and, given the chance, to invade.

OUR INVASIVE SPECIES

The first record of garlic mustard in North America is from the Brooklyn Botanical Garden in the late nineteenth century. The plant was probably brought to the United States as a culinary herb. It tastes a bit garlicky and a bit mustardy. Back home in England, we call it Jack in the Hedge. It's a short-lived biennial of modest stature, common enough but never weedy. You wouldn't pick it as an invader. You'd expect an invader to be of sturdier stock. Bigger, perhaps, or faster growing or in possession of sharp spines or woody thorns. More vigorous, somehow. Garlic mustard is an unremarkable English wildflower. Honestly, it looks like a bit of a wimp.

In England, that is. In America, garlic mustard is a monster.

Once established on the Eastern Seaboard, garlic mustard began to spread through the eastern deciduous forests until by the end of the twentieth century it had colonized nearly every patch of deciduous woodland from Maine to Missouri. And it was causing damage. Garlic mustard emerges early in the spring and forms thick stands that shade out the lovely ephemerals of the spring forest: trilliums, bloodroots, Dutchman's breeches, toothwort, trout lily, and bluebells. What's more, there's evidence that garlic mustard can inhibit the germination and growth of tree saplings, which means that this wimpy English wildflower might be changing the structure of American forests.[16]

There's nothing special about garlic mustard. It is small. It is a wimp. What causes it to invade is the simple fact that it has moved from one continent to another. The environment it moved to is very much like the environment it came from, but while the flora and fauna of Europe have lived alongside garlic mustard for millennia, its new neighbors in North America had never seen it before.

Garlic mustard, it turns out, is a fighter. (Well, of course it's a fighter. Everything that has emerged from four billion years of evolution is a fighter. The selfish genes demand nothing less.) Garlic mustard's particular tactic is to attack the friends of its enemies. It attacks the fungal symbionts that its competitors use to acquire nutrients from the soil.

The fungal symbionts of Europe have been busy evolving defenses against garlic mustard, but the fungal symbionts of North America haven't had time. The chemical weapons that had been neutralized in the relentless European theater of botanical war found new unwitting targets on a new continent. Its weapons were suddenly toxic again, and garlic mustard launched its invasion. It will invade through long generations until its novel weapons are no longer novel, and only then will it become a naturalized American.

I tell the long story of the invasion of North America by garlic mustard not to make you care about garlic mustard, although I hope you do. This unremarkable English wildflower reminds us that nothing in nature is unremarkable and shows how strikingly similar this plant invasion of the Americas is to the human invasion that preceded it.

The human equivalents of garlic mustard's novel weapons are discussed in Jared Diamond's *Guns, Germs, and Steel*.[17] The patterns of human migration and colonization, argues Diamond, were largely predestined. Consider the fate of the Inca ruler Atahualpa at the hands of Francisco Pizzaro. An Inca army in the tens of thousands was defeated by a few hundred Spaniards with some novel weapons. That Pizzaro would devastate Atahualpa at Cajamarca was not inevitable, but that devastation was coming in many forms when Europeans invaded the Americas was inevitable.

So, are humans just like garlic mustard? Well, we're similar in more ways than you might think. We are a biological species with skills and limitations, but there is one nontrivial difference. We evolved a brain that can resist the urge to conquer if it chooses.[18]

We know what we're doing and do it anyway. Why do we invade and colonize? Just because we can?

This way of thinking can sanitize history and bleach out the violence, and I don't want to do that. No matter how biologically inevitable the European invasion of the Americas might have been, we must remember that it was orchestrated by real minds and carried out by real people. Choices were made, and actions were followed. Humans find it hard to resist conquest and control, especially when they see an opportunity to fulfill their cravings and desires.

Colonialism is one of the defining features of the modern age. We live in a world that was captured, exploited, and reordered by western Europe (primarily Spain, Portugal, Britain, France, the Netherlands, and Belgium) beginning in the long sixteenth century. The United States and Japan got in on the act in the long twentieth century, and China became a major force in the last half century. The first era of colonization primarily concerned the capture of territory by military means. Today's colonialism, or neocolonialism, is primarily an exercise in the capture of capital by economic means. Fundamental to colonization, whether military or economic, is the consumption of cheaply acquired nature and people and their conversion into capital.

Colonialism has been central to the development of the wealthy nations of the world and embodies some of our most awful truths. The sudden economic flourishing of the West did not come primarily from enlightenment, as we like to tell ourselves, but instead came from genocide, enslavement, and a continent-scale land grab. How to square this with the West's view of itself, emerging in parallel, as "civilized?" Civilization and the Enlightenment emerged from brutality and exploitation, a fact that can cause significant cognitive dissonance. How do we validate ourselves as moral in the face of this paradox?

One way is to create a story: a mythology. While establishing a system of rules and norms for the enslavement and sale of Africans, sing "Rule Britannia, Britannia rules the waves. Britons never, never, never shall be slaves!" When invading westward across North America, perpetrating a genocide against diverse Indigenous peoples, declare it to be your manifest destiny. While brutally suppressing resistance to your colonization of North Africa, do so with *liberté, égalité, fraternité.* To enshrine your mythology and embed it deeply in the minds of your group, have a representative of your mythology—Prince Dodgy or Princess Dowdy—show up to cut a ribbon every time you open a new hospital, or smash a bottle of champers on the bow of every new ship you launch. Or sing to and salute your mythology before every sporting event. Since we are all heroes in our own stories, the easiest way to feel like a hero is to write your own story.

To live honestly and find new ways to inhabit our environment, we must learn to slough off these mythologies—these lies:

Bear the nation's humiliations to become worthy of its fertile soil and abundant harvests. (v. 78)

Imagine a small country with few citizens. . . . Their food is nutritious, their clothes are comfortable, their customs are cheerful. Other nations are very close—dogs can be heard barking, roosters can be heard crowing—but imagine these people: they can grow old and die without feeling the needs to explore. (v. 80)

The wise do not hoard, but by serving others receive more and by giving to others they gain more. (v. 81)

THE CAUSES OF WAR

When the world is on the Path fine stallions leave their manure in the fields. When the world loses its way, mares are bred for warhorses. (v. 46)

We say we want peace but act in ways that suggest otherwise. We crave more: more land, more water, more oil, more sugar, more coffee, more cotton, more rubber, more people to enslave. We find ways to justify taking the things we want from others. We act particularly violently when like-minded in-groups coalesce around their hatred of out-groups.

There is a long history of books on the causes of war, from Thucydides and Sunzi (Sun Tzu) to Niccolo Machiavelli and Geoffrey Blainey. Blainey's *The Causes of War* argues that wars break out when two groups calculate that they have more to win by fighting than succumbing.[19] Since they can't both be right, war becomes the test of it. War will always demonstrate one of them was wrong. It usually demonstrates they both were. *Weapons, no matter how beautiful, are the tools of violence. All men should detest them. . . . In victory, be solemn. To glorify victory is to glorify killing. If you glorify killing you can never be whole. When people have been killed, hear their pitiful cries of sorrow. Treat victory as a funeral*" (v. 31).

One way to avoid war is to succumb to aggressors, and this seems to be what Laozi is suggesting: *If a small country yields to a great one it will be annexed. If a small country conquers a large one it will eventually be absorbed. Some who yield conquer. Some who yield are conquered. . . . Both can have their way. It is fitting to yields and merge* (v. 61). Fitting to yield and merge? Go preach that in Bakhmut, Ukraine. People have fought to the death for their group or country throughout history rather than be dominated by an aggressor. We frequently decide we have less to lose by fighting than surrendering and by death than defeat. Laozi disapproves:

Compassion in battle brings victory. Compassion in defense builds strength. Heaven protects with compassion. (v. 67).

Advance without advancing, reach out without striking, confront without attacking, hold your ground without weapons. (v. 69)

The human proclivity for war is quite the conundrum, and Laozi struggled with it. In some ways he sounds rather like his contemporary Sunzi, author of *The Art of War*, when he gives strategic and tactical advice. But how to give strategic and tactical advice on war when your philosophy is based on pacifism? Laozi invokes battle tactics based on *wuwei* and yin-yang but this is unconvincing from a military perspective:

Be straightforward in ruling a nation. Be unpredictable in war. (v. 57)
A good commander doesn't rush ahead. A good warrior doesn't lose his temper. A good leader overcomes without confrontation. (v. 68)
The master of war says, "I dare not strike first, but prefer to defend. I dare not advance an inch, but prefer to retreat a foot." . . . No mistake is worse than underestimating your enemy. . . . When well-matched armies clash the side that yields will win. (v. 69)
So hard and stiff belong to death and tender and gentle belong to life. Thus is the unyielding army shattered and the unbending tree splintered. (v. 76)

He is more convincing when he advocates resisting violence: *Rash courage can be fatal. The courage to resist can be liberating* (v. 73).

The violence inherent to the human psyche is troubling, and it troubled Laozi: *Controlling by force of arms is in opposition to the Dao. It invites retribution. Where armies bivouac, thorn bushes grow. Where armies clash, harvests fail*" (v. 30). Our cultures have perpetrated great violence against each other.

Are humans the only species that engage in war? We've established that colonization shares commonalities with biological invasions. Humans expand their territories in ways similar to other invasive species, but war is different. There are clashes in and among other species that resemble war, such as battles between colonies of social insects, and there is intense competition in nature that frequently leads to violence, but human wars have some very special characteristics.

It seems to be uniquely human to escalate conflicts beyond direct competition. We hunt down our competitors and attempt to destroy them. We fight preemptively. We even fight indirectly by doing such things as destroying our enemies' food resources. No other species does all this. Humans seek to not only compete but also control and dominate:

The wise limit wastefulness and pride and temper the desire to control. (v. 29)
When people have been killed hear their pitiful cries of sorrow. Treat victory as a funeral. (v. 31)

The combination of colonization and control is dangerous. It separates us from the realm of nature, a milieu in which organisms coevolve, and locks us into stasis. To be under control is to be stagnant. To be apart from nature is to relinquish the capacity to evolve as part of it. Our wars against each other are a subset of larger wars we are fighting against nature. We perceive ourselves as having dominion over other people and over nature, and we commit violence to maintain thar perceived position.

We often wonder if humans are innately good or bad. We are neither, of course, and both. We need help to be the best versions of ourselves, and if we are to curtail our baser tendencies and nurture the better angels of our natures, we need to build societies conducive to these goals. We must find ways to act in the common interests of the group with an understanding of shared rights and responsibilities. A basic need is to find social mechanisms that protect and share resources.

THE TRAGEDY OF THE COMMONS

Without guidance the upright revert to evil and confusion and anarchy reign. (v. 58)
To big or small; to many or few, respond to vice with virtue. (v. 63)

The tragedy of the commons is a fraught concept. It seems reasonable at first glance, masquerading as a compelling explanation of why people trash the shared resources upon which their lives depend, why commoners (peasants) fail to join in common cause to curtail their greed, and why people take resources without concern for sustainability and destroy their environments and their communities.

Garrett Hardin was an interesting character, at once both insightful and blinkered, whose contribution was a sequence of works in which he stressed that some ecological problems had only social solutions, not technological ones. His seminal work was the essay "The Tragedy of the Commons."[20]

Tragedy, as used by Hardin, is more than merely tragic. It comes from the remorseless unwinding of things and has a distinctly Shakespearean edge to it. The headline, "Child killed by lightning on playground swing" is tragic, but not tragedy in this sense. It could only be true tragedy if it was inevitable that the poor kid would get zapped. Tragedy is what befalls *Hamlet*, *Macbeth*, and *Romeo and Juliet*. When Hamlet ruminates "To be or not to be," we are in the midst of tragedy. Numerous not-to-be's are sure to follow. The feud between the Montagues and the Capulets is going to destroy Romeo and Juliet. We don't know how exactly, but destroy them it will. The [spoiler alert!] sleeping potion ruse is pure Shakespeare, but if Old Will hadn't given us lovers-die-together-in-tomb he would have given us something equally satisfying. Romeo and Juliet were screwed from the get-go. And when the Great Birnam Wood marches on Dunsinane

Hill? This is more than merely tragic for poor old Macbeth: it's pure tragedy. Macbeth was doomed from the first *damnèd spot* to the last tomorrow, and tomorrow, and tomorrow . . .

The tragedy of the commons describes the unfolding of environmental tragedy as a result of the everyday selfishness of humans, and its painfulness comes not only from the destruction wrought and the suffering caused but also from its inexorability. What's more, the tragedy of the commons is not caused by unwitting, irrational fools; it is caused but by intelligent people making rational choices. Wrong choices, for sure, and selfish ones, but choices made in the clear light of day.

The scenario invoked by Garrett Hardin is a grazing commons—a sheep pasture—shared by multiple herders. The pasture starts to become damaged by overgrazing. What to do? The obvious solution is for everyone to reduce their flock in order to bring the impacts of grazing back under control, but the herders' dilemma presents them with the following decision tree:

1. If I add another sheep to the pasture, the profits from that sheep will all be mine.
2. It seems unlikely that one more sheep would do much damage to the pasture.
3. If my extra sheep does damage the pasture, I won't be the only one who has to deal with it. The cost will be shared by everyone.
4. If my neighbors add sheep and I don't, I'll be left out.

The tragedy of the commons is caused not by thoughtlessness but instead by thought-out (and yet selfish) decision-making. Each herder weighs the above calculation and decides to add the sheep to the pasture. When many herders make the same decision, the flock increases further, the degradation worsens, and the tragedy deepens, and as it deepens and despite the fact that the degradation of the pasture is worsening, the calculation remains the same. Indeed, the tragedy may soon seem locked in. To remove sheep from the degraded pasture once each herder's situation has become dire is even more risky. In Hardin's words, "Ruin is the destination toward which all men rush each pursuing their best interest in a society that believes in the freedom of the commons. Freedom in a commons brings ruin to all."[21]

The second thing to understand about the tragedy of the commons is that it is not caused by people who fail to consider their neighbors. Indeed, a central mental calculation is this: "If my neighbors add sheep and I don't, I'll be left out." Consideration of neighbors is not discounted; it is central. Concern about neighbors' suffering might alleviate the tragedy, but concern about neighbors' excesses will exacerbate it.

The tragedy of the commons does not unfold by people being either irrational or ignorant; it unfolds by people making economic and psychological calculations, by making choices. We choose to prioritize clear, short-term, selfish gains over unclear, long-term, communal ones—and we choose to do this again and again and again. Like I said, perhaps our species is not as evolved as we think we are.

The tragedy of the commons provides an excellent baseline for understanding a number of gnarly social conundrums. It is in effect the basic challenge of civilization. How can people organize themselves into societies that will cause selfish individuals to cohere in altruistic groups? How to mitigate the tragedy of the commons is an important instrument for thinking about how societies fail or succeed: a blunt instrument, for sure, but one that can't be ignored. *The wise keep their part of the deal but don't insist on all their rights. It is virtue to attend to your own obligations. It is not virtue to insist others do the same"* (v. 79).

Enter Elinor Ostrom, the Indiana University professor and Nobel Laureate in Economics whose hopeful and gentle counters to Hardin's apocalyptic and bombastic tragedy of the commons catalyzed one of the most important intellectual wars you may never have heard of. Ostrom showed us that communities *can* manage common pool resources. Indeed, given time and left to their own devices, they usually will.

Ostrom studied a wide range of different commons systems from Bangladeshi fisheries to Philippine irrigation systems and West African forests and found that successful commons management systems have their own peculiarities involving unique combinations of rules, regulations, moralities, and taboos. Although there are some overarching themes, each is unique to its place.

Trust is required among stakeholders, of which there may be many. Reciprocity is required. If local communities are to be mobilized in a regional conservation effort, for example, they must gain something more tangible from their participation than just vague gratitude for serving some abstract "greater good." Frameworks of organization are required, through which all stakeholders can buy in and play their part. There must be punishments, broadly accepted, working through trusted systems of justice, and those punishments must be enforced. The thing Ostrom stressed the most was the need to keep local communities at the center of decision-making.

There is no one-size-fits-all solution to the tragedy of the commons. Indeed, an important premise of Ostrom's approach was that overly simple prescriptions would always be flawed. From this, the informal Ostrom's law emerged: "Whatever works in practice can work in theory."

So, with sufficiently comprehensive systems in place, a commons can be effectively, rationally, and altruistically managed—but we knew that all along. This close linkage of a community to its environment is very difficult to design, but it has repeatedly emerged in cultures long associated with a place. Cultures living fully within their environment seem to eventually learn how to live in balance with it. There will be failures and realignments, disasters and recoveries, but cultures can coevolve and be sustained in place. It may take a very long time, however, for colonizers to be naturalized.

The irony of all this is that the truth was there to be seen in the very system Hardin invoked. The medieval grazing commons that he used as his model persisted for centuries and were maintained by complex arrangements such as those described by Elinor Ostrom. People didn't run amuck; they organized. And this brings us full circle to the original complaint about the tragedy of the commons. The eventual collapse of the medieval grazing commons did not come from overgrazing and degradation—not from the so-called tragedy of the commons at all—but from the enclosure movement and industrialization. The biggest threat to the commons is not the commoners but rather encroachment from outside: from colonizers.

Ostromistas and Hardinites don't get along, and part of the reason is that they envisage different actors in different systems. Much of Ostrom's work investigated the management of common pool resources in the homelands of Indigenous and peasant communities. Those invoking her work argue for the community-based protection of resources in well-defined areas. Hardin, in contrast, tends to be invoked when more unwieldy systems are at stake: huge common pool resources such as global oil reserves, deep ocean fisheries in international waters, and greenhouse gas emissions into our shared atmosphere. The irony, then, is that it's not commoners who perpetrate the tragedy of the commons; it is colonizers and corporations. Commoners are not the problem. Commoners are the solution and have been all along.

So, as Raj Patel explains in *The Value of Nothing*,[22] the view that humans sharing common pool resources will robotically cheat each other because it's the "rational" thing to do is simply false. He compares this notion to the concept of *Homo economicus*, "rational-economic human," that has been advanced be free market economists. People can be predictable consumers, but we're not as predictable as economists would like to think.

Corporations are thoughtless and selfish, so Mitt Romney was partially correct when he snapped at a voter during the 2012 US presidential campaign and said that "corporations *are* people, my friend!" Corporations are *Homo economicus*. They are economically rational drivers of environmental tragedy.

The tragedy of the commons gives us another peek into the animating mythology of global capitalism. If we fear the foolish and backward commoners, we are much more likely to cede control to the capitalists. The tragedy of the commons also illustrates a group cooperation problem stripped down to its simplest form. Will you free ride on the back of others? Will you add sheep or will you not? Larger, less personal, less trusting, and less cohesive communities—fake communities of businesses and bureaucracies—add the sheep and the pesticides, plastics, and petroleum and whatever can turn a profit. Smaller, more personal, more trusting, and more cohesive communities—true communities of people, especially peasant communities—can resist.

The tragedy of the commons should be renamed the tragedy of the colonizer or the tragedy of the corporation.

The tragedy of the commons gives us a fascinating insight into the problem of cooperation among large groups of humans. Cooperation can fail catastrophically or can succeed magnificently. The failures come from direct, rational, simplistic thinking, especially thinking imposed from the outside. The successes rely on complex thinking and the hard-won trust that has been built within cohesive communities.

THE MIDDLE PATH OF DEMOCRACY

> *The Way of heaven is like a stretched bow. Its higher tip is bent down. Its lower tip is bent up. It takes from what has too much and gives to what has too little. . . . The way of people is not so. It takes from those who already have little and gives to those who already have much.* (v. 77)
>
> *The people are hungry. Their leaders tax them too hard: that is why they are hungry. The people are unruly. Their leaders interfere with their lives: that is why the people are unruly.* (v. 75)

The country that supposes itself to be the paragon of democracy and pinnacle of human freedoms saw its government assailed by an angry mob on January 6, 2021. The mob called themselves patriots, defenders of democracy. After nearly 250 years of democracy, we watched in horror as a mob tried to overpower the US Capitol in the name of, er, patriotism, or democracy—or something. *When the country falls into chaos, the patriots present themselves* (v. 18).

There is a pervasive sense that all is not right with the world. I certainly have this sense. My analyses of climate change, peak oil, biodiversity loss, resource depletion, and human nature lead me to conclude that our societies are in peril at all levels, from local to global. Politics is pivotal because it would be really great if people could work together on big environmental and social challenges, but we are fracturing rather than coalescing. We share a sense of doom but see different demons lurking in different shadows. We have polarized into distrustful, competing political tribes, and our polarization threatens civic failure and social breakdown just when we need cooperation the most. Many of us have been clamoring for an overhaul of our systems of government and economics, a revolution of some kind, but the revolution that is arriving is not what we had all hoped for.

Fear is bringing out the worst in us as it so often has in the past, just like Yoda, George Lucas's little green Laozi, warns: "Fear is the path to the dark side. Fear leads to anger. Anger leads to hate. Hate leads to suffering."

Political disagreements have become increasingly angry and ineffectual. The debates over abortion and gun control in the United States are particularly instructive.

People agree on many aspects of these debates, but you wouldn't know it from listening to the loudest voices. Instead of negotiating policies that find some reasonable middle path, we argue extreme positions that inhibit the development of reasonable policy. Most people want to protect the health and welfare of mothers and newborns and reduce the number of unwanted pregnancies. Most people want to reduce the ravages of gun violence, especially mass shootings in schools, and are supportive of reasonable rights of gun ownership. But these reasonable arguments are drowned out by shouting from the fringes. We seem to be afraid of the middle path. Perhaps our gratitude that the middle path is close enough to our own position is bested by our bitterness that it seems too close to our opponents' position.

Most of what occupies the news and social media is peripheral to the danger confronting our democracies. The issues we are angriest about are smoke screens that obscure a power struggle. The biggest threat to democracy is the accumulation of wealth and power and the disenfranchisement of regular people: an imbalance between organized money and organized people. Democracy is weakened by attacks against democratic systems and institutions. *The palace is full of splendor while the fields are choked with weeds and the granaries are left bare. They dress in extravagant clothes sporting fine swords at their side, gorging on exotic food and drink, accumulating wealth in abundance. This boastfulness and vanity is robbery by people who have most certainly left the Path* (v. 53).

Democratic government recognizes that people are not perfect and that robust systems must be deployed to keep one group from overpowering others. History displays a sequence of stories of sovereigns, dictators, oligarchies, and military juntas who exploited and disenfranchised a populace and of the desperate, violent revolutions against them. *The more heavily the government arms itself the more the people will riot* (v. 57). Democracy promises to give a voice to different political ideas, create an arena in which they can be discussed, and then protect a system of electing preferred representatives. The process should create balance among different systems of government. Let people propose different means of government, says democracy, and then let them choose. The ideal outcome is a middle path between competing ideas, but ideas can morph into ideologies, and ideologies can be terrifying.

Alexandr Solzhenitsyn explains this in *The Gulag Archipelago*:

> MacBeth's self-justifications were feeble—and his conscience devoured him. Yes, even Iago was a little lamb, too. The imagination and spiritual strength of Shakespeare's evildoers stopped short at a dozen corpses. Because they had no *ideology*. Ideology—that is what gives evildoing its long sought justification and gives the evildoer the necessary steadfastness and determination. That is the social theory which helps to make his acts seem good instead of bad in his own and others' eyes.... That

> was how the agents of the Inquisition fortified their wills: by invoking Christianity; the conquerors of foreign lands, by extolling the grandeur of their Motherland; the colonizers, by civilization; the Nazis, by race; and the Jacobins . . . by equality, brotherhood, and the happiness of future generations. . . . Thanks to ideology, the twentieth century was fated to experience evildoing on a scale calculated in the millions.[23]

Ideology cuts a path through democracy toward a pathology of victory, control, and domination. Democracy requires that there only be temporary winners, never final ones. A democracy should limit political struggles and maintain constant negotiations to find ongoing compromises along a middle path. *Do good work and then step back. This is the Way of heaven* (v. 9).

Plato described democracy as "a charming form of government, full of variety and disorder, and dispensing a sort of equality to equals and unequals alike." Winston Churchill said, "Many forms of Government have been tried, and will be tried in this world of sin and woe. No one pretends that democracy is perfect or all-wise. Indeed, it has been said that democracy is the worst form of Government except for all those other forms that have been tried from time to time." Laozi says nothing about democracy, and it seems that the idea never crossed his mind, but he gives lots of advice on leadership. He advocates for responsible self-government at the village level but always sees a king at the regional and national level. Laozi challenges the king to be the best he can be and challenges the people to keep the king honest to the extent that they can:

> *When the humble leader has done her work the people will say, "Look! We did it all ourselves!"* (v. 17)
>
> *When government is restrained; unobtrusive, the people will be simple; genuine. When the government is severe; prying, the people will be needy; cunning. . . . Without guidance the upright revert to evil and confusion and anarchy reign.* (v. 58)
>
> *If the people weary of authority a great force will be unleashed. Don't constrict their lives. Don't limit their livelihoods. Don't show them contempt, and they will not weary of you.* (v. 72)

We are reminded of the antiquity of the concept of De, which was inscribed on the Oracle bones of the Neolithic Shang dynasty. De confers superior powers of virtue and divinity on kings, giving their position at the top of a hierarchy a legitimacy that is difficult—and dangerous—to challenge.

Laozi's views on leadership and government sound a little naive in light of our last few centuries' experiments with democracy. He gives us an idea of his utopian society in the penultimate verse of the *Daodejing*: *Imagine a small country with few citizens . . . well equipped with tools, but few of them are used . . . boats and carts, but they are seldom ridden . . . armor and weapons, but no need to display them. . . . They can grow old and die without feeling any need to explore*" (v. 80).

In representative democracy we have found an adaptive form of government with the potential to be versatile, fair, and capable of engaging large numbers of people in leadership. It can be nimble enough to act decisively and yet be responsive to change, and I think Laozi would be deeply impressed and would revise his thinking. And his reaction to the cavalier attitude with which we are currently treating a social system centuries in the making? I think he would be horrified to see us treat something so precious with such carelessness.

It took our species a very long time and great sacrifices to form democracies. Surely we can see how important they are, and surely we should be able to sustain them now that the hard work of establishing them is done. Now that the masses have wrested power from the clutches of the powerful few, shouldn't they be forever motivated to defend it?

It seems not—which is absolutely fascinating.

There are three pillars of democracy. The first pillar is a system of political decision-making, particularly a system of electing people to represent the masses. If the wealthy and powerful can subvert this system by disenfranchising voters or buying off representatives, they can expand their power. Many democracies suffer from systemic fraud. The US Congress is largely bought and paid for.

The second pillar is a fair system of law and order. A healthy democracy requires equal access to a fair system of laws. If the wealthy and powerful can capture this system and skew it in their favor, they can use the system to protect them for being accountable for their misdeeds. Compare the punishments for blue-collar and white-collar crimes. Why are the penalties for bank robbery so high while those for bank theft are so low? Why are our structures of justice so racist?

The final pillar is freedom of information, and this too has been captured. Too many people are ill-informed and subverted by biased media owned by the likes of the Murdochs. Social media in particular can capture people in reinforcing cycles of skewed information. People can't unite if they don't recognize the same problem. Dividing the masses into angry factions serves the needs of the wealthy and powerful all too well.

When democracy is under attack, we should know instinctively from whom. Democracy is most precious to the poor and powerless and most threatening to the wealthy and powerful. To find the villains, we need only follow the money and power, and when we do we will find billionaires who manipulate the system to protect their parasitic businesses. We will find media moguls who peddle power to control the flow of information and generate a flow of misinformation to gain power. We will find people riding revolving doors between government and industry: a stint here to develop financial policy, a stint there reaping the rewards of lax policy. We will find many of the world's worst polluters reaping profit from the commons and pouring pollution back into it. Most of all, we will find corporations.

Corporations exhibit all the cravings and desires of people but none of the restraint. Why do we afford them so much power? Corporations never seek the middle path; all they ever seek is more. They won't come back onto the middle path of their own volition. They must be regulated back onto it.

Here are some of the remarks Laozi makes about government. They are suffused with wisdom but have limited application to the business of building democracies:

Therefore the wise govern by emptying hearts and filling bellies, weakening ideology and strengthening bones. (v. 3)

Great leaders are barely known. Next are the leaders people admire. Next are the leaders people fear. Worst are the leaders people despise. (v. 17)

The palace is full of splendor while the fields are choked with weeds and the granaries are left bare. . . . This boastfulness is robbery by people who have most certainly left the Path. (v. 53)

Cultivate yourself to develop genuine virtue. Cultivate your family to foster a wealth of virtue. Cultivate the village to support enduring virtue. Cultivate the country to promote abundant virtue. (v. 54)

Be straightforward in ruling a nation[;] . . . the more prohibitions and laws are enacted the poorer the people become. The more heavily the government arms itself the more the people will riot. . . . The more calls are made for law and order the more robbers and bandits abound. So the wise say, Practice not-doing and the people will thrive independently. (v. 57)

In governing show moderation. . . . With abundant virtue everything can be overcome, anything can be achieved, and you are fit to rule. (v. 59)

Governing a big country is like cooking a small fish. Govern in accordance with the Dao and the evil spirits will be left asleep. (v. 60)

[I]t is deceitful to use trickery to govern. Governing without trickery is a great blessing. (v. 65)

The best leaders put themselves below the people. This is the virtue of noncontention, the source of power of strong leaders, in harmony with heaven's Way. (v. 68)

CAPITALIST REALISM

Fantasy and science fiction rarely use democracy in their world-building, preferring to conjure Sauron, Emperor Palpatine, President Snow, Shaddam IV, and Voldemort. It's simpler and cleaner. Here's your enemy: a cruel, greedy, and selfish human, humanlike, or near-human being. How do we fight this evil? Well, with courage, selflessness, and sacrifice.

But what do we do when there's no king to dethrone? Who do we challenge in a democracy? We have put our own leaders in place, and we can replace them, so what should we do if that doesn't change things?

My concern here is the effectiveness of democracy in a system of so-called free markets. In 1992 soon after the fall of the Berlin Wall, Francis Fukuyama declared "the end of history."[24] The Cold War was over, the Soviet Union had collapsed, and the reckless follies of its communist (so-called) economic system had been laid bare. The centralized Soviet economy couldn't compete with US and European capitalism because it generated less productivity and innovation. Communism and capitalism were claimed as the only two competing ideologies. Communism had suffered a crushing defeat and capitalism had emerged triumphant, so this was the end of history.

In truth, the dictatorships of the Cold War weren't remotely communist, and the centralized economies of the Soviet Union and China were never a challenge to the capitalist systems of the United States and Europe. Nonetheless, capitalism was anointed the uncontested champion of economic thought, and it was assumed that the marriage of democracy and capitalism would be blissful.

But all is not well. Capitalism, as currently configured, insists on growth in a finite world and is trashing the planet. A quote commonly attributed to Exxon executive turned environmentalist Øystein Dahle might have summed up our predicament best: "Socialism collapsed because it did not allow the market to tell the economic truth. Capitalism may fail because it does not allow the market to tell the environmental truth."[25] Capitalism also fails to tell the social truth. It can generate massive inequities between rich and poor—people and countries.

Capitalism is the system of economics employed by all the wealthy democracies of the modern world, and it's not working. What to do?

The first dimension of our dilemma is what Mark Fisher called "capitalist realism," in which he posits the reflection that "it's easier to imagine the end of the world than the end of capitalism."[26] I hear it all the time, especially in the United States. "Well, it might be a mess, but it's all we've got." "I know—but there's no alternative."

Maybe, but we shouldn't concede so easily. The first thing to recognize is that capitalism and democracy are not the same thing. This seems too obvious to need saying, but I think many people, especially Americans, conflate them. Democracy and capitalism have come together in the West because the Western democracies have all chosen some version of free market economics. (Americans have always chosen an aggressive form.) But a democratic system could choose a different economic system: socialism, perhaps, or even communism. Maybe we are too close to the system to be able to see it. Consider David Foster Wallace's two young fish:

> There are these two young fish swimming along and they happen to meet an older fish swimming the other way, who nods to them and says, "Morning boys, how's the water?"
>
> And the two young fish swim on for a bit, and then eventually one of them looks over at the other and goes, "What the hell is water?"
>
> This is a standard requirement of US commencement speeches, the deployment of didactic little parable-ish stories. The story thing turns out to be one of the better, less bullshitty conventions of the genre . . . but if you're worried that I plan to present myself as the wise old fish explaining what water is to you younger fish, please don't be.
>
> I am not the wise old fish.
>
> The immediate point of the fish story is merely that the most obvious, ubiquitous, important realities are often the ones that are hardest to see and talk about.[27]

A quick recap of capitalism reminds us that its modus operandi is to scoop up cheap nature and cheap lives and convert them into capital. There are a number of subsystems. Capitalist food systems scoop up cheap soil, water, fuel, and lives to make money. They can make food, of course, but the fact that generating money, not food, is the goal is evidenced by the fatty ground beef, chicken breasts, Pop-Tarts, and soda foisted upon us. Capitalist health care systems scoop up cheap care, food, education, and fuel to make money. They can deliver good health care, but they can also produce complicated, expensive, capital-intensive health systems that serve the rich extremely well but exclude the poor.

What drives a system of capitalism forward is its consumption of cheap nature and cheap lives. A capitalist system must always grow and consume, and it is rapacious.

A second significant feature of capitalism is that it emerged through colonization, which is a fancy word for invasion, murder, and theft.

Capitalism was the operating system of colonialism and the transatlantic slave trade, and plantation industries were the first organized systems of global capital. The countries that stole cheap nature and cheap lives from around the world in the long sixteenth century remain rich while those they impoverished remain poor. The rich now preside over a neocolonial system of global capitalism that continues to extract cheap nature and cheap lives from these same countries. Industrial capitalism is an optimization function. It optimizes the conversion of cheaps into capital, and it seems to be functioning optimally.

Those of us living in democracies enjoy a political system in which ordinary people have the power to design the economic system under which they will live their lives. So, when we look at our capitalist systems, which deliver short-term wealth, comfort, and social inequities and long-term environmental peril and ask "Is this the system we want?," the short answer must be "Yes, it is." An economic system that enriches the self above the other and leaves the other impoverished seems to be exactly what we want. A system that protects short-term comforts but causes long-term environmental destruction is what we have chosen. We have chosen this system and voted it into place. There is no dictator to overthrow but ourselves.

This leaves us in a bit of a pickle.

We must entertain the following flow of logic: Democracy is worth fighting for, and people should have the opportunity to determine their own destinies, but in the process of doing so people reveal inherent weaknesses in the capability of our species. We are unable to develop systems that promote sufficient altruism to other beings. Our species may lack the capacity to avert our modern crises.

When we peer into the animating mythology of the modern world, we see that capitalism is much more than just an economic idea: it's the ideology that won the Cold War; it's the ideology that many see as the source of our democracies, of our greatness, of our systems of law and order. Capitalism is not just an economic system. It's an ideology, a mythology. Why do we give capitalism the credit for all this rather than democracy? We tell ourselves stories of a fair system that maintains our greatness and offers it to everybody, but the story is riddled with holes. We need to unshackle ourselves from this mythology. We need to see through its lies and find new stories.

Are other stories possible? We know that many bad stories are possible, of course. History is littered with tyrants. Dictators and would-be dictators govern most people in the world today. Democracies can stall under the spell of people such as Turkey's Recep Tayyip Erdoğan and Hungary's Viktor Orban. They sputter and die like the Arab Spring. They can show growth, like Mikhail Gorbachev's Soviet Union, and then regress and descend into kleptocracy like Russia under Vladimir Putin. We are also acutely aware that the fate of the United States is uncertain with the return to power of Donald Tramp.

But yes, we also know that good stories are possible. The Scandinavian democracies have employed well-regulated capitalist economics coupled with far-reaching social services. And there are hints of other possibilities. Cuba's communist experiment showed signs of flourishing until the US embargo crushed its economy and Fidel Castro refused to yield power. Yugoslavia's communist experiment was also remarkable in its own way, charting a precarious path between the economic wisdoms of both the West and the Soviet Union for a while.

Many emerging former colonies, from Algeria to Zambia, tried different economic experiments and social systems but were obstructed by Western military or economic repression. Who knows what economic and political systems might have been possible had the capitalist West allowed it.

Further back in history, we consider the social and political systems that existed before 1492. There are myriad different ways of organizing a society. Why do we insist that the system we have is the only option? We'll find it hard to develop better societies until we can imagine that such a thing is possible.

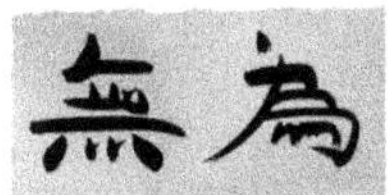

4

SHAPE THE PATH

It only takes the least scrap of sense to stay on the broad Path—but I fear wandering off. The broad Path is flat and straight—but people are fond of detours. (v. 53)

NOT ONLY DOES THE MODERN WORLD APPEAR TO BE IN CRISIS, BUT ALL our crises appear to be urgent. We must act *now*, we must restore our democracies *immediately*, and we must develop new renewable energy sources *within ten years*, and if we don't act before atmospheric carbon dioxide passes 350 ppm (spoiler alert: it did, in 1989) or mean surface temperature rises by more than 1.5°C (spoiler alert: we're hitting that number now),[1] all bets are off, we fail, everything collapses, and it's apocalypse now.

Maybe. Or maybe too much urgency is part of the problem. Maybe we need to slow down not only with the planet-trashing thing but also with the planet-saving thing. Maybe we need to settle in and shape the path. A quick fix may not be what we're looking for. *Movement overcomes cold. Stillness overcomes heat. Calmness keeps the world in order* (v. 45).

There is more than one path; indeed, there's a network of paths. The first path can't be improved by shaping: it is the Dao, writ large; nature; the cosmos; the ecology of everything. *The path that can be trodden is not the Eternal Path* (v. 1). We should relinquish control and shape ourselves to nature rather than shaping nature to our desires, and where environmental impacts are inevitable or necessary we should think of our role as integration with nature rather than control over it. Our guiding principle for living in the world should be to limit our impacts. We don't need flashy new technologies for sustainable growth. Growth has brought us to the edge. We need to step back. We need to slow down and do less.

The second path is that of our societies, which must be shaped by people cooperating. Healthy societies need constant tending. There is always something to be maintained or repaired, but what is rarely needed is urgent, drastic action followed by urgent, drastic reaction. The coming decades are going to be difficult enough no matter how well we cooperate, and if we refuse to cooperate, we may end up with horrific societies by century's end. Our societies do best when they have steady, unselfish hands on the tiller. *Tackle the difficult in its simplest form. Tackle big problems while they are small* (v. 63). *Act before problems develop. Govern well before disorder emerges* (v. 64).

The third path is our inner path: the path of our minds. Shaping our minds to promote kinder, calmer neural networks and to tamp down reactive thoughts and aggressive behaviors can make us happier and kinder. The foundation of psychological well-being is to accept things as they are and to shape the path gently with patience, compassion, and equanimity. Only when we have attained a calm and thoughtful mind should we attempt to shape any kind of society. Only *the person who tends to their self can be trusted to lead people and care for the world* (v.13).

NONVIOLENT RESISTANCE

> *So here is a simple rule: The violent die violent deaths.* (v. 42)
> *Advance without advancing, reach out without striking, confront without attacking, hold your ground without weapons.* (v. 69)

Mohandas K. "Mahatma" Gandhi organized mass acts of nonviolent resistance against the British in India in 1930 known as the Salt Marches, or Salt *Satyagraha*. Nonviolent resistance has deep origins in India. Ahimsa, a key tenet of Hinduism and Buddhism, means nonviolence, and satyagraha, also Sanskrit, is derived from *satya*, meaning truth or love, and *agraha*, meaning force or insistence. Being kind and peaceful does not mean you can't be persistent and assertive. And nonviolence does not mean accepting victimhood.

Gandhi's announcement that he was mobilizing Indians to protest salt taxes was initially viewed by the British with derision, an example of yang tyrants underestimating the yin forces that were about to be arrayed against them. Salt taxes seemed insignificant to the British, being such a tiny source of income, but the taxes were a hardship to the poorest Indians and symbolic. Meanwhile, salt could be harvested for free from extensive marshlands on the Gujarat coast. Gandhi and his fellow marchers would simply walk to the sea and harvest its salt. The British were brought face-to-face with an act of defiance that openly challenged their control, and they did what tyrants do when insulted: they tried to bully their way out of trouble. But their bullying didn't demonstrate their strength; it revealed their vulnerability.

A particularly dramatic event occurred at the Dandi salt factory. Thousands of protesters marched on the factory to confront the British police and were beaten with sticks. But they kept marching. Protester after protestor approached the gates to the factory and was beaten. And the protesters kept coming. Eventually the protest was repelled, and perhaps the British could claim to have won the day by repelling it, but the protesters won in every other way.

The salt marches gave the lie to the British pontification that the "poor, backward" Indians were better off and perhaps even happy to be ruled by the "enlightened" British. And the salt marches showed Indians the source of their power. Tens of thousands dressed in traditional white khaddar flowed as a "river of white" and brought the British face-to-face with the truth of their brutality. The Indians were nonviolent but resisted, and the British were brutish and bested.

Gandhi's Salt Satyagraha has inspired many people since, notably Martin Luther King Jr. and Nelson Mandela. King visited India in 1959 and went to see the place where Gandhi had stood firm against the British and then returned to the United States to use nonviolent resistance in the American civil rights movement. What King learned was that nonviolent resistance forces oppressors to see their own violence and confronts them with their own tyranny. "Hatred never ceases by hatred," said the Buddha, but nonviolent resistance implies not hatred but rather calculated strategy and tactics. "Get in good trouble; necessary trouble, and redeem the soul of America," said John Lewis.[2]

I visited Tibet in 2010 and 2011 and found a police state. Almost nowhere in the city of Lhasa was beyond the net of CCTV. Even the tour buses had CCTV cameras. The monasteries had them. The police and the military were everywhere, and they carried fire extinguishers following a spate of self-immolations by monks protesting the police state that has existed since the 1959 Chinese invasion. The Dalai Lama, Tenzin Gyatso, at the time a young man, fled over the Himalayas in 1959 and set up a government-in-exile in Dharmsala, India. He is now in his eighties and is a Nobel Peace Prize winner, and he remains the undoubted spiritual leader of Tibet.

Tenzin Gyatso has spent decades navigating the narrow paths between peace and conflict and compassion and resistance. He is a true master, and we are compelled to believe that his mastery of speech and behavior comes from the mastery of his emotions and his mind. He has maintained a clear and firm stance of opposition against an overwhelmingly powerful oppressor, but he has done so with compassion and equanimity. He is a master of nonviolent resistance. He often speaks with great kindness of the Chinese people, whom he sees as cousins to the Tibetans, and he shows compassion for their plight even in the face of his own plight. As the Tibetan people suffer from the cruelties of an aggressive Chinese regime, he recognizes that the Chinese people suffer from the same regime. Here is an excerpt from an interview with Ann Curry in 2008:

TENZIN GYATSO: I appeal with my whole hopeful hand to the millions of Han brothers, sisters.... [R]espect you, admire you.... [W]e feel sympathy with them.

ANN CURRY: You have sympathy for China?

TENZIN GYATSO: We pray together. No differences. Same human beings.

Vaclav Havel taught us an important lesson in nonviolent resistance with his famous samizdat, *The Power of the Powerless*,[3] published in 1973 during the Soviet occupation of his native Czechoslovakia. When faced with the specter of Nazism, fascism, or any dictatorial regime, we can learn from Havel's greengrocer. "The manager of a fruit-and-vegetable shop places in his window, among the onions and carrots, the slogan: 'Workers of the World Unite.' Why does he do it?" And thus begins the central metaphor of *The Power of the Powerless*. There are many possible motivations, explains Havel, but the greengrocer does it because "these things must be done if one is to get along in life." The problem, however, is that by playing his part in this tragedy of the commons, the greengrocer is "living inside a lie." Havel continues. "Ideology... is one of the pillars of the system's external stability. This pillar, however, is built on a very unstable foundation. It is built on lies. It works only as long as people are willing to live within the lie.... Let us now imagine that one day something in our greengrocer snaps and he stops putting up the slogans" and "begins living within the truth."

The truth is dangerous for the greengrocer. Speaking truth to power is always dangerous, and the greengrocer is likely to be persecuted, but when enough people resist the lie and start living in the truth, the oppressive regime is doomed. Before they can gain a full political reconstruction, societies need some degree of moral reconstruction.

The eloquence of Havel's ideas in *The Power of the Powerless* is witnessed by the way he led Czechoslovakia through the nonviolent Velvet Revolution and then the peaceful Velvet Divorce of the Czech Republic (Chechia) and Slovakia. The full meaning of *The Power of the Powerless* is diluted, however, if we think of it only as an anti-Soviet pamphlet. It actually calls on all cultures to consider the ways in which they live inside a lie. *The Power of the Powerless* does not suggest that the end of the Cold War was a victory for the truth of capitalism over the lies of communism. Capitalism, too, is rife with lies.

A rising tide of wealth floats all boats?

The free market is free and open to all?

It's perfectly reasonable that the colonizers should dictate the rules of global trade?

The system policed by the rich protects the wealth of the poor?

The lives of the poor are more valuable than the property of the rich?

International treaties protect the environment from whom, exactly?

Nonviolent resistance is an expression of equanimous minds. It is possible to follow only with a thoughtful and persistent eye for the Middle Path. Seeking truth takes courage and requires being honest with yourself and speaking truth to power.

The character Adam Ewing (masterfully portrayed by Jim Sturgess in the movie adaptation) closes David Mitchell's panoramic novel *Cloud Atlas* with a lovely scene. Ewing, a junior lawyer, has been out on the high seas suffering at the hands of an arsenic-wielding Dr. Goose, (played by Tom Hanks, no less), among other depredations, representing his father-in-law's slave trading business. The trials of Adam's journey have enlightened him to the horrors of slavery. He quits his position and burns the documents from his travels in the fireplace in front of his father-in-law.

> I hear my father-in-law's response. . . . "You'll be spat on, shot at, lynched, pacified with medals, spurned by backwoodsmen! Crucified! Naive, dreaming Adam. He who would do battle with the many-headed hydra of human nature must pay a world of pain & his family must pay it along with him! & only as you gasp your dying breath shall you understand, your life amounted to no more than one drop in a limitless ocean!"[4]
>
> Yet what is any ocean but a multitude of drops?

So, rapacious capitalism, the many-headed hydra that grinds down cheap lives and cheap nature and crushes them together to create capital, must be resisted.

Don't comply.

Be difficult.

Refuse to participate.

Practice nonviolent resistance.

Practice passive resistance.

Don't be Sisyphus, pushing some stupid rock forever up some stupid hill because that's what's expected of you. Step aside. Let the rock fall.

Be August Landmesser in that famous photo from 1936, arms conspicuously folded amid a seething crowd, the only person refusing to offer the Nazi salute to Adolf Hitler.

Heed what civil rights leader and clergyman William Sloane Coffin suggested: "At the edge of the abyss, the only progressive step you can take is backward."[5]

Or, when you reach the edge of the abyss, turn around and see what new paths can be shaped.

BUILD RESILIENCE

The term "sustainability" has been greatly abused in recent decades. Any Tesco, Dick's, or Harrod's can claim a sustainability agenda. Organic lettuce, recycled plastic bags, and LED lights are an indicator of sustainability. Driving a Tesla is a surefire badge of sustainability.[6] We use the word to mean "slightly less shitty than a possible alternative." The bigger problem is that not everything should be sustained. Sustaining biodiversity and an unpolluted environment is desirable, yes, but sustaining this modern economy? No. We tend to think that we could sustain both the environment and the economy by substituting less sustainable products for more sustainable ones, but we can't. Electric cars are not going to sustain biodiversity, and wind turbines aren't going to save the world's coral reefs.

A new buzzword has emerged in recent years, and I'm rather drawn to it: *degrowth*. I like the degrowth crowd because they recognize the great peril we are in and have been brave enough to refuse the usual sustainability platitudes. They know that the environment will never be protected as long as our first priority is economic growth. They recognize that economic growth can no longer be accepted as an inevitable and necessary goal.

The degrowth movement seeks ways to slow down economic growth without causing social ruptures. I admire the people of the movement and hope they're right and I'm wrong, but I see no such path. I don't think it's in our natures to slow down voluntarily. Growth may well be coming to an end, but precious few of those with power and privilege will accept it gladly, and fewer still will embrace it. We need to slow down and do less, but you need to know that if you do you will be in a precarious minority.

Our modern crises are going to wreak havoc. Climate change will devastate critical infrastructure. Resources will be stretched and depleted. Lots of things will stop working. Much social chaos is likely. Wars will break out in unexpected places. The focus for maintaining coherent societies through the coming decades should be on building resilience.

Resilience is sometimes conflated with sustainability but is not the same thing at all. Resilience accepts that change is an essential part of truly sustainable systems and is necessary if they are to flex and move. Rather than having the goal of sustaining its structure and function despite shocks, resilience has the goal of accepting damage but recovering. If sustainability has the strength of brick, resilience has the strength of rubber. It's the ability to bounce back from shocks. It's also the ability to adapt to change—to bounce back different, if different is required.

A system built for resilience should consider what kind of shocks it is likely to face. If the shocks are known, it might have a specific feature than can absorb them. We freely adapt to seasonal change in a way that resembles resilience adaptation. Knowing that crops will not grow in the winter, we store food. Periodic shocks are harder to manage, but we are familiar with many of these. Knowing that tornadoes are common in the central plains, those who can afford them have tornado shelters in their houses even though the probability of a tornado hitting them is relatively low. Unexpected shocks cause us more trouble. Pandemics continue to catch us unawares, but many governments have ramped up their pandemic response systems since COVID-19. We don't know what pandemic-threatening organism will come next or when or where, and we accept that we can't stop it from happening. Therefore, we need good systems in place so we can respond nimbly.

The most difficult future shocks to prepare for are those we can't predict. The coming collision of environmental, economic, and civic crises will spawn many challenges to our systems, and we can't predict what they will all be or when they will strike. A generalized crisis requires a generalized response, so how do we build general resilience into our systems? What are the principles we should follow?

On a recent trip to Ireland, I visited the Famine Museum in Skibbereen in County Cork. I already knew a good deal about the Irish Potato Famine (so-called),[7] but there was one story that struck me particularly hard on this occasion.

I asked the tour guide why fishing had not been more of a feature of the famine period. Ireland is surrounded by abundant oceans and has many inlets and estuaries and rivers and lakes. Why hadn't the Irish been able to stave off starvation with fishing?

"They sold their boats," she said.

"They did what?"

Assuming, or hoping, that their problems would be temporary, Irish fishermen, struggling for cash, sold or pawned their boats and nets. As the famine dragged on and the shorelines were stripped of seaweed, moss, clams, and anything else edible and as people collapsed and died across the landscape on seashores and lakeshores, abundant fish swam nearby. A fishing industry might have saved many lives, but *they had sold their boats.*

Rather than building resilience into systems and maintaining them in good condition, we are tempted to strip our systems down for parts when trouble encroaches.

The Irish Potato Famine offers a classic history lesson in shocks. Things went very wrong in Ireland over a short time frame. A million people died and a million more migrated over a period of only about seven years, from 1845 to 1852.

So, what "caused" the Irish Potato Famine? Well, potatoes, you'd think, and people most often blame a potato disease, late blight of potato, *Phytophthora infestans*, that swept across the country blighting potato crops and rotting stored potatoes. That seems logical enough: the Irish eat potatoes, the potatoes become blighted, and the Irish starved. Peel off the flimsy scab of that simplistic story, however, and a system lurks beneath. While late blight was the proximate cause of the famine, the deeper cause was the selfishness and cruelty of the British Empire.

When we think of the British Empire, we tend to think of its global reach, particularly its domination of India, its insane Opium Wars with China, its colonization of large swaths of East Africa, and its invasion of North America. What we tend to forget is that Britain's first colonial expansion was into Ireland.

Ireland was Britain's first imperial "possession," and it was in Ireland that the British first practiced the capitalist art of taking cheap nature and cheap people and grinding them down for profit. The British took the best land, from which they exported food. The Irish became wage workers on British estates and were pushed onto smallholdings on the worst land.

Late blight arrived in an Ireland already on the brink. Since Irish peasants farming tiny rocky plots could only subsist on potatoes, that was the vast majority of what they grew. The disease was devastating to smallholder peasants, and the British could have saved them, but the British continued to export tons of pork and other commodities throughout the famine. Why did they let the Irish starve? Well, for the same reasons we let a billion people starve today. . .

. . . But what about those fishing boats? What could be more important than food in a famine? Well, cash, I suppose, and I suppose it depends on who's buying, who's selling, and who's starving.

The sacred cow is a strange thing. I visited India on a work trip a dozen or so years ago with my friend Guri Johal, and I was struck by the cows. You'll find emaciated cows scavenging for trash in the middle of a city. It's very off-putting. A cow will putter out into the road, amble between the cars, bring a motorcyclist to a screeching stop, and then wander off. There are millions of stray cattle roaming India.

The taboo against hurting or killing cows is an integral part of the Hindu religion and is deeply embedded in the Indian culture. You don't mess with the cows? Why? You just don't.[8] What is also in-your-face obvious in India is the relative lack of meat in the diet and the malnutrition of the poor. Not even the starving poor will kill a sacred cow.

Marvin Harris examines sacred cows in his fascinating book *Cows, Pigs, Wars, and Witches.*[9] His hypothesis boils down to the idea that making cows sacred is a resiliency strategy. It may have become an anachronism in the modern Indian city, but "never kill your cows" made perfect sense over the long term and for centuries in rural India, argues Harris. The strategy doesn't seem to make sense every year. It's not always a problem to eat your cows, but the full value of cows is not obvious in the good years. It only becomes clear when times are tough.

Cows are the source of milk, which is the source of yogurt. Cows are also the source of oxen, which are essential to the planting of next year's crop. When you reach a point so desperate that you are willing to eat your cows, you're in deep trouble. Your situation has passed beyond precarious, and you have eroded your capability to recover from shocks. So, make this a rule: never eat your cows. Now embed that rule into religion. Into culture: make it a taboo. Make the cow sacred.

> Never eat your cows.
> Never sell your boats and nets.

Joseph Campbell reminds us to pay attention to myths and legends. They transmit neither truth nor fact down through history untrammeled, but they do offer insight:

> Mythologies and their deities are productions and projections of the psyche.... What gods have there ever been that were not from man's imagination?... Essentially the same mythological motifs are to be found throughout the world. There are myths and legends of the virgin birth, of incarnations, death, and resurrections, second comings, judgements, and the rest, in all the great traditions. And, since such images stem from the psyche, they refer to the psyche. They tell us of its structure, its order, and its forces, in symbolic terms.[10]

I come from North England, where we have one of the coolest features of a natural-looking human-modified landscape in the world: the dry stone wall. One of my favorite places, to which I keep returning and hope I always will, is Great Langdale in the Lake District. Stop on a curve on the road just west of Chapel Stile and take in the view.[11] The road wends its way down into a quilt of emerald and lime green pastures and disappears among oak and beech copses and hawthorn hedgerows. Raise your eyes slowly, and the quilt of greens merges into a patchwork of squares and rectangles of olive, umber, ocher, and auburn. Raise your eyes yet farther, toward the walls of the valley, and the patchwork of squares and rectangles dissembles into gray, mossy walls of scree, crag, and peak.

Now, head down into the valley, grab a pint at either the Old Dungeon Ghyll pub or the New Dungeon Ghyll pub or both, and then head up into the fells. You'll soon come across a dry stone wall; there are miles and miles of these walls. Take a good look at the wall. It's solid. It's a great big thick pile of interlocking stones. No mortar (hence "dry" stone), just largish, smallish, roundish, and flattish stones cleverly interlocked so that they will hold together in a sturdy wall.

As you climb the mountain and look back at the valley, you'll understand two things about the dry stone walls. First, this is what gives the landscape its quilted and patchwork appearance. Each square and rectangle is surrounded by a wall.

Second, you'll notice that the grays of the dry stone walls are the same as the grays of the crags and screes. Millions of stones have been moved to make these walls, and most of them have been moved by hand, a feat that staggers the imagination at first, but then you understand that most of the stones have been gathered from nearby and have been gathered one by one over long generations. People are a part of nature here and have been for a very long time. There was no sudden mad effort of wall building but rather a slow and constant tending of the landscape that began in the Neolithic and continues to this day.

As an aside, the dry stone wall is the key piece of infrastructure that shapes this landscape, and it does so in essentially the same way that barbed-wire fences converted the Great Plains from bison habitat to cornfield and feedlot, but while the barbed-wire fence feels wrong, this feels right.

As another aside, why choose a dry stone wall rather than a hedgerow? The fertile pastures in the bottom of the valley are often delimited with hedgerows rather than dry stone walls. The answer is simple: it makes sense to work with what the landscape has to offer. While dry stone walls emerged from a landscape scattered with rocks that needed to be cleared out of the fields anyway, living hedgerows of hawthorn, beech, or blackthorn emerged naturally from the rich soil, which was deep and lacked rocks.

Many pastures are enclosed not by hedgerows or dry stone walls these days, of course, but instead by wood,[12] metal, or concrete fences and walls. These emerged from a landscape of different cheaps, and I'll place a bet with you. Come the end of the long emergency,[13] the much older hedgerows and dry stone walls will still stand, and the newer concrete barricades will have collapsed.

Elinor Ostrom, the Nobel Prize–winning sociologist who challenged Garret Hardin's "Tragedy of the Commons" (see Chapter 3 in this volume), conducted a fabulous study of irrigation systems in Nepal.[14] There appeared to be a problem with the Nepalese peasant farmers. They kept cutting irrigation channels to bring water to their mountainside plots, and the rains kept damaging them. The farmers were forever clambering into the hills to repair their irrigation channels, poor bastards. Surely something could be done. Well-meaning nongovernmental organizations blundered in and built good, solid, concrete irrigation channels. Problem solved. The water flowed, the crops were irrigated, and all was well. The peasants could occupy themselves with other things.

Until the concrete channels failed. And when they failed they failed big, and the social systems through which the older, simpler channels had been maintained had been lost. The peasants who had cooperated in long-standing traditions of shared work on these community projects were now off in the city working in bike shops and bakeries. The irrigation channels remained unfixed, the erosion worsened, and peasant irrigation systems that had been effective for generations were destroyed by experts. They had been made more robust but less resilient.

Off to another place, strikingly different and yet oddly similar: the Longji Rice Terraces of Guangxi Province, China. Entire mountainsides have been sculpted with thousands of narrow, fertile ride paddy strips.[15] This place is incredible, or at least it was when I was last there, in 2017. I hope it has continued to thrive.

People moved into the mountains of Guangxi seven centuries ago to escape conflict in the flatlands, and they set up shop in the Longji Valley. Lacking flatland for rice cultivation, they cut terraces into the mountainside above the village. The village grew, generation by generation, and as more terraces were cut, generation by generation, rice cultivation climbed the mountain.

Soils are being degraded and eroded on farmland all around the world, and soil loss is such a pervasive problem that we've come to think of it as almost automatic. We tend to start losing soil as soon as we begin to cultivate the land. Consider the Fertile Crescent that is no longer so fertile, the collapse of the Mayan Empire, and the Fall of Rome.[16] And yet the Longji terraces have persisted for centuries. And what's more, they have persisted on steep mountain slopes in an area of thin soils and despite frequent abundant rains. How can this be?

The key to understanding why Longji is special is to acknowledge that people are a force of nature and that communities of people can be diverse ecological features. People can destroy the environment, but they can also shape and protect it.

The critical feature of Longji that has supported rice terraces for centuries is the continuity of its community. An unbroken line of dozens of generations of people has tended to these terraces. The terraces are built on steep mountain slopes where it does rain, and they are vulnerable to erosion. They do erode. They erode every year. But the people who tend them are equal to the task. The terraces constantly erode, and the farmers constantly repair them. The terraces aren't in the slightest bit robust, but the system that maintains them is deeply resilient. Eroded soil carried down the mountains by running water is carried back up the mountains by people. When the soil of a terrace is damaged, it is repaired with soil. The mountain is in constant flux, its soil constantly moving, its shape a constant negotiation with gravity.[17]

There is great hope in places such as Longji. The Altes Land in Northwest Germany has supported productive agriculture on fertile land for centuries. Chateau Vollrads has been producing wine from the same vineyards for over eight hundred years. Sustainable and resilient landscapes are possible.

SLOW DOWN, DO LESS

I've started telling people at work the truth about how busy I am or am not. Honestly, my job as a professor of horticulture is not that hard. I am required to prepare classes, teach, and then assess my students' level of adequacy. The job gets easier with time, and I've been doing it a long time. Meanwhile, I avoid as many of the pointless make-work chores of the workplace as possible because, well, most of them are pointless. So, I'll pass a colleague in the hallway and get a long list of their overdue grant proposals and papers and all the other things that are running them ragged, and when they ask how I'm doing I'll say, "Yeah, good. Not too busy." It's strange how strange that sounds, and it doesn't always go over well. It's almost an affront to tell a coworker you're not stressed and overworked. What the hell are you doing with your time, Steve? Well, for one third of it I'm doing my really easy job; for the second third I'm reading, writing, or fiddling around with hobbies, taking a nap, cooking, and eating; and for the final third I'm asleep.

Economists insist that we need more: more consumption if we want more jobs, more productivity, and more growth. But we know that the environment needs us to produce less of just about everything and that we need to slow down. But the idea that we would solve a problem by slowing down and doing less runs counter to our natures. We are fixers. Problems are solved by doing more, innovating, and working harder. If we want to do less, we will first reach for some innovative new efficiency or some new-fangled do-less-ing machine. The idea of actually doing less seems so hard.

The British economist E. F. Schumacher tackled this in his 1973 masterpiece *Small Is Beautiful*,[18] in which a particularly wonderful chapter titled "Buddhist Economics" was inspired by his travels in Burma. Buddhist economics seeks an economic Middle Way between economic asceticism (stagnation; suppressed innovation, mundanity) and economic hedonism (greed, selfish accumulation, wide wealth gaps). Its principles are to consider people as interdependent with each other and with nature. Its methods require a populace whose desires and cravings are attenuated. For an economic group to be sustainable, argues Schumacher, each individual must be reasonably of a mind to cooperate and share.

One of the reasons we find it hard to share is that we care deeply about our status in the world and spend a lot of mental energy worrying about it. Gaining status is one of our most fervent desires. Losing it is one of our greatest fears. *Be equally wary of honor and disgrace. Honor can demoralize. We are apprehensive about gaining it. We fear the disgrace of losing it.* (v. 13). Will Storr explains three genres of status game in his book *The Status Game: On Human Life and How to Play It*.[19]

The first type of status is *dominance* and is basically a pecking order based on violence or the threat of violence—encompassing social violence such as ostracism and canceling. This status game is generally not subtle and is never progressive. *The wise do not hoard, but by serving others receive more, and by giving to others gain more. . . . The way of the wise is to serve without competing* (v. 81).

The second type of status is *success*. In this case, social status is gained by those seen to be competent. Being good at your job and recognized for it is generally a good thing, but success-related status seeking can get a little strange when coworkers vie to be promoted. The competition to be promoted from associate regional vice president to senior regional associate vice president can be as intense as it is ridiculous. Success can mutate into status symbols such as expensive houses, flashy cars, and ostentatious jewelry. The status game of success, taken too far, becomes sociopathy and can encourage rapacious consumption:

> *Diminishing celebrity limits striving. Moderating wealth limits theft. Restraining desire limits yearning.* (v. 3)
>
> *Hoard wealth and your home will be a target for thieves. Amass prestige and you invite downfall and disgrace. Do good work and step back. This is the way of heaven.* (v. 9)
>
> *So the wise act without laying claim and accomplish without claiming credit. They do not flaunt their worth.* (v. 77)

The third status game is *virtue*, and here's where we get into some seriously messed-up mind games. The status gained by virtuous behavior is generally a good thing, but while status can be gained by good deeds and acts of kindness, selflessness, and bravery, it can also be gained by fakery. It's more important to your status to be seen to be virtuous than to actually be virtuous, which can lead to all manner of Machiavellian antics:

> *True virtue is higher than virtue: unassuming, and therefore virtuous. Fake virtue is simply for display and therefore not virtuous at all.* (v. 38)
>
> *It is virtue to attend to you own obligations. It is not virtue to insist other do the same.* (v. 79)

Adherence to religious doctrine can be a play in a virtue game. To demonstrate that you will go along with the irrational dogmas of your religion is to give a nod to your faith community. The more illogical the belief, the stronger the virtue play. I'll submit Joseph Smith's golden tablets as my first exhibit.

One amusing subset of status games is fashion. People go to great lengths to dress in ways that signal their status. The medallioned uniforms of generals are obvious dominance plays, and the tailored suits and silk ties of the C-suite mob are obvious success (and dominance) plays, but dreadlocks, Doc Martens, or tattoos are status symbols of their own. Fashion can be a statement of individuality but is more often a declaration of status. I'm richer, more powerful, or more punk than you.

Status games are no joke. Playing them well is good for your health, and playing them poorly can cause great stress. Feeling secure as a member of communities promotes mental health. Feeling insecure is deadly. Humans will go to great lengths to fit in with their communities. Again, Joseph Smith's golden tablets. "We are today as we've always been: tribal," says Will Storr. "We have instincts that compel us to seek connection with coalitions of others. . . . [W]e strive to achieve their approval and acclaim."[20]

So, we find ourselves yet again to be not quite as evolved as we had thought. I'm suggesting that you slow down and do less, but be warned: this may require you to sacrifice status, and you need to be pretty secure in your own skin to do that.

We have discussed *wuwei* a few times, particularly in relation to relinquishing control of nature. *Wuwei* is translated as not-doing, inaction, or not forcing. It advises us to leave things alone, to no tamper with things, to trust the course of nature, to be comfortable with uncertainty, and to relinquish the desire to control:

> *The softest things in the world override the hardest. The formless infiltrate the impenetrable. Thus we understand the influence of doing without doing; teaching without telling.* (v. 43)
>
> *Do without doing. Act without acting. . . . Tackle the difficult in its simplest form. Tackle big problems while they are small.* (v. 63)

Wuwei is the ultimate iteration of slow down, do less.

Robin Wall Kimmerer's *Braiding Sweetgrass* is a masterpiece of *wuwei*.[21] What a lovely book. It meanders gently at all levels: its sentences, paragraphs, and chapters and its concepts and themes. It explains little and yet teaches much. It tells relatively little but shows a different way of being. Each chapter builds toward a beautiful coherent picture that comes slowly into focus as we work our way through the book. Much sweetgrass is braided, among it the yangs of modern scientific knowledge with the yins of Indigenous knowing.

A favorite chapter is *The Honorable Harvest*, in which Kimmerer shows us how to ask nature what it's okay to take and what should be left untouched. The example she uses is a patch of plants in the forest. She pauses and asks whether or not it is okay to take some. Nature might say "no," she explains, whereupon you should obey. As a general guideline, take some but leave more behind. What you harvest should be honorable. Harvesting a renewable resource need not cause any damage; it simply has to be done in a way that allows the resource to renew. A broader vision of the honorable harvest might be to consider the concept of the ethnosphere,[22] which reminds us that human technologies, cultures, thoughts, and ideas—dreams even—are part the biosphere. *The space between heaven and earth is a bellows. Empty and yet inexhaustible. The more it is pumped the more it produces* (v. 5).

Cultural guidelines such as habitual adherence to an honorable harvest appear to have been a common feature of Indigenous societies. Kat Anderson explains how the Wintus of California, when collecting tubers with a digging stick, would collect the large tubers but simultaneously replant the smaller ones.[23] Similarly, the Miwoks knew that the rhizomes of riverbank sedges should be harvested from the same patch only every three or four years to allow time for regrowth, while the growth of bunching deergrass was encouraged by harvesting, so an entire patch might be pruned back whenever a harvest was made.

The basis of *wuwei* is to slow down and do less, but *wuwei* also invokes effortless action: that state of beautiful unconscious or semiconscious brilliance we call flow. Flow is when a pianist rips out a Beethoven sonata. There's no way a human brain can actually calculate all the correct placements of fingers on keys. The pianist has to train the brain and the hands—and then trust them to find their own way across the keys. The way Daniel Barenboim detonates those double fistfuls of rapid chord triplets at the end of the first movement of Beethoven's Appassionata? Unthinkable.

A skilled, well-practiced tennis player finds herself "in the zone," and every shot is suddenly easy. Each first serve goes in, every dropshot sneaks just over the net and dies, and each passing shot goes right down the line. But beginning to think, letting the conscious mind interfere and disrupt the flow, she starts to miss.

Entire teams catch and lose flow. Five skaters on a hockey team, with five independent minds, can experience flow together and give the impression of being linked as one. They have the momentum. They pass faster, intuit each other's moves, skate more freely, and score! Then they start thinking. They lose their flow, and the momentum switches to the other team. Suddenly, the team who couldn't string two decent passes together is ransacking their goal. Practice, practice, practice, yes, because practice makes permanent, but the time for too much thinking ends when the game begins. Stop trying to control things: just play:

> *A skilled tracker leaves no trace. A skilled speaker leaves no doubt. A skilled bookkeeper needs no gadgets.* (v. 27)
>
> *Those who act cause harm. Those who snatch fumble.* (v. 64)

Slowing down and doing less doesn't necessarily result in achieving less. Indeed, it may result in achieving more. But I am not proposing "slow down, do less" as a productivity hack. The most important gains are relaxation, saved resources, and higher quality of output.

QUALITY AND BEAUTY

It feels at times like our culture is engaged in some kind of efficiency-fueled race to the bottom. Big box stores such as Walmart and fast-food restaurants such as McDonald's were corporate America's dubious gift to the late twentieth century, and now we have Amazon. Let's hope we have reached the nadir of this soul-sucking homogenization of culture. In 2005, Thomas Friedman claimed that "the world is flat."[24] He meant economically flat, leveled through globalization, but I think it's going flat like a stale soda. The world is less beautiful. My monstrous HD TV can show me the Great Barrier Reef in luminous color, for sure, but the real thing is fading into monochrome. We can watch the Amazon Basin burn on Amazon Prime.

Think of the angst endured, the pain suffered, and the drudgery borne to produce our food. We grow vast monocultures of corn and soybeans on tens of millions of acres to feed hundreds of millions of animals that we "finish" in vast, stinking feedlots and slaughter on an industrial scale. We mine, ship, synthesize, and spread ton upon ton of fertilizer and spray gallon upon gallon of pesticides to enact this miracle. We support the agricultural industry with billions of dollars of subsidies; a network of public and private researchers, economists, marketers; and a massive education system. We exploit millions of farmworkers, many of them so desperate for work that they will cross a rattlesnake- and vigilante-infested border to be overworked and underpaid on farms with lax safety protections because it's the least bad of their awful options. We have destroyed millions of acres of habitat to do this. We pollute the waterways of North America to do this. We have created a vast dead zone in the Gulf of Mexico to do this. And for what?

For a hamburger.

And for epidemics of obesity and type 2 diabetes.

Consider this: there was just as much biomass of buffalo on the vast, beautiful, diverse prairies than there is of cattle produced off the same land now plowed and planted with corn and beans. So, this entire war against nature waged in the name of productivity (and what claim other than productivity could possibly be made?) has caused productivity to decline. Nature produced more by doing nothing.

The cornfield and the feedlot are natural extensions of the efficiency solution. We allow ourselves to be convinced that we need more and that it's acceptable to make sacrifices to produce more, and so quality and beauty fall to the sacrificial knife. Efficiency speeds things up. Quality and beauty slow things down. Who wins from this race to the bottom? Neither those who farm nor those who eat. We are living within the greengrocer's lie.

Robert Pirsig speaks often of quality in his glorious book *Zen and the Art of Motorcycle Maintenance*, and he capitalizes the word: Quality is the center of his metaphysics.

> The city closes in on him now, and in his strange perspective it becomes the antithesis of what he believes. The citadel not of Quality, the citadel of form and substance . . . in the form of steel sheets and girders, concrete piers and roads, . . . of asphalt, of auto parts, old radios, and rails, dead carcasses of animals that once grazed the prairies. Form and substance without Quality. That is the soul of this place. Blind, huge, sinister and inhuman: . . . into the neon of BEER and PIZZA and LAUNDROMAT signs and unknown and meaningless signs along meaningless straight streets going off into other straight streets forever. If it was all bricks and concrete, pure forms of substance, clearly and openly, he might survive. It is the little, pathetic attempts at Quality that kill.[25]

Pirsig presents us with Quality in a way that resembles the Dao. Like the Dao, Quality is hard to define, but we all sense its presence and recognize its absence. It is art or motion, or motorcycle maintenance, produced with beauty, enhanced by a state of *wuwei*. It is the great sculpture carved from the block, and it is the uncarved block. Or as Aldo Leopold said, "A thing is right when it tends to preserve the integrity, stability, and beauty of the biotic community. It is wrong when it tends otherwise."[26]

BE LIKE WATER

> *The highest good is like water. Water benefits everything without fuss. It settles in the lowest places. This is how it shows us the Path.* (v. 8)

The *Daodejing* loves to point us in the direction of nature, and if it has a single overarching message it might be "Let nature be your guide." A fancy modern word for this is "biomimicry." Velcro was an early example, inspired by the burrs of common burdock, but much more interesting than things that mimic nature, however, would be systems that could mimic the ways of nature. In our search for sustainable systems, what better guide than ecosystems?

Sustainable systems are bounded by natural constraints. They receive a constant supply of energy, recycle all their component parts, and are adaptive. They evolve. They bend and shift with the changing world. They *are* the changing world. Identify any form in nature and it will disappear unless you can observe it for long enough, in which case you'll see it morph into something else.

Try to catch hold of water and you will drown, try to pull yourself up through water and you will sink, and yet stay still and you will float. And you can swim through water, of course, an activity best achieved by moving with rather than struggling against.

If we want to adopt *wuwei* to recalibrate our relationships with each other and with nature and if we want to refrain from victories and dominance and settle, seek beauty, and shape a quiet path between yin and yang, what better guide could we have than water? Water simply flows downhill without guile or judgment, follows the most natural path, and shapes and reshapes the path as it flows. It shifts from trickle to torrent. It goes where it must go, and as it goes it makes streams, rivers, and valleys. None of these things are water; they are all made by water. The water simply flows through, and its flowing through, molecule after molecule, forms a waterfall here, a rapids there, or a whirlpool, each of them a process, a flow. Water has no control over where it will flow, what shapes it will create, or what process it will form. *The seas and rivers are the kings of the hundred valleys and ravines. They rule by lying below. Water flows down to them giving the valley shape* (v. 66).

THE PATH HAS NO BEGINNING AND NO END

All this striving. Gah. All those goals and targets. All those things we must get done. Always working toward some final achievement. I will be happy when . . . When what? The world will be saved when . . . When what? The United Nations Sustainable Development Goals are a case in point. Seventeen targets to achieve a sustainable world by 2030. Everything will be good when we, #1, "End poverty in all its forms, everywhere"; #6, "Ensure availability and sustainable management of water and sanitation for all"; #13, "Take urgent action to combat climate change and its impacts"; and #16, "Promote peaceful and inclusive societies [and] . . . justice for all." Part of the implication in most calls for action, whether they be political protest, climate action, or social justice activism, is that the action concerned will help bring about the end of some problem or other: end hunger, rid us of corruption, end poverty. And once the problem is ended, all will be well. The reason for these urgent action, immediate action, and act now movements is, I think, that it's too dispiriting to imagine that the problem can never actually be fully solved. If you can't win the game, that means that the game never ends, and that means that you will be playing the damned game forever.

This seems bad at first, but settling in to play the game forever is exactly the right approach. There is no end point, the destination is not final, and the journey is all there is. There's no point in trying to reach the destination or change it; the thing to be working on is the path itself. We don't live at the destination; we live on the path. The obvious thing to do, then, is to shape the path.

James Carse encapsulated this idea beautifully in his book *Finite and Infinite Games: A Vision of Life as Play and Possibility*, which is presented in 101 short lessons, including the following:

> #1 A finite game is played for the purpose of winning, an infinite game for the purpose of continuing the play.
>
> #2 If a finite game is to be won by someone it must come to a definitive end. It will come to an end when someone has won.
>
> #100 Infinite players are not serious actors in any story, but the joyful poets of a story that continues to originate what they cannot finish.[27]

Laozi, of course, has been begging for us to see the Path this way:

The path that can be trodden is not the Eternal Path. (v. 1)

Face it and you see no beginning. Follow it and you see no end. (v. 14)

The Path maintains eternal nonaction and yet leaves nothing undone. (v. 37)

5

THE WAYS OF THE MIND

The wise love themselves without vanity; know themselves without arrogance. (v. 72)

JUST AS THE UNTENDED BODY WILL WEAKEN AND SOFTEN, SO WILL THE untended mind. We (well, they) go to enormous lengths to train the body with physical exercise, to build this or that muscle, to increase cardiac capacity, to improve endurance or speed, but we train the brain in only a few very specific ways. The brain is the most remarkable, intricate, vulnerable, and trainable part of our bodies, so it seems a shame that we don't give it the attention it deserves. We know that the brain can be trained because we do train it extensively in schools and colleges with knowledge, but there is so much more on offer.

Everything we sense, calculate, say, or do is processed by the brain. Everything we experience is experienced by the brain. Everything we think is thought by the brain. The brain is our interface with the world. It's also our interface with imaginary worlds. As Shakespeare said, "Nothing is either good or bad but thinking makes it so."[1] The whole of our lives happens in our brains.

Let's think of humans as having three brains.[2] The first brain is the mesencephalon, crudely the brain stem, even more crudely the "reptilian brain." It is old, skilled, and deeply evolved, and we only become conscious of its work when it causes us to do something against our will, such as vomit, jump in fear from a snake (or a coiled rope), or become sexually aroused.

The second brain is the diencephalon, crudely the limbic system, even more crudely, the "mammalian brain." It is more recently evolved, nestled around the mesencephalon, and enables subtler analyses of the environment and more nuanced responses. The mammalian brain is particularly skilled at handling memories and emotions.

The third brain is the telencephalon, crudely, the cortex, even more crudely, the "human brain." The cortex is the most recently evolved part of the brain. It grows out over and around the top of the diencephalon and brings abstraction, analysis, and higher-order cognition to the party. We tend to think of this third brain as *the* brain: "the brains of the operation." It feels like the seat of consciousness and feels like it houses the "self."

Different areas of the brain specialize in different functions. The cortex, for example, has two hemispheres, and each hemisphere has four lobes. The occipital lobes specialize in vision; the temporal lobes specialize in speech, music, and short-term memory; the parietal lobes specialize in pain and touch, spatial orientation, and contribute to the analysis of speech; and the frontal lobes specialize in personality, decision-making, much of the olfactory system, and speech. The frontal lobes are headlined by the prefrontal cortex, which is further subdivided into areas that include the dorsolateral prefrontal cortex and the ventromedial prefrontal cortex, which have a strikingly yin-yang, us-them, mood-balancing relationship to each other. The specialization is partial, however, because different parts of the brain collaborate in networks.

Perhaps the most fascinating aspect of the brain is its plasticity. It creates memories, performs calculations, and learns by changing its structure, particularly its networks of neuronal connections. People can change their minds—change their brains—which can increase their knowledge, analytical ability, behaviors, and even their personalities.

You can get a sense of the plasticity of the brain by taking a test, doing something that uses the brain, and then retaking the test. Work hard to learn something—a new language, say French—and you can see obvious measurable changes in the brain. You can go from *Bawnjoor* to *Je t'aime* in no time. You can also boost your math or chemistry or memorize poems. We're familiar with these forms of brain training, which influence conscious brain activities, but the type of brain training that influences unconscious brain activities is less widely understood. Well, of course it is. You can't be conscious of how you've changed the unconscious brain even when you've changed it.

The plasticity of our brains beyond cognition is harder to assess, but an indication can be given with a different kind of test. The tests are limited, but they can give some valuable insights. The CliftonStrengths assessment will categorize your work styles: Are you a strategist, a learner, or a team builder? The commonly used (and probably most flawed) Myers-Briggs Type Indicator will indicate which of sixteen personality types you most resemble by testing your tendency toward introversion versus extraversion, intuition versus sensing, feeling versus thinking, and judging versus perceiving. The Intercultural Development Index will assess your competency in intercultural settings along a continuum from denial of cultural differences through polarization, minimization, and acceptance, to a full adaptation to cultural differences. The Harvard Implicit Bias tests use response speeds to analyze your innate biases to various dimensions of human difference. Do you have an implicit (innate/unconscious) bias against men versus women, Black people versus white people, old people versus young people? You probably do. (I do.)

These tests are far from perfect and can only give a pinhole vision of the workings of your mind, but they are useful. Any insight into the workings of your mind is valuable. With suitable brain training, you can change your scores on these tests but within limits. You can improve substantially in some areas, only a little in some, and not at all in others.

Yes, you can train your brain, but your overall personality type will likely remain rather stable. You can become less racist and more accepting, and you can train yourself to be less anxious or more assertive. Even the subtlest rewiring of your brain can have significant effects on your relationships (to others but also to your "self") and your orientation with the world. Laozi speaks often about brain training, notably the mitigation of desires and cravings:

> *The greatest mistake is desire. . . . The greatest curse is craving.* (v. 46)
> *With desire managed all is quiet. The world settles into peace.* (v. 37)

The ancients had no knowledge of neuroscience as we understand it, and yet their philosophy was centered on brain training over two millennia ago. How can that be? It is striking how closely the modern neuroscience wisdom "neurons that fire together wire together," coined by Donald Hebb,[3] echoes one of the earliest wisdoms of the Buddhist canon: "Whatever a person frequently thinks and reflects on becomes the pattern of their mind." What the Buddha understood millennia ago and prescribed practical methods to exploit now has a neuroscientific mechanism. Modern science has learned enormous amounts about how the brain works, and what we have learned confirms the utility of many of the propositions and prescriptions of ancient China and India.

We shouldn't be surprised. The machinations of the mind have always been a source of suffering and fascination. The ancients had neither scientific tools nor published research to build on, and yet they came up with some astonishing insights into the functioning of the mind and effective methods for its training.

Absent any knowledge of brain biology or even how the spongy blob in the cranium is linked into itself and the rest of the body, the ancients challenged ideas of mind and body, thought and emotion, self and no-self. They may not have had fancy laboratories, but they did have minds of their own as research tools to use and observe. What that means, of course, is that we can, each of us, run their experiments whenever we want and test their findings.

THE ELEPHANT AND THE RIDER

Having previously discussed the brain as having three parts—reptilian, mammalian, and human—I'm now going to confuse things by talking about the mind as having two parts. All these three-brain and two-brain metaphors are crude, of course. The brain is an integrated network of electrical impulses and chemical signals, but forgive me, I find this particular model the most useful.[+]

Jonathan Haidt offers the elephant and the rider as his metaphor for the divided mind. The ancients used similar conceptualizations. The Buddha compared the mind to a wild elephant. Plato compared the mind to a charioteer trying to control a chariot pulled by one tame horse and one wild horse. Zen Buddhism uses the image of the ox. A fascinating series of ten paintings from the fifteenth century by Tensho Shubun illustrates the stages of enlightenment through the finding, taming, and freeing of an ox. (It is probably no coincidence that Laozi is said to have left China and headed off into the West on an ox.) Centuries later, Sigmund Freud would develop the idea of the id, the ego, and the superego. The mind is not a simple place, and it doesn't manifest as a singular place.

The elephant, broadly speaking, represents the older parts of the brain responsible for memory, emotional "control," and a range of automatic behaviors; crudely, it's the limbic system: the "mammalian brain" and parts of the "reptilian brain" from earlier in the chapter. The elephant is old and well tested by evolution, effective and reliable, and set in its ways: the elephant is certain and stubborn.

The rider (again, only in the broadest terms) represents the shiny new brain, the neocortex—the "human brain" from the beginning of the chapter—evolved in the last few million years. The rider is responsible for analytical and abstract thought, is less well tested by evolution, and is more likely to be a bit glitchy.

So, the elephant and the rider travel together. Where one goes, the other must go too. The rider appears to be "the brains" of the operation, but there are actually two brains operating here, and the elephant has the bigger, better-functioning, and more reliable one. If the rider and the elephant want to go in different directions, they are more likely to end up where the elephant chooses. The rider has limited control over the elephant, and how much control the rider has depends on how well she can train the elephant.

Let's say we want to travel a path that may conceal tigers. The rider is more able to plan a tiger-free route, but the elephant is more likely to smell any tiger that appears. Both skills are valuable.

We don't know our minds very well, but we do have some knowledge and awareness of the rider. We know how to teach her, for example: we give books to the rider and send her to school so she can learn to analyze math problems. (We'd be better off if we taught her less math and more ecology, in my humble opinion, but let's let that go for now.) A formal and informal education provides the rider with maps she can use to chart a path. The rider is the easy part.

The elephant is the difficult part because we're seldom conscious of him, and yet as our default setting, he is in charge. This doesn't seem right. Surely the smart rider should be in control of the dumb, automatic, subhuman elephant, right? But that's not how it is, and we shouldn't expect it to be. The elephant is old, deeply evolved, and tested. The rider is young and a naive work in progress. The rider evolved to serve the elephant, who was already in place serving his selfish genes.

One of the roles of the elephant is to handle our autopilot systems. Did you ever head out to the grocery store and find yourself in the parking lot at work? The elephant took you there. (Notice, by the way, that "he" didn't crash the car even though "you" were off in Lalaland.) The tennis player who practices a shot until it becomes automatic will nail it more and more often. Training develops unconscious skill and delegates tasks to parts of the brain that operate beneath our attention. Developing these advanced skills might give the expert a sense of "flow," or "being in the zone," when the body performs beyond its capability to calculate: the concert pianist whose brain seems to be wired directly into the piano, the tennis player who smashes the instinctive volley down the line at full stretch. It's not even clear to them how they're doing what they're doing—and, in a sense, "they" aren't, if by "them" we mean the rider, or the self.

I find the elephant and rider metaphor a clear and concise way of thinking about and conceptualizing the mind and recognizing the link between cognition and emotion, body and mind. Understanding minds is one of the most important things we can do to face our modern crises. It can help us to find ways to build cooperative, supportive communities and find stability, strength, and peace through the storm. We can move minds, and we must. We can inoculate minds against reactiveness and greed. We can support minds to act bravely and wisely. Much work is to be done through the ways of the mind.

So, in learning to navigate a path, our best bet is to teach the rider and train the elephant. What we're most interested in training, however, is not the elephant's sense of direction but rather his memories and emotions. Our best bet is to try to *motivate* the elephant. As Anil Seth, professor of neuroscience at the University of Sussex put it, "We are not cognitive computers, we are feeling machines."[5]

The work of training elephants is not easy. Like most difficult jobs, it requires serious planning and intention, but we are in the happy situation of having more than two millennia of useful advice, or as Jonathan Haidt said, "[The] Buddha made a psychological discovery that he and his followers embedded into a philosophy and a religion. They have been generous with it, teaching it to people of all faiths and no faith. The discovery is that meditation tames and calms the elephant."[6]

MEDITATION AND MINDFULNESS

Can you focus your vital breath until you are as supple as a newborn? Can you polish your inner mirror until its reflection is pure? (v. 10)

Perhaps it will come as a revelation to hear that meditation can shape the brain. Shape the brain? Wow, that's amazing. I should try that! But everything shapes the brain. Learning a language shapes the brain, as does playing the violin. Golf shapes the brain. Making breakfast shapes the brain. The question isn't whether to shape the brain or not but instead is how, how much, and into what shape. The brain will be shaped by our behaviors, emotions, and actions whether we take an active role in the shaping or not. Better to have it molded into shape than bent out of shape.

Different people understand the terms "meditation" and "mindfulness" quite differently. They are unfamiliar terms in some cultures, or recent and trendy, and commonplace in others, with deep cultural roots. Where mindfulness and meditation have heritage, they are practiced in different ways by diverse traditions. Meditation tends to refer to focused practices performed in a controlled, usually quiet, setting. Mindfulness tends to refer to meditation-like techniques used during everyday life. If you're sitting cross-legged, silent and still, on a lotus flower–inscribed zafu cushion in your backyard tea house, you're probably meditating—or intending to meditate. If you're aware of the smell of detergent and warm steam rising from the dishwasher while you're removing squeaky-clean, bright-white plates, you're being mindful.

There are many forms of meditation, but the practice has just a few basic ideas. The simplest form of meditation is to settle somewhere and be still. This is meditation in the Daoist tradition, and nothing much else is required. A quiet room or outdoor space is best. Simply go there, sit comfortably, settle, and be still. This practice is sometimes called mindfulness meditation. Simply observe the contents of your mind. Don't worry about trying to achieve anything. Do this for a while, and you'll begin to notice that your mind does have certain contents, and you'll likely want some more specific ideas about what to do with them.

Many techniques have been suggested, but a few are particularly interesting because they match up well with the findings of modern neuroscience. *Vipassana* meditation is powerful and simple. The requirement is simply to observe the mind and notice different types of thought. Notice little drifty thoughts, do nothing more than notice them—"Huh, cool: little drifty thoughts"—but noticing ugly or domineering *trains of thought*, learn to drop them. This is most easily achieved by bringing one's thoughts to a mental anchor, ideally a bodily sensation—most commonly, the breath.

Depending on your individual set point or current state of agitation or stress, trains of thought may come thick and fast when you first settle down to meditate. An example:

You have been passed over for a promotion. Your mind heads off investigating all the different ways you are going to reprimand your boss, dynamite the Human Resources office, and wrestle Karl, the sniveling cur who was promoted ahead of you, to death in a pit of rattlesnakes. Or your partner has—again!—again, I tell you!—not done the damn dishes. Your mind spins out into some fantasyland picturing all the things you do around the house and how wonderful you are and remembering all the times your partner—again and again!—didn't do the damn dishes. Just notice these trains of thought and bring your mind back to the observation of your breathing or other anchor, and the trains of thought will drop out. That's all. Then do it again. And then do it again.

Dropping thoughts and returning to the breath trains the brain. You'll remember the phrases of the Buddha, "Whatever a person frequently thinks and reflects on becomes the pattern of their mind," and Donald Hebb, "Neurons that fire together wire together."[7] That's what we're doing here. Spend a little time every day or two to train the brain. Research suggests that frequent practice is effective even if brief. It's a bit like trampling a rough track through the woods. It will remain trampled if you walk it often enough and will become clearer the more it is walked. Practice doesn't make perfect: practice makes permanent.

The beauty of *Vipassana* is that you can always get the sense of doing something useful. If the trains of thought just keep coming and coming you might think you're making no progress, but more trains means more practice, so you're doing lots of productive work, and if the trains of thought are few, well, then, you're already kinda Zen. Enjoy!

Returning from trains of thought into a bodily anchor appears to be particularly powerful because it links the "human" brain into the "mammalian" and "reptilian" brains, which means it's linking the cognition-focused parts of the brain into the emotion-focused parts of the brain. It's teaching the brain to calmly douse smoldering trains of thought rather than heating the emotions up into a forest fire.

There are a number of simple additions. One is to label your thoughts as they arise as negative and positive. When a positive thought arises, identify it and hang with it. Give it a little smile. When a negative thought arises, identify and ditch it. Another similar approach is to leave your awareness open, wandering from observation to observation, mood to mood, and thought to thought, as the mind chooses. Only return to your anchor when the crazy trains come, and then wander off again, watching the mind do its thing. Through time, you'll start to witness a few things about how the mind works. After a little practice, try looking for yourself—your *self*, right?— while this is all going on. You won't find it, of course, because it doesn't exist, but noticing this for yourself might eventually give you the feeling of no-self to go with the intellectual recognition. We'll get back to that.

So, mindfulness and meditation can give you a more honest appraisal of the condition of your mind, which can lead toward a reprogramming of sorts, a deprogramming from some of the mental and emotional baggage that can make life angsty, and an overall attitude adjustment. As a result, mindfulness and meditation can improve focus, assist in anger management, reduce greed and craving, and help you become calmer, more patient, and more equanimous. It can, as Laozi promises in the first verse of the *Daodejing*, also become the gateway to a spiritual awakening.

A lovely form of meditation, *Metta*, has the express purpose of developing compassion. This is the form of meditation that seems most similar to prayer, in the Abrahamic traditions. Create specific foci of meditation, perhaps three people: someone you love or admire, someone you dislike or who frustrates you, and someone for whom you have neither positive nor negative feelings or barely know. The meditation is to direct positive, loving, compassionate thoughts toward visualizations of each of these people. Again, the theory is that neurons will eventually wire together, and you will develop the habit of compassion. Be angry, and you become angrier. Be kind, and you become kinder and happier. Be patient, and you become more persistent. Be compassionate, and you become calmer. Do these things intentionally and focus on them, and you shape your brain toward a configuration that makes it more natural for you to be more compassionate, patient, and persistent.

To engage in meditation is usually called to *practice* meditation, and this is a useful term. It should be taken in the sense that we practice something like a sport or a musical instrument to improve, but it should also be taken in the sense of practicing medicine, or high ethical standards, as something you do as a part of how you live. To practice meditation is to be attentive to how one's thoughts, feelings, and actions shape the mind.

There are many practical reasons to meditate. It's generally good for your mental health, and since mind and body are linked, it's also good for your physical health. The health benefits are found in many areas, including parts of the body that seem rather unconnected to the mind. Meditation has been shown to improve cardiovascular function. But why would we expect the heart and mind to be disconnected? We say that sadness gives us "heartache" and can even "break our hearts." In Chinese, the character *xin* is interpreted as mind, heart, or heart-mind.

The neuroscience of meditation is relatively new but has generated a flood of findings. The technique that has taught us the most about how meditation affects the brain is functional magnetic resonance imaging, or fMRI,[8] which detects the flow of oxygen in the brain indicating increased activity. Meditation can affect activity, connectivity, and even the size of certain parts of the brain, notably the anterior cingulate cortex and amygdala.[9] This knowledge has significant clinical applications, and the support for using meditation in clinical settings is growing. There is a range of therapies explicitly using mindfulness and meditation, including integrative body-mind training, mindfulness-based cognitive therapy, and mindfulness-based stress reduction. The guru of this field is Jon Kabat-Zinn.[10]

Meditation can't transform you into a happy, calm, kind, compassionate Tenzin Gyatso overnight. That level of expertise takes long hours of practice and isn't for everyone, but even the biggest asshole can benefit from being a bit less of an asshole, and anyone can benefit by taking the edge off their arrogance, anger, or anxiety.

Mindfulness is sometimes considered to be the same thing as meditation and sometimes considered to be something quite separate. I think of mindfulness as meditation on the go. Formal meditation may be more focused, but what happens "off the cushion" is much more varied because real life presents the mind with more varied and more quickly changing experiences. You can look more closely at the mind in quiet solitude, but there is more to look at as you move through the world. Mindfulness is the practice of paying attention to whatever is going on and how the mind is responding to it. I think of mind-full-ness as the opposite of mind-less-ness, or distractedness. It also has the potential to help you understand and accept your emotional responses to what is going on around you in a more patient way, operating as a sort of *wuwei* for the mind and helping to act on things calmly rather than reacting to them irrationally.

Alan Watts uses the analogy of floodlights and spotlights to contrast different ways of opening or directing the mind.[11] An observing mind can allow for an open awareness of the external world or the mind and (some of) its contents. The image is of a floodlight that illuminates a wide visual field. A concentrating mind can focus on a specific observation, calculation, or thought. It will tend to illuminate a very small mental field and leave the rest unobserved, like a spotlight. The ability to recognize when one is spotlighting or floodlighting and the ability to toggle between them at will (rather than being unmindfully dragged under spotlights) is valuable in meditation, mindfulness, and everyday life—three things that are, of course, the same thing.

I finally learned to love long-haul flights when I had to travel from the US Midwest to East Africa a few times for work. The journey from West Lafayette, Indiana, to Eldoret, Kenya, involves a three-hour drive to Chicago O'Hare; a nine-hour flight to Frankfurt, Germany; a long layover; another nine-hour flight to Nairobi; another layover at Jomo Kenyatta International Airport; and a short-hop flight or long drive to Eldoret. It takes a day and a night and plonks you down eight time zones away. This journey is many people's idea of hell, but I enjoy it. I use trips such as this as opportunities for quiet time to read, write, meditate, and practice mindfulness.

Most people seem to do almost anything they can to distract themselves from what's going on when they fly—to make themselves mind-less. Me, I am absorbed. I study the airport, watch the people, and look out of the plane window onto a great moving map of the world. Why would you want to distract yourself from this? It's truly incredible to look out on top—*on top!*—of the clouds and to see the curve of Earth. It's so clearly a sphere bumbling through space, and the colors of the sky can be remarkable. Why on earth—above Earth at 500 mph and thirty-five thousand feet in a recliner!—would you want to distract yourself by watching some crap movie? Watching the movie is mindlessness. Watching the world and your mind in it is to be mindful.

There's a lovely little scene in David Lean's *Lawrence of Arabia* in which the enigmatic T. E. Lawrence, played by the equally enigmatic Peter O'Toole, extinguishes a match with his fingers. One of his colleagues, the rather less than enigmatic minor character William Potter, tries to copy Lawrence's "trick" and burns his fingers:

POTTER: "Ooh, it damn well hurts!"
LAWRENCE: "Certainly, it hurts."
POTTER: "Well, what's the trick, then?"
LAWRENCE: "The trick, Mr. William Potter, is not minding that it hurts."

This is by no means a definitive encapsulation of mindfulness, but it is an amusing illustration. Mindfulness is primarily concerned with paying close attention.

One of the practical benefits of mindfulness that is particularly valuable to me is sneeze control. I have a very nasty allergy to something—I can't pin down exactly what, certain kinds of dust I think—that sends me into paroxysms of sneezing. It has happened since I was a kid. Once triggered I sneeze hard dozens of times, turn red, and sweat like I'm in the sauna. I learned to control these fits with mindfulness. When a sneezing fit starts, I close my eyes and pay attention. I observe the nose tickles, manage my breathing, focus, quiet down, turn inward, and shut the sneezes off. It takes all my focus, but it feels pretty cool to be able to shut down an automatic physiological response with mind control.

Meditation and mindfulness are neither pervasive magic nor simple trickery. They can achieve mental transformations that appear magical, such as reducing outbursts of anger, and they can perform neat tricks, such as controlling sneezing fits, but whatever changes they bring come from small and subtle changes to the brain. What's fascinating is that they can act on the unconscious mind and help find more beneficial mind states. The practice is simple, more or less effortless, the changes at a physiological level are minuscule, and the benefits are mostly subtle, but the practice improves your brain by training parts of it to which you have no direct, conscious access and can significantly improve your life.

Meditation and mindfulness influence the way your neurons wire together in networks and can promote ease of mind and a more compassionate outlook. They also give you a much better chance of achieving various kinds of insight and enlightenment.

MANAGE YOUR MONKEY-MIND

To know yourself is to be enlightened. . . . To master yourself takes strength. (v. 33)

So much mental busyness. So much stress, or self-doubt, or self-loathing, or imaginings of things as they could have been, your future greatness, perhaps. What should have been, might be, chattering in your mind: who has wronged you, why such a thing is unfair, not your fault, chatter, chatter, chatter, what you'll do if she does this or that, or when you graduate or get that promotion, oh boy, he'd better not do that or you'll, you'll . . . you'll what? Stop! Stop with this chatter-chatter monkey-mind.

The mind can do beautiful things—create gorgeous images, give and receive love—but it can also create suffering. Most of our suffering is indeed caused by our own minds, and one of the best visualizations of this is the concept of the second dart, attributed to the Buddha.[12]

You are struck by a dart. It might be an actual dart or other pointy thing, or it might be pain from falling off your bike, crashing your car, or it could be a sharp word, an insult, an abusive sneer, or it could be a disappointment, failing an exam, or missing out on a promotion. The first dart is largely out of your control. It strikes. First darts happen. They cause suffering, sometimes mild, sometimes severe. They are part of life, and many of them can't be avoided. What happens next, however, can be avoided. How will you respond to this first dart? If you respond with magnanimity and equanimity, your suffering will end when the first pain passes, but we often respond to first darts by throwing a second dart at ourselves.

The second dart is our own monkey-mind reliving the pain of the first dart, blaming whoever threw it, feeling wronged for being targeted, judging ourselves, wallowing, and on and on. Second darts can reproduce themselves, creating entire cascades of mental suffering. These sufferings and disappointments are a large part of what the Buddha called *dukkha*, which is the centerpiece of his teachings, expounded in the Four Noble Truths.

The First Noble Truth states that *dukkha* is a characteristic of human life, and it keeps us trapped in samsara.

Dukkha is usually translated as suffering, but it's tricky to define. It does not imply suffering from physical pain but instead implies mental suffering and not necessarily acute or severe suffering but rather general unhappiness or mental discomfort—unsatisfied-ness. *Dukkha* can be anxiety or discontent. The first noble truth is often simplified to the phrase "life is suffering," which is a workable translation in the context of the normal, humdrum, everyday human sufferings of life. Samsara is the wheel of life to which Buddhists imagine we constantly return until we figure out how to free ourselves from *dukkha* and escape to nirvana. Daoism and Buddhism have very similar ideas about *dukkha. The mind devises its own suffering, but without a physical self how can it be conscious of suffering?* (v. 13).

The Second Noble Truth states that the origin of *dukkha* is tanha.

Tanha—surprise!—is difficult to define with precision, but its definition is somewhere in the mental patchwork of cravings, thirsts, greeds, desires, and longings and is equivalent to desires and cravings as described in the *Daodejing*. So *dukkha*, suffering, is the kind of suffering that is caused by tanha: cravings. The dangers of tanha are stated clearly in the *Daodejing*:

> *The five colors blind the eye. The five notes deafen the ear. The five tastes dull the palate. . . . The wise tend to the belly, not the eyes.* (v. 12)
>
> *The greatest mistake is desire. The worst misfortune is discontent. The greatest curse is craving.* (v. 46)
>
> *Succumb to the desires of the outer world and you will suffer to the end of your days.* (v. 52)

The Third Noble Truth states that the cessation of *dukkha* comes from the relinquishment of tanha and leads to nirvana.

If *dukkha* is the constant, generalized suffering that occupies so much of our headspace and if it's caused by our own unwarranted cravings, the pathway to nirvana is simple. Get a grip on your mind, don't crave, and don't release second darts. Be grateful for the beauty around you. It's exactly as easy and as tantalizingly difficult as it sounds. Having a path to follow is helpful. The Dao is Laozi's Path:

> *Know when you have enough: there's no disgrace in that. Know when to stop: there's no danger in that. The key to lifelong contentment.* (v. 44)
>
> *Subdue your senses, constrain your desires, blunt your sharpness, unravel your knots, soften your glare. Be as dust.* (v. 56)
>
> *The wise do not desire desire. They learn to unlearn.* (v. 64)

Giving up cravings is easier said than done, and I have some doubts about the wisdom of overstating this advice for young people. It's all well and good for us old'uns, with the experience of age, to tut-tut foolish young'uns, but part of what helps us see the road to wrack and ruin is the experience of having wrecked and ruined. Perhaps a healthy quota of early-life screw-ups is required for us to appreciate the gentler, kinder path. Dao knows I've had my share. Tanha has been my obdurate fellow traveler, and I have developed a healthy respect for *dukkha.*

The Fourth Noble Truth is that the route from samsara to nirvana follows the Noble Eightfold Path.

Recognizing that the relinquishment of tanha, the cessation of *dukkha,* and finding nirvana is not as simple as it sounds, the Buddha gave further guidance. His eight guidelines are organized into three categories.

First, ethical conduct is composed of right understanding, right thought, and right speech. The path to nirvana requires more than just good intentions. It requires one to live out those intentions. Such requirements are common among religions and philosophies: don't cheat, steal, lie, be cruel, or be mean. Thou shalt not covet thy neighbor's sheep. Here is a smattering of relevant phrases from the *Daodejing*:

> *The wise put themselves last, and yet advance; keep to the outside, and yet remain centered.* (v. 7)
> *Live in connection with the earth. Love generously. Speak the truth.* (v. 8)
> *The ancient masters were . . . [c]ourteous, like polite house guests.* (v. 15)
> *The opinionated are not bright. The self-righteous are unaware.* (v. 24)
> *The wise help everybody, ignoring none.* (v. 27)
> *The wise limit wastefulness and pride and temper the desire to control.* (v. 29)
> *The wise are sharp without cutting, pointed without piercing, assertive without bullying, and brilliant without dazzling.* (v. 58)
> *To big or small; to many or few, respond to vice with virtue.* (v. 63)
> *I have three treasures. . . . The first is compassion. The second is moderation. The third is humility.* (v. 67)
> *Truthful words are not pretty. Pretty words are not true.* (v. 81)

Second, mental discipline is developed through right action, right livelihood, and right effort. This is a particularly noteworthy part of Buddhist practice. To Westerners, Buddhism and Daoism may appear to be entirely focused on mindfulness and meditation, but this is a false perception. The Buddha also pointed out that the pathway to nirvana is paved by simple goodness.

Right livelihood can be particularly challenging and is easier for some to achieve than for others. I have been very fortunate with my career. As a tenured professor I can do more or less what I want, so I choose to create classes that reflect my beliefs and that I think will be of service. We don't all have this flexibility, but we can all work with the choices we have been presented. If you must tend bar, tend it well. If you have capital to invest, don't invest it in weapons of war.

One valuable piece of advice is to do what you love, because when you put your heart into your work it is more likely to produce beauty and quality and serve others:

Do good work and then step back. This is the way of heaven. (v. 9)
Be simple like undyed silk; like the uncarved block. (v. 19)
The wise get results and then withdraw. They don't presume to take by force. (v. 30)
What is well rooted is not easily pulled. What is firmly attached is not easily separated. (v. 54)
Governing a big country is like cooking a small fish. (v. 60)
Do without doing. Act without acting. . . . Tackle the difficult in its simplest form. Tackle big problems while they are small. (v. 63)
Those who act cause harm. Those who snatch fumble. (v. 64)
The way of heaven is like a stretched bow. . . . [I]t takes from what has too much and gives to what has too little. (v. 77)
It is virtue to attend to your own obligations. It is not virtue to insist others do the same. (v. 79)

Third, wisdom is developed through *right mindfulness* and *right samadhi*.

Here is where we find the vast practical difference between Eastern and Western approaches. Samadhi, for our purposes, is synonymous with meditation:

Can you unify the elements of your soul . . . ? focus your vital breath . . . ? polish your inner mirror . . . ?" (v. 10)
The wise tend to the belly not the eyes. (v.12)
Attain complete emptiness. Maintain absolute stillness. (v. 16)
To know others is to be wise. To know yourself is to be enlightened. To master others takes force. To master yourself takes strength. (v. 33)
The greatest mistake is desire. The worst misfortune is discontent. The greatest curse is craving. (v. 46)
Know the world without leaving your front door. Know heaven's Path without looking out of the window. (v. 47)
To now this harmony is to know the eternal. To know the eternal is to be enlightened. (v. 55)
Subdue your senses, constrain your desires, blunt your sharpness, unravel your knots, soften your glare. Be as dust: a profound unity. (v. 56)
The wise do not desire desire nor value valuable treasures. They learn to unlearn. (v. 64)

THE MIDDLE PATH FOR THE MIND

The wise cleave to the one as their foundation. Not conceited, they shine. Not emphatic, they are reliable. (v. 22)
"Steadiness is the master of frivolity. Stillness is the ruler of impatience. (v. 26)

Bipolar disorder is the epitome of a mind far from the Middle Path. Formerly known as manic depression, it is characterized by mood swings from low (depression) to high (mania) extremes. In high mood, people may feel euphoric but also out of control, irrational, and irritable. They may engage in impulsive and risky behavior. In low mood, they may suffer great sadness, lethargy, and depression and experience an elevated risk of suicide. Bipolar disorder is pathologically related to attention deficit/hyperactive disorder and post-traumatic stress disorder (PTSD), and all these disorders are linked to impaired functioning of the limbic system.

Conditions such as bipolar disorder, attention deficit/hyperactive disorder, and PTSD make it particularly difficult to bring the mind into balance, and people with these disorders tend to need drugs to assist. This might give the impression that so-called neurotypical people who must have typical brains, should find maintaining mental balance easy. But no such luck. Even in the absence of trauma and with mood swings within normal range, whatever that means, the human mind is a hot mess.

Happiness teeters above misery. Misery lurks beneath happiness. Who knows which is in the future? (v. 58)

Hinduism in the time of Prince Siddhartha Gotama prescribed extreme asceticism as an antidote to indulgence and a path to spiritual awakening. Religions have often promoted behaviors such as asceticism, renunciation, and abstinence:

"It is easier for a camel to pass through the eye of a needle than for a rich man to enter the kingdom of heaven." (Mark 10:25)
"For all that is in the world—the desires of the flesh and the desires of the eyes and pride in possessions—is not from the father but is from the world." (1 John 2:16)

Many have chosen a path that renounces the pleasures of life. If sex, drugs, and rock 'n' roll are the sinful, indulgent path, perhaps abstinence, sobriety, and asceticism are the true path? Not so, said the Buddha. Asceticism is its own form of indulgence.

Siddhartha abandoned the palace and roamed the countryside as an ascetic for years seeking enlightenment. Finally, starving and emaciated after a grueling spiritual quest of self-imposed austerity, he settled beneath the Bodhi tree in Bodh Gaya to do battle with Mara. He found the Middle Path, was enlightened, and became the Buddha.

The true path avoids both extremes and is shaped through balance and equanimity. A similar principle is elucidated in the *Daodejing*:

> *Be equally wary of honor and disgrace. Honor can demoralize. We are apprehensive about gaining it. We fear the disgrace of losing it.* (v. 13)
>
> *Be as dust: a profound unity. Those who attain this cannot be seduced or rejected, promoted or impeded, honored or disgraced.* (v. 56)

The Middle Path for the mind should also acknowledge that the mind has different needs at different stages of life. Hinduism considered this and defined four life stages in the ashrama.

The first stage, brahmacharya, is that of the student. In the education of a Hindu yogi, a student would study science and the scriptures and self-discipline, both physical and mental. In a secular context, we can think of brahmacharya simply as the early stage of life during which receiving care and education should be a person's first priority.

The second stage, grihastha, is that of the householder. A person enters society, works, marries, and raises children or follows some analogous path. The ashrama seems to acknowledge that life is going to "get in the way" of things, and the key roles of grihasthas are to produce food and provide for the material needs of one's family and community. Grihastha are likely to be knotted up in the busyness of life but should orient their actions to serve, such as by providing care and education to others.

The third stage, vanaprastha, is that of the "forest dweller." At some stage, and this can happen earlier or later, a person comes to understand that much of the grihastha's life is a treadmill. Moving from the household to the forest imagines a form of spiritual liberation and a move toward enlightenment.

The fourth stage, sannyasa, is that of the renunciate. Usually imagined as the final of four stages, it can also be discovered at any stage of life. For monks, sannyasa might be sought directly from brahmacharya and is the stage of detachment from property and material wealth, the renunciation of cravings and desires, and the move toward settling into a focus on moksha: peacefulness and spirituality.

The four stages of the ashrama remind us of the well-known but seldom honored difference between two types of happiness: *hedonism* and *eudaimonia*.

The idea of *hedonia* comes to us from Aristippus of Cyrene (435–356 BCE), who made a philosophy out of pleasure-seeking. Hedonic happiness comes from activities and things and represents most of our distractions, amusements, and material goals. It's by no means all bad. We get great pleasure from a new car, going to the movies, sex, a feast, a feast of sex in a moving car. It's all good, in moderation, but the traps are obvious. Laozi speaks often about cravings and desires, and we have discussed them at length in other parts of the book. It's not the hedonism that is bad per se but rather the craving of it.

Hedonism tends to crave more hedonism, and we can get caught on a hedonic treadmill. When we have experienced a number of roller coasters we might get attached to the buzz of them, and we seek more and faster roller coasters to keep the buzz. Attachment is the precursor of addiction. Hedonic happiness is good but only in good measure.

The check to *hedonia* is *eudaimonia*, which comes to us from Aristotle (384–322 BCE). *Eudaimonia* is a little harder to pin down, but rather than the happiness that we associate with excitement and the pleasures of the senses, it's the happiness that comes from a sense of well-being and flourishing. It has less of a buzz to it and more of a warm fuzz. It's the satisfaction that comes from helping others, from feeling "in the right place," or from having a sense of purpose. *Eudaimonic* happiness tends to be fallen into rather than sought, and it tends to be fallen into when we are selfless and compassionate and when we are able to slow down and do less.

THE MIDDLE PATH BETWEEN YIN AND YANG

Existence and nonexistence arise together. Difficult and easy become each other. Long and short shape each other. High and low incline toward each other. Sound and tone harmonize each other. Before and after follow each other. (v. 2)

The Buddha described the eight vicissitudes of life: gain and loss, praise and blame, fame and disrepute, and pleasure and pain. The eight vicissitudes lie on four continua of yin and yang, and moderation is the preferred path in each case, steering away from either pole. Take pleasure and pain, for example. It might seem obvious that we should steer away from pain and toward pleasure, but that's not what the Buddha advised. Craving pleasure can become its own form of pain, and a fixation on dulling pain or distracting oneself from it can make it harder to bear. The Middle Path steers calmly between pain and pleasure, accepting both.

A common Western perception of a Buddhist is an unassuming person with a shaved head and saffron robes who spends an awful lot of time sitting cross-legged on a cushion meditating—whatever that means. The whole thing looks terribly boring and uncomfortable and a lot like asceticism. This perception makes sense because most of us are likelier to veer toward indulgence rather than abnegation when we stray from the

Middle Path, and so we are more likely to need an adjustment in the direction of asceticism, but no suffering is actually required. Too many people have suffered at the hands of so-called teachers who told them that spirituality was be found through pain.

The Middle Path is unique to each individual, but a key mental characteristic is equanimity, which is a robust form of mental evenness or neutrality. Equanimity is not indifference, disconnectedness, or disengagement but instead is the maintenance of mental and emotional balance, engagement, and awareness without reactiveness. Equanimity deals with pain stoically and resists the craving of excessive pleasures. It is to be humble when praised and composed when blamed, generous with gaining and magnanimous with loss, and wary of fame and undaunted by reputation. Laozi speaks of equanimity frequently in the *Daodejing*:

> *Tempering desire, you see the depths. Embracing desire, you see the surfaces.* (v. 1)
> *Overfill a bowl and it will spill. Oversharpen a blade and its edge will brittle.* (v. 9)
> *Be equally wary of honor and disgrace.* (v. 13)
> *To be content is to be rich. Be persistent, develop willpower, hold your place, remain steady, and you will endure.* (v. 33)
> *With desire managed all is quiet. The world settles into peace.* (v. 37)
> *Know when you have enough—there's no disgrace in that. Know when to stop—there's no danger in that. The key to lifelong contentment.* (v. 44)
> *The greatest mistake is desire. The worst misfortune is discontent. The greatest curse is craving. When you are content with enough there is always enough.* (v. 46)
> *Seal the openings, close the doors, and life will always be easy. Succumb to the desires of the outer world and you will suffer to the end of your days.* (v. 52)
> *Subdue your senses, constrain your desires, blunt your sharpness, unravel your knots, soften your glare. Be as dust.* (v. 56)
> *The wise love themselves without vanity; know themselves without arrogance.* (v. 72)

Yin-yang thinking acknowledges the importance of the dark as well as the light, the feminine balanced with the masculine, and the complementarity of rigidity and flexibility. Yin-yang thinking recognizes the futility of seeking the permanent victory of one ideology over another. The forces of good tend to see the extermination of bad as progress, but whose ideology is good and whose is bad? Yin and yang are not opposites but instead are poles, and you can't have one without the other. The *taiji* symbol tends to be thought of as a symbol of dualism, but its intent is to convey the idea that that all apparent opposites are complementary parts of a nondual whole.

Yin-yang thinking demands respect for the other and a recognition that ideologies other than one's own have a role in creating a balanced polity. Who are Democrats in the absence of Republicans? Who are conservatives in the absence of liberals?

The extermination of one side by the other does not lead to victory but instead leads to tyranny. Laozi appears to take sides, speaking frequently about the power of yin, but his point is not to elevate yin above yang but rather to regain balance. Yang is generally perceived as dominant, but yin, although softer and gentler, is of equal influence. The power of yin against yang is conveyed by the metaphor of water against rock illustrating the power of persistent yielding motion against the tough and inflexible. Adversaries will usually benefit from respecting each other's differences—and there is often more to respect than we think:

> *Know the masculine but cleave to the feminine. . . . Know the light but cleave to the dark.* (v. 28)
>
> *The strong and big are inferior. The soft and weak are superior.* (v. 76)
>
> *Nothing is softer or gentler than water and yet nothing is more potent for attacking the hard and rough. . . . Soft gets the better of hard. Gentle gets the better of rough.* (v. 78)

Our minds jump to simplistic, often negative conclusions. Given time, however, and training, our minds become more able to consider more nuanced ways to proceed. This problem is encapsulated in the title of Daniel Kahneman's wonderful book *Thinking, Fast and Slow.*[13]

Fast thinking is intuitive, emotional, and often unconscious. It makes us jump away from a snake or pull our hand away from a flame. It's essential, but it's also rife with heuristics and gravitates to the emotional poles. Fast thinking decides that things are wonderful or terrible but seldom ordinary. When making important decisions, it's beneficial to slow down enough to give our deliberative thinking some time to consider other ways of thinking. Developing patience and equanimity is a process of training the mind to slow down and develop properly considered opinions. Fast thinking is yang. It exaggerates. It leads us to see our enemies as evil. It wants to win and dominate. Slow thinking is yin. Given the chance, it can be thoughtful and reasonable and can see things through different eyes. Yin and yang thinking are both needed to find the Middle Path for the mind.

RESILIENCE FOR THE MIND

> *Yield to become complete. Be twisted to be straight. Be emptied to be full. Be broken to be whole.* (v. 22)

It's important to protect our mental health, not just in general but also to prepare for psychological shocks. As with all forms of brain training, there's only so much that can be done since we are all endowed with a genetic setpoint and have limited control over our environments, but there are some things we can do to build our mental resilience. Importantly, we can also help others build their mental resilience, particularly our children. Or at least, we can keep ourselves from eroding it.

Having achieved great success, many admirers, and precious few detractors with *The Happiness Hypothesis* and *The Righteous Mind*, Jonathan Haidt, with coauthor Greg Lukianoff, decided to go ahead and piss a few people off by writing *The Coddling of the American Mind*.[14] Its premise is that modern parents, particularly the baby boomer and GenX parents of millennial and GenZ kids, have become far too protective. Terrified of psychopaths and pedophiles lurking on every corner, parents have reined in their kids to keep them safe, too safe according to Lukianoff and Haidt. Meanwhile and perhaps fearing the wrath of overprotective parents, schools, colleges, and universities have begun to pander to students who feel attacked or triggered too easily. This coddling and pandering, they argue, is making our kids soft-minded. It is robbing them of the psychological trials necessary for the development of mental resilience. Finding the balance, the Middle Path, between protection and pandering is not easy, but there are costs to veering in either direction from the Middle Path. Here are some great quotes from the book:

"Avoiding triggers is a symptom of PTSD, not a treatment for it."

"Teaching kids that failure, insults, and painful experiences will do lasting damage is harmful in and of itself. Human beings *need* physical and mental challenges and stressors or we deteriorate."

"Prepare the child for the road, not the road for the child."[15]

The Stoics were a great source of wisdoms on mental resilience. Originating with Zeno of Citium around 300 BCE and followed by many ancient Greeks, including Chrysippus and Cleanthes, Stoicism stands alongside Aristotle's *Ethics* as one of the great classical contributions to the philosophy of virtues and ethics. Although a Greek philosophy, Stoicism probably had its greatest flourishing in ancient Rome, and its most famous and influential adherents were Epictetus, Seneca, and the "Philosopher Emperor" Marcus Aurelius.

Marcus Aurelius's *Meditations* are a glorious hodgepodge of passing thoughts, ideas, and reminiscences that combine to offer a treatise on Stoicism, and Marcus Aurelius is eminently quotable:

"Shame on the soul, to falter on the road of life while the body still perseveres."

"Drama, combat, terror, numbness, and subservience. Every day these things wipe out your sacred principles, wherever your mind entertains them uncritically or lets them slip in."

"If thou art pained by an external thing, it is not this that disturbs thee, but thy own judgement about it. And it is in thy power to wipe out this judgement now."[16]

The last quote is a perfect statement of the Buddha's second dart, and the Stoics probably represent the classical world's closest approximation to Eastern philosophy. Their philosophy emphasized a naturalistic ethics with logic and rationalism. Their practice involved the honest and open investigation of difficult truths.

An archetypal Stoic meditation is the contemplation of death. Since we are all destined to die, we should recognize the need to live fully now. As Marcus Aurelius said, "Think of yourself as dead. You have lived your life. Now, take what's left and live it properly."[17]

Our usage of the word "stoic" has shifted in modern times and now tends to have the narrower meaning of someone who does not show their feelings. A stoic approach to cold weather, for example, is to bear the cold without outward emotion. The usage loses much from the breadth of Stoic philosophy, but it does retain an important kernel. A stoic approach to training the mind is to train it for bad things—illness, despair, and death—so that when they arrive, as they will, you will have more mental resilience:

What is well rooted is not easily pulled. What is firmly attached is not easily separated. (v. 54)
Be as dust: a profound unity. Those who attain this cannot be seduced or rejected, promoted or impeded, honored or disgraced. (v. 56)
Have deep roots and a solid base. This is the Path of longevity and clarity. (v. 59)

LET YOUR SELF GO

The wise . . . , through selflessness, find themselves. (v. 7)
The mind devises its own suffering, but without a physical self how can it be conscious of suffering? (v. 13)

Robert Zemeckis made a lovely movie, *Cast Away*, which seems like a simple plane crash desert island survival movie but on closer examination turns out to be a gentle and unassuming story of the spiritual path of a man. Tom Hanks's character, Chuck Noland, a fast-living FedEx executive, washes up on a Pacific atoll after surviving a plane crash. He is stranded for years, and the experience brings him to a spiritual awakening. He passes through various stages of the death of the self to an eventual rebirth.

First, he has to abandon the island, the boundary within which he has been trapped. Next, he has to abandon Wilson, the volleyball that represents his ego; his self. Finally, lost, a speck drifting in a vast ocean, he lets the oars to his battered makeshift raft slip away, gives up all control over his life, and accepts his fate. When he has finally shed all the vestiges of the old Chuck Noland—soft, shallow, ruled by time, materialistic, blind to the beauty around him—a ship can now come and pluck him from his raft. He can live honestly and openly and in the present. Life still won't be without its challenges, but he knows what to do now, as he explains in a pristine monologue filmed as an uninterrupted four-minute panning shot: "And that's when this feeling came over me like a warm blanket. I knew, somehow, that I had to stay alive . . . keep breathing, because tomorrow the sun will rise. Who knows what the tide could bring?"

We tend to have a sense of ourselves as a self, a being, a soul. There appears to be something—some *thing*—that is not just our head and body but exists at some deeper level that is *us*. This self appears to be immutable. It seems to have been the same all our lives: since last week, last year, since we were young children. You remember baby-you as you, you consider yourself to be you now, and you assume you will still be you as you grow old.

This unchanging you is a mirage. Everything is change: both yourself and your self. There is no permanent soul. There is no self.

The illusion of self is part of a greater illusion of everything. Consider that nearly every cell in your body has been replaced since you were an infant. Your thoughts are different; even your style of thought is different. The structure of your brain has changed, and the connections among the neurons in your brain have been rearranged. You are demonstrably not the same you that you were: there can be no unchanging "self." Everything changes. This is not to suggest that you don't have a body, presently, and that the shoes at the door aren't yours and don't fit your feet, but it does suggest that you should see yourself as a process rather than a thing. This might seem like a scary idea, but it's also a liberating one.

It feels like our self is thinking our thoughts, but is our self beating our hearts? Digesting our food? Growing our bones?

Try this. Our mental constructions of the world are both poorer and richer than the real thing. Consider color, for example, which is simply a mental construct based on the proportion of electromagnetic radiation with wavelengths of 420, 530, and 560 nanometers entering our eyes and exciting our retinas. Nothing in nature actually has color. We see blue, green, and red (usually) and construct a vibrant, technicolor mental model of the world. We see a colorless world in color—which means that our conception of the world is greater than the world itself! But wait. Our visual construction is based on three midrange electromagnetic signals out of a continuum of signals from gamma rays to radio waves. So, our visual world is depauperate. Would the world "look" more beautiful if we could access and process more wavelengths? Not relevant. We don't see with our eyes. We see with our minds. Cats' eyes "see" only in monochrome. Insects' eyes "see" ultraviolet light. Do they live in a world that is differently colored than ours?

Or try this. A human life is like a candle flame. The flame draws materials to it—oxygen from the air and combustible volatiles from the heated candle wax—that flow through, producing heat and light. The flame is not a thing, certainly not a static thing. It holds a beautiful, bright, flickering shape, but the stuff of which it is made is not to be found in the flame but instead is moving through it. The flame is not a thing but rather a dynamic process; not an object but a flow. The candle flame, by the way, is one of the more common foci of meditation. Picture a monk in a Tibetan monastery watching a yak-butter candle and meditating on impermanence—or try it yourself. *Great means always flowing. Always flowing leads to reaching far. Reaching far results in returning to the root* (v. 25).

Or try this. A strange group of protists in the genus *Dictyostelium* grow a stalk with a button on top that resembles a tiny mushroom. The button bursts to release cells, like a mushroom cap releasing spores. Their mushroom-like appearance caused them to be named slime molds, but closer inspection reveals that the basic unit of a slime mold, what you might have expected to be a spore, is an amoeba-like single-celled blob-looking thing that wanders around hunting bacteria. Each amoeba-like blob thing acts independently, as its own organism. You'd think that each blob is an amoeba, its own self, until an environmental trigger causes the amoebae to crawl toward each other, link up, and form a new mushroom-like stalk-with-blob thing. So, which is the organism, the amoeba-like single cell or the mushroom-like blob on a stalk? Where is its self?

Or try this. An egg hatches to release a caterpillar, which crawls around munching leaves until it decides to pupate, at which point it melts itself down to its constituent elements and rearranges its *self.* When it breaks back out of the pupa it is no longer a fat, wingless, crawling caterpillar but instead is a skinny airborne butterfly. Same self, metamorphosed, or new self?

Or try this. There are no borders. I know: tell that to someone living in Rafah or stuck in Ciudad Juarez, but nobody understands this better than a Palestinian or Central American. Borders are not barriers; they are edges, ecotones, zones of exchange, transition zones, and selectively permeable membranes. Consider the broad edge between the Amazon rainforest and the Cerrado and between the North American woodlands and prairie. Consider the boundary between axon and dendrite in the nervous system, nephron and capillary in the kidney, and oxygen moving from lung to blood. None of these borders is a fixed boundary. Each is fluid: a zone of exchange, a diverse and active zone, a negotiation. And so it is with you. Your skin is not a border that separates you from the world but instead is a mediator with it.

Or try this. An ant is not an organism. The ant colony is the organism. Each ant is just a body part. The colony's body just has large spaces between its parts. (Bear in mind, there's usually only one queen.) So, where's the ant's self or the ant colony's self?

Or try renaming the self and the words related to it. This might change how you think about it. The self can be selfish or selfless. The self might also be thought of as the soul, so you can be soulful or soulless. On the other hand, call the self the ego and you become egotistical, which is to say self-centered.

Our selves are not what they seem. There is no we; there is no self who does all our thinking and deciding. We are a hodgepodge of selves at best. Understanding this brings us closer to an acceptance of our transience. We are fabricated from the matter of the planet and then subsumed back into it. Earth is a candle, and we are one of its flames. To know this intellectually is not particularly difficult. It takes only a basic understanding of ecology to recognize organisms as brief way stations in the dynamic flows of the living planet. From that understanding, it's a simple leap of humility to recognize ourselves as standard-issue earthlings and to fully embrace our transience. All cultures have grappled with this: "Earth to earth, ashes to ashes, dust to dust."[18]

Research by Marcus Raichle and others identified a neural network in the early 2000s that has become known as the default mode network.[19] It is a strongly interconnected network of brain regions with its principal nodes in the prefrontal, parietal, and temporal parts of the cortex. The default mode network was revealed following the surprising discovery that the brain didn't seem to slow down when it rested or, rather, that it didn't slow down when we stopped concentrating on something "important." We had assumed that the brain would be less active when "we" weren't "thinking," but this is a classic assumption of the self. The brain's job is not just to do the thinking that we think is important; it has other tasks in mind beyond our awareness.

The modus operandi of the default mode network is to quieten down when other brain activities are brought online but then swing back into action whenever there's nothing more pressing going on. So, the brain will emphasize its salience network when something fearful is detected, its executive control network when making decisions, or its task positive network when directing focused attention, but it won't then go quiet; it will turn its default mode back up. The default mode, at least in terms of energy use and oxygen consumption, is not a resting state but rather a state of activity that we don't fully understand. (We probably shouldn't be surprised that the brain is always busy when we're awake because we know that it sets off neurological fireworks in our sleep.) The brain is definitively not "ours." Most of its work is unbeknownst to us.

So, what does the default mode network do? What tends to activate and deactivate it? Well, since it is activated in default and is the "nothing special is going on" mode, it tends not to be called-on per se but returned-to. It probably has specific tasks, but we don't understand much about what they are. What we do know, however, is that the default mode network spends most of its time in self-referential cognition. It is involved in thinking about our recent actions and interactions, thoughts and feelings, and interpersonal relationships. It seems to engage in a good deal of storytelling and memory compilation.

Our sense of self seems to be located, in significant part, in the default mode network. So, if you want to think of yourself as having a self, the default mode network is as good a referent as any. Dan Harris talks about "the asshole in your head" in his book *10% Happier.*[20] That asshole, your monkey mind, might be centered on the default mode network.

The default mode network presumably serves a vital role in the activity of the brain, but it also seems to be linked to depression and loneliness, and one of the neurological effects of meditation seems to be in attenuating its activity. This makes sense. Quieting the self—the monkey mind, the asshole in the head—is good practice.

Understanding the absence of a specific "thing" that is the self is considered to be a critical step in the Dharma, the Middle Way, of Buddhism. The Buddha said, "Just as a snake sheds its skin, so we must shed our past again and again." An important stage along the path to enlightenment is to attain emptiness, sunyata, which is synonymous with discarding the self and the absence of a self need not be a fearful thing: *A flower grows, blooms, returns to the root. . . . [T]hough the self is ephemeral, there is no fear* (v. 16).

Sam Harris speaks often of the illusion of the self in his book *Waking Up* and meditation app of the same name: "So what would a spiritual master be a master *of*? At a minimum, she will no longer suffer certain cognitive and emotional illusions—above all, she will no longer feel identical to her thoughts."[21]

There are some human tendencies that stem from an overdeveloped sense of self. For example, we have unrealistic expectations that people should have fixed morals. We probably shouldn't trust people whose moral compass changes with the tides, but surely we want people to learn and grow. This hang-up is evident with politicians, whom we lambast for changing their minds, as if changing your mind is a bad thing, but we honor being "true to their selves."

We find it easy to hold onto our judgments of people who have committed certain misdeeds, and we sometimes feel justified (self-justified, righteous) in maintaining a negative judgment against people for a very long time. If someone has done a bad thing, we label them as a bad person. Badness is their self, and since the self is some basic, underlying truth, certain people, we feel, can never be trusted.

When we assume that people can't change—a leopard cannot change its spots, and a tiger cannot change its stripes—we fall into the trap of glorifying the unchanging self.

People do change and do improve, and their learning should be honored—and there is great hope in this. Be kinder to others; they *can* change. And so, by the way, can you. There is significant practical value in overcoming the illusion of self. Abraham Lincoln put it well: "It is said an Eastern monarch once charged his wise men to invent him a sentence, to be ever in view, and which should be true and appropriate in all times and situations. They presented him the words: "And this, too, shall pass away." How much it expresses! How chastening in the hour of pride! How consoling in the depths of affliction!"[22]

Being angry does not make you an angry person; it makes you a complex being who is currently feeling anger. You are not bad just because you have done a bad thing. You are a complex being who is currently feeling unworthy—and this too shall pass away. Discarding one's sense of an immutable self can make personal change easier and more dynamic.

One way people can change and for which they should be honored is in their ability to accept, understand, and honor people of different racial, ethnic, and cultural heritages. I have certainly changed in this regard—and thank goodness. The culture of my first formative years, in Oldham, England, in the late 1970s and early 1980s was overtly racist. The casual use of racist language was normal. Educational, housing, and employment opportunities were blatantly segregated, and since White Oldhamers and South Asian Oldhamers tended to live in different communities, a pervasive sense of us and them persisted. The climate of Oldham worsened through the end of the twentieth century until race riots broke out in 2001. Persistent and patient work has been undertaken by many dedicated people, but Oldham continues to struggle. I wonder to this day to what extent my evolution as a human being required me to leave Oldham. Its problems were much more evident to me from the outside once I had left than they had been from the inside.

People can become racist and they can become antiracist, and the process is one of changing minds. Fascist leaders capture minds with ruthless efficiency using messaging that reaches into the emotion-responsive, tribe-defending, fearful parts of the brain. When Donald Trump keeps demeaning Mexicans and Muslims, he is engaging in the business of conditioning unenlightened brains toward racism. Antiracists try to save people and bring them back with hope and rationality. The battle for the hearts and minds of people—the *xin*, the heart-mind—is a constant struggle.

Another area in which the power of mental change becomes obvious is addiction, both when people become ensnared by addiction and when they release themselves. The most unyielding addictions are to drugs such as nicotine, cocaine, and heroine, which bind to receptors in the brain. The brain becomes accustomed to having its receptors sated by the drug and sends out messages of craving when the drug dissipates. The addict must find a way to cope with the cravings if he is to go clean.

But addiction requires no drug. We can be addicted to all kinds of craved or desired things, such as danger, sex, gambling, and social media. No drug is needed for addiction because the brain supplies its own.

The brain uses a suite of chemicals to modulate its activity. They include glutamate and gamma-aminobutyric acid, which interact to affect memory and regulate agitation versus calmness; serotonin, which is a kind of chill pill, although too much of it can cause depression; noradrenaline, which acts mostly in the sympathetic nervous system regulating fight-or-flight responses; and endorphins, of which there are dozens, that impact pain relief and relaxation. Some of them are more potent than morphine. The most fascinating neurochemical in this context, however, is dopamine, which regulates arousal and stimulation and can lead to dependence.

If the Buddha had known that neurons that fire together wire together, his teachings would have been so much clearer, and had he known about dopamine they would have been clearer still. We now understand a good part of the science behind the Buddha's wisdom: "Whatever a person frequently thinks and reflects on becomes the pattern of their mind." Fixation and addiction are created in the mind by the formation of new connections among neurons and by the synthesis and deployment of neurotransmitters, particularly dopamine.

Being lazy and weak-minded now has a neural mechanism. When we give the brain what it wants, it wants more. To be strong and determined is to stand up to our own minds. *To know others is to be wise. To know yourself is to be enlightened. To master others takes force. To master yourself takes strength* (v. 33).

Recovered alcoholics, recovered sex addicts, and ex-smokers haven't recovered; they have simply improved. They don't have their "old self" back. They have simply changed again, for the better, this time. A smoker is not a smoker; he is simply a person who currently smokes. Likewise, a nonsmoker simply doesn't smoke. He has changed his mind.

And there's one last addiction, the granddaddy of them all. Most of us are addicted to thought. In particular, we are addicted to self-destructive thoughts, which come often, and uninvestigated thoughts, which can come like a torrent. Getting this last addiction under control is to take a peek at nirvana.

AWAKENINGS AND ENLIGHTENMENT

When the weakest student hears of the Path she laughs out loud, but then, without laughter, it wouldn't be the true Path. So, it is said: The brightest Path appears dark. . . . The clearest things are opaque." (v. 41)

"Enlightenment" is one of those awkward words. We can fall into the trap of thinking we and ours are more enlightened than they and theirs. Europeans feel enlightened. The Enlightenment was a European thing after all, so the West is enlightened and the East is, what, lagging behind? But, Buddhists, Hindus, and Daoists consider enlightenment to be found on a path that requires a certain character of mind that, let's be honest, one is less likely to find in selfish Westerners. To become enlightened is to see the right way to think and be. We become enlightened when we have an epiphany, when we change in a way that enables us to see the world in a new way, in a new light, and in the right light. Becoming more enlightened is better than becoming less enlightened, but the term is freighted.

I think my biggest objection to the idea of enlightenment is when it is spoken of as an instantaneous transition and a permanent transformation to a final mental destination. We can certainly have moments of sudden enlightenment, but I distrust any expectation that they would be permanent and doubt there is any knowable final destination. We may think we have suddenly figured it all out in a moment of brilliance and are now an enlightened being. Yesterday we saw the world one way, but the veil has now been lifted. We realize that we had been looking through fog all our lives, and now our knowing is clear.

Staring at a window you see only your reflection because the light is bounced back from the glass. Then your point of focus shifts and you can see through the glass into a new dimension. These enlightenments are real and wonderful.

Saul of Tarsus headed out on the road to Damascus intending some dastardly anti-Christian deeds but was struck down by a light that "shined around him like a light from heaven." He was brought back to his senses by Ananias: "'Brother Saul, the Lord, even Jesus, . . . appeared unto thee . . . that thou mightest receive thy sight and be filled with the Holy Ghost.' And immediately, there fell from his eyes as it had been scales: and he received sight forthwith, and arose, and was baptized" (Acts 9: 3, 17–18). And thus did Saul of Tarsus, persecutor of Christians, become Paul, principal author of the Christian faith.

Rather than the term "enlightenment," I prefer the term "awakening." From a sleepy life that misunderstood the world, we suddenly wake up. *Aha! Now* I see. But why, even in the most enlivening aha moments, would we expect to suddenly see everything? And why would we trust our minds to tell us that? No, I think we can wake up to insights, but I also think we need to keep waking up to them and can always wake up to more.

The moment of awakening is wonderful, and waking from your stupor, from your fixed, rigid, simplistic way of seeing the world, is an unalloyed good. The problem is when it comes with a sense of finality. Awakenings do not bring us to some level of the fully enlightened but instead merely advance the ball.

One gets a better sense of this with age. I have spent most of my life fairly certain that I had it all figured out. At each aha moment, I have seen with perfect clarity that I had been wrong and knew, with equally perfect clarity, that I was now right. I was now enlightened and so much better than the previous foolish me. (What *had* I been thinking? Never mind, we're good now.) Only now, a few more awakenings along, have I learned to distrust my awakenings. You're still a fool, Steve, but you're getting better.

A quick note to Buddhists on the subject of ultimate enlightenments. I don't think that nirvana exists as an ultimate destination. I think that moments of visitation are the best you can get, so just enjoy them in the moment. They will pass away, and that's okay. There is no final enlightenment. There are always more enlightenments to be had. The moment you think you've reached it, think again. Everything changes. The Buddhas weren't fully and finally enlightened, not even Siddhartha Gotama. Why would we expect such a thing? Indeed, who is to say any person, even the Buddha or the Dalai Lama, is or was more enlightened than you?[23] To understand your own mind is hard enough. To know another's is impossible.

Let me suggest a sequence of awakenings that might be beneficial in these modern times of crisis. Each awakening involves changing minds in a different way.

The first group of awakenings is intellectual. Knowledge, understanding, and analytical thinking are necessary places to begin, and much work is required. People need to understand at least the basics of how the world is, how it is changing, and how it is threatened. We need good, effective, well-trained teachers at all levels to transfer knowledge and encourage analysis. We need to understand the truth about our crises.

At the same time, however, we need to recognize that the truth is not always singular. How we understand science is influenced by our emotional, behavioral, and cultural set points, and although it is necessary, an environmental science education is not a cure-all. After all, our understanding of carbon emissions and the carbon emissions themselves have increased in step.

The second group of awakenings is ethical and moral, which is going to be fraught. Whose ethics? Whose morals? When people suggest that others should behave more ethically and morally, they tend to be moralizing in an way that is unhelpful and counterproductive. What I'd like to suggest instead is an awakening to the validity of the ethics and morals of others and to the problems with our own.

Unexamined, morals draw bright lines between "us" and "them," and although it's relatively easy to learn about other cultures, it's difficult to embrace new ethics and morals. Doing so requires a learning deeper than knowledge, and I consider the development of this orientation as central to the process of human awakening because it engages both the conscious and unconscious parts of the brain. It requires us to want to change our minds, to be willing to work at it, and it may require courage: people are prone to defending their group's ethics and morals with social punishments and violence. To go against them can be dangerous. (More on morals in Chapter 6.)

The third group of awakenings is spiritual. "Spiritual" may not be the best word because the word is entangled with religious. Religion seems to lead many people toward a spiritual connection (although it probably dissuades others), but it isn't integral to the way I understand spirituality, which has closer synonyms in numinous, metaphysical, mystical, and sacred.

This is something of a change of direction for me, coming from a series of small awakenings over the last decade or so. I spent most of my young adulthood as an argumentative atheist. I'm still an atheist but less argumentatively. It took my science-trained self a long time to awaken to an openness to spirituality, for which there seems to be a significant place in the human psyche.

So much about religion is fictional, even fantastical, and it can be hard to take adherents seriously. They can't possibly believe in extinction-averting boat zoos, talking snakes, flying horses, or real flesh-and-blood (or wafer-and-wine) humans springing back from the dead and ascending to the heavens—to the sky, the clouds, Kolob. Can they? Yes, actually, they can and do. I choose to read the stories of Jonas in the belly of the whale ("Great Fish!"), Cain killing Abel, Mohammad splitting the moon, and Arjuna finding his battle nerves as metaphorical, but others treat them as real. However, the question is peripheral.

The human tendency to seek spiritual connection is so widespread that it seems likely to have evolved as an adaptation or exaptation (by-product) of the evolving brain. It is closely related to human emotions such as empathy, and the evolution of empathy seems likely to have played an important role in building the cohesiveness of human communities. The ability to connect with people is derived from sophisticated brains tapping into networks of analytical, behavioral, cultural, and emotional cues. We have an almost magical ability to connect with each other. How different, fundamentally, is connection with a god? Empathy machines seek connection and find it in lots of places.

The feelings that come through spirituality are deeply moving. Connect with your god, your cosmos, or whatever you connect with. Don't refuse its presence just because people so often link it to things you find hokey. Midichlorians are definitively fictional, but may the Force be with you anyway.

The fourth group of awakenings is ecological. We seem to suffer when we are disconnected from nature and thrive when we are reconnected. In a modern world that is majority urban and whose distractions are frequently digital, we have come increasingly apart from nature. Time in nature, separated from our urban lives and unplugged from our digital ones, awakens us to our place. We cannot be apart from nature; we are a part of it. We awaken, step by step, as we deepen our connection to nature and the cosmos. We are impermanent processes of life passing through. We are the whirlpool, the candle flame. We are the river, flowing to the sea. We can learn about our place in nature from classes or books, but we also need to come fully awake to our true nature.

All four groups of awakenings can arise together as we open ourselves to a path of honest learning about the true natures of our minds and morals, our orientation toward others, and our place in the cosmos. So, is this how we are to save the world, through mindfulness and meditation, education, community spirit, and ecology? Hardly. This knowledge has been available for millennia, and there's no reason to think that the whole of humanity would suddenly change and get all of this right . . .

. . . But you can.

Tending to life's tasks with quality and beauty, relating to other people with understanding and compassion, and living in the world as both a temporary, insignificant speck and an integral part helps us take less from the world and give more. You can't do as much as you would like to change others, but you can change yourself, and only by first tending to yourself can you hope to change others for the better. *In myself I see the self. . . . In my village I see all villages. . . . In the world I see everything under heaven* (v. 34).

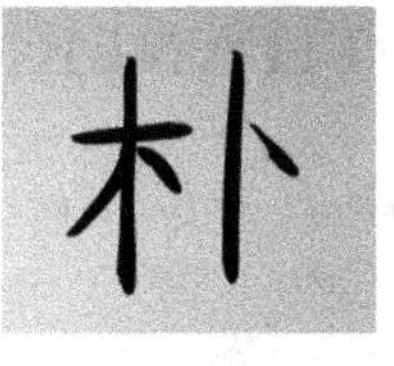

6

MEETINGS OF THE MINDS

The wise engage with the world and remain simple at heart. (v. 49)

So the wise are sharp without cutting, pointed without piercing, assertive without bullying, and brilliant without dazzling. (v. 58)

FOR A SPECIES WITH SUCH INCREDIBLE INTELLECTUAL CAPACITY (OR SO we tell ourselves), humans seem to have inordinate trouble getting along with each other—which is absolutely fascinating. We do dumb stuff, repeatedly, even when we know it's dumb. Our brains must be more glitchy than we think—which is absolutely fascinating. The evolution of our brain, the monstrous computer atop our necks that supports phenomenal powers of calculation and communication, is what selected us as a dominant species in the first place, but just how effective is this three-pound blob of Jell-O?

Humans have an incredible capacity to read each others' minds, and this capacity has made us the only truly social creature on the planet.[1] We are borderline telepathic, not in a sci-fi, magic show kind of way, but with a highly evolved capacity to analyze postural and facial cues. We interpret the finest facial tic to understand the emotional state and motivations of other people. We can detect embarrassment from the slightest turning away of the face, or a blush; a microaggression from a momentary scrunching of the eyebrows; attraction—invitation, even—from a meeting of the eyes that lasts just that moment longer or is just that fraction more intense. We are empathy machines. That we are so good at this is amazing. That we are not as good as we think we are is a problem. The societies we form are shaped by brains attempting telepathy. The successes are remarkable. The failures range from the embarrassing to the disastrous.

LOVE THY NEIGHBOR

To know others is to be wise. To know yourself is to be enlightened. To master others takes force. To master yourself takes strength. (v. 33)

Biologically speaking, it makes sense for most animals to treat most other animals as potential threats. Selecting a few friendlies from among a horde of potential hostiles is fraught. Most species are limited to cooperating with kin groups and play it safe by distrusting all outsiders. This evolutionary legacy is the antagonistic bedrock upon which human social systems are scaffolded, so it should come as no surprise that complex societies have their glitches. To cooperate outside kin groups is contrary to deeply evolved parts of our nature, and it takes work.

Richard Dawkins's *The Selfish Gene* instructs us to place genes, rather than individuals or populations, at the center of evolution. Our genes have an ancestry that reaches back billions of years through untold generations of a vast back-catalog of species that have served as their survival and replication machines. Organisms evolve to complement an ever-changing world and serve their selfish genes. Each organism is used, abused, and then discarded so that the selfish genes will live on. Selfishness runs deep. It's in our genes. It *is* our genes.

Selfish genes make selfish organisms, and even organisms with brains use those brains to navigate the bloody, brutal, predatory world selfishly. Even the most advanced brains serve selfish ends: how to avoid being killed, how to kill, how to replicate those selfish genes. So, brains too have evolved to be selfish. The human brain, however, can break the rules, sometimes, and in some ways.

Evolution led the brain in a strange direction when primates began to cooperate. In cooperation, the success of one set of genes in one body is dependent on the success of other sets of genes in other bodies, which means that selfish genes need their organisms to cooperate—that is, to be unselfish: altruistic.

True altruism is rare among animals and is unstable under normal forces of natural selection because altruistic individuals tend to be raided or outcompeted by selfish ones. Free-riding: profiting from the work of others in a group, stealing, being lazy, is the default setting for selfish individuals and selfish genes. So, how can selfish genes evolve altruistic organisms?

Imagine you are the eighth rower in a boat with seven other rowers. You don't much care for rowing, you have been rowing for a while, it's cold, it's rainy, the boat is uncomfortable, and you are tired. Why not ease up a bit? The other seven rowers will make up for your lack of effort, and it's unlikely anyone will know you're the lazy one. Indeed, idleness will give you all the benefits of being in the boat with less of the pain. This tendency for individuals to free-ride always threatens the stability of group cooperation.

There is, however, a situation that stabilizes cooperation: competition with other boats.

Things are different if your boat is racing against another boat. Your success is now more immediately tied to the success of your boat. Your selfish genes now benefit more from cooperating to win, and if boat races are common, natural selection will select not only for successful genes and individuals but also successful boats—selfish boats rowed by altruistic people.

Evolution stabilizes this altruism by selecting genes that—quite selfishly—cause their organisms to cooperate, and a powerful way to make organisms cooperate is to give them traits such as empathy. Individuals who can respond to each other with empathy cohere as a group and row the fastest boats. And by fastest boats, of course, I mean most effective group hunts, disciplined armies, school boards, government agencies, tribal councils, and football teams. *The wise do not hoard, but by serving others receive more, and by giving to others, gain more* (v. 81).

All of this sounds great, but planted within this success story are the seeds of some of our most troubling paradoxes. It's remarkable that we evolved to cooperate so effectively and develop tight bonds that can extend beyond kin groups, but the key condition that selected for altruism—the constant threat of competitors—weaponized in-groups. The adaptations that shaped our altruism toward "friend" were sharpened on the harsh anvil of antagonism against "other." We are, by nature, vulnerable to classism, sexism, and racism. We can love Liverpool and hate Everton even though their football grounds are only eight hundred yards apart across Stanley Park. We can create political or religious enemies in our heads. We can become enslavers and exploiters. We are capable of kindness and cruelty, generosity and greed, altruism and selfishness. We are yin and yang.

People tend to find it more difficult to join together in sensible, calm, progressive action than reactive, aggressive, combative action. People can behave as though they were joined at the brain when they assemble into cohesive in-groups. Consider a Nazi rally. The fascist leader salutes: tens of thousands respond. But that's not you, right? Consider a football crowd. Strangers chant together, unscripted. They cry tears of real anguish when their team loses. They scream at the referee together. Sometimes they fight the fans of the opposing team. Still not you? Consider a church service, a concert, or the way you move through a library. We all have our tribes, usually a small collection of them, and these tribes compel our allegiance both consciously and unconsciously.

Group behavior is influenced by the way emotions affect thinking. We tend to think that our rational, thinking selves are in control of our emotional selves, but our emotional states change the way we think. When we are part of a group, we can sometimes be led to believe what the group believes even when, absent the group, we would have believed something quite different. We are unconscious of this because we are unconscious of the parts of the brain that mediate our emotions. We think we are in control, with our thinking brain, but the vast majority of the brain is outside our knowledge—know-ledge, think-age—and it gets up to all sorts of shenanigans. The brain feels (thinks) like it's a conscious thinking machine, but most of its work is performed as an unconscious sensing, emoting, motivating machine.

Are humans basically good or basically evil? This is a very old question but not a very good one. Many people think we are basically good but can be seduced by the "dark side," but that's not right. Other people think (and Christian doctrine argues) that we are fallen and that we must find forgiveness to transcend our innately evil natures, but that's not right either. We are both good and evil, each of us capable of both, and we are shockingly malleable.

Stanley Milgram performed a series of psychology experiments at Yale University in the 1960s to investigate how people respond to authority.[2] He made people think they were helping out a researcher with an experiment, but it was all a hoax: *they* were the experiment. They were given the task of delivering electric shocks to people they thought were experimental subjects. These poor people actually chose to electrocute people, sometimes thinking they were inflicting intense pain, sometimes even death, and they did this simply because they were told to do so by an authority figure in a white coat. Some people were traumatized by what they were doing, but to their own horror, they kept pushing the button. Humans tend to be weak-minded in the presence of authority.

Phillip Zimbardo showed us more of this with his evil-genius (and thoroughly unethical) 1971 Stanford Prison Experiment.[3] Zimbardo selected twenty-four young men and assigned them randomly to the role of prisoner or guard in a mock prison in the basement of the psychology building at Stanford University. The young men adapted to their roles with shocking ease. Within days, some of the "guards" became tyrants and some of the "prisoners" became demoralized victims. The experiment was supposed to run for two weeks but was abandoned early when the abuse inflicted by the guards began to border on torture.

Experiments such as these put the lie to the common platitude we hear when things go wrong in real prisons or when abuses are perpetrated by authority figures such as the police, who might say something like "We regret the behavior of these *few bad apples* and assure you that they do not represent our values." This is not how it is. Most of us are capable of both beautiful and ugly behaviors. Alexsandr Solzhenitsyn said it best in *The Gulag Archipelago*:

> If only there were evil people somewhere insidiously committing evil deeds, and it were necessary only to separate them from the rest of us and destroy them. But the line dividing good and evil cuts through the heart of every human being. And who is

> willing to destroy a piece of his own heart? During the life of any heart this line keeps changing place; sometimes it is squeezed one way by exuberant evil and sometimes it shifts to allow enough space for good to thrive. One and the same human being is, at various ages, under various circumstances, a totally different human being. At times he is close to being a devil, at times to sainthood. But his name doesn't change, and to that name we ascribe the whole lot, good and evil. Socrates taught us: *Know thyself.*[4]

A few bad apples? No.

It was not a few bad apples that tortured at Abu Ghraib prison in Iraq during the early stages of the Iraq War. It was a rotten culture in the US military that led people to commit abuses contradictory to their better natures.

It's not just a few bad apples who kill Black men in traffic stops. It's structural racism in American police forces, and it's poor training that causes police officers to behave irrationally and fearfully and act on implicit biases.[5]

No apple is either good or bad, but storage makes it so.[6]

The Milgram and Zimbardo experiments are the most famous experiments on conformity, but they're not actually the best. The most revealing and one of the earliest was performed by Solomon Asch in the 1950s.[7] The Asch conformity experiments showed how easily people yield their beliefs to the group. Experimental subjects were given a card with three lines on it and asked which of the three lines was the closest in length to a line on a second card. When answering independently, the error rate was less than 1 percent. When performing the experiment among a group of confederates who were deliberately giving the wrong answer, the error rate was more than 50 percent. "That intelligent, well-meaning young people are willing to call white black is a matter of concern,"[8] said Asch in history's greatest understatement since Emperor Hirohito.

This is the species that we are. We are weak-minded and weak-willed in the presence of authority figures or peer pressure, and we are self-deceptive. We are who we have been shown to be, not who we pretend to be, and it is this weak-minded and weak-willed creature who must buckle down to build communities that can thrive through our modern crises. We need to be humble in the face of what our minds can and can't do. This humility is particularly important when we judge others. One of our mental glitches is to find fault in others more easily than ourselves. Jesus was familiar with this glitch: "Why do you see the speck in your neighbor's eye, but not the log in your own eye?" (Matthew 7:3). And so was the Buddha: "One shows the faults of others like chaff winnowed in the wind, but one conceals one's own faults as a cunning gambler conceals his dice" (Dhammapada 352). And so was Laozi: *He who tiptoes will be unsteady. He who strides will not walk far. The opinionated are not bright. The self-righteous are unaware* (v. 24).

Hannah Arendt offers one of the most important insights into the nature of human evil with her analysis of the trial of Adolf Eichmann, one of the key organizers of the Holocaust.

She described a thoroughly boring, weak-minded, terrifyingly ordinary person, a bureaucrat, who had condemned millions to terrible suffering and death. She coined the term "banality of evil."[9] The idea that evil might be somewhere out there in the world to be confronted, rooted out, and stopped is comforting compared to the realization that evil might be lurking within our ordinary selves, living in our ordinary minds, and destroying others as we putter through life "doing our job" and "minding our own business."

> *Braggarts achieve little of value; boasters are eventually exposed. To the Dao, such people are leftover food; pointless exertion* (v. 24)

We don't live in the world in the way we think we do. We live in our minds. We don't see the world as it is but instead create it in our minds as the backdrop for our lives. Our imagined selves perform on the stage of our minds, or in the words of Will Storr, author of *The Status Game*, we engage in grandiosity when we cast the stories of our lives on our own minds: "We don't feel like players of games. We feel like heroes in stories."[10]

Earlier in the chapter we considered the evolution of human altruism through the selective advantages of empathy. I likened it to cooperation among eight rowers in a boat. When we are empathically connected, we can row more effectively as a group. Empathy is a social glue that makes us want to support the group, but there's much more than empathy going on in the minds of the eight rowers.

Each rower is feeling, emoting, and thinking, both consciously and unconsciously. Each of their minds is calculating, worrying, ruminating, scheming, and running scenarios that imagine their place in the story of their lives. They might be rowing poorly and worrying that the other rowers will look down on them. If so, they might be busy justifying their poor performance to remain adequately heroic in their own minds. On the other hand, they might be rowing particularly strongly, in which case they might be glorifying themselves as the hero of the boat. Many different things will be going on, but one thing is certain: each rower will considering their status in the boat. And not only in the boat but in dozens of status games they are playing (in their minds) in the world.

Much of our lives are spent comparing ourselves against others, and unexamined, these comparisons will tend toward self-justification and grandiosity. "Life," explains Will Storr, "is a game.... This game is inside us. It *is* us. We can't help but play.... Culture conspires in the dream of human life. Cultures are built out of billions of brains: billions of neural storytellers working in concert. They fill their religions, novels, newspapers ... with simplistic stories of moral heroes and evil villains. ...We all live the dream of the mind."[11]

THE RIGHTEOUS MIND

The opinionated are not bright. The self-righteous are unaware. (v. 24)
The wise love themselves without vanity; know themselves without arrogance. (v. 72).

The term "theory of mind" is used to describe how people assess the emotions and motivations of others. It's the "borderline telepathy" I mentioned earlier. We base a lot of our decisions on what we think others are thinking and feeling. (Well, if *he* says it's okay I guess . . . well, he's a scientist, right? I thought line "a" was the longest, but they all seem to think it was . . . what? They all selected line "b." I guess that's probably right, then. What *was* that smile? Affection? Pity? Will she laugh if I ask her out? What will she think if I *don't* ask? Future happiness? Instant humiliation? Did I leave the gas on?[12] The human mind is a torture chamber.)

In his elegant and deeply disturbing Vietnam War novel *The Things They Carried*, Tim O'Brien is drafted into the army but does not want to go to Vietnam. He is afraid of the war and morally opposed to it. He takes off north, heading toward Canada, intending to flee, but his mind is tortured by imagining what people will think. At one point he's in a boat in the Boundary Waters of northern Minnesota, mere yards from the Canadian border. All he has to do is jump across to safety, but he balks: "All those eyes on me—the town, the whole universe. . . . I could hear people screaming at me. Traitor! they yelled. Turncoat! Pussy! . . . And right then I submitted. . . . I would go to the war—I would kill and maybe die—because I was embarrassed not to."[13]

Laozi encourages us to be courageous enough to resist fighting: *Rash courage can be fatal. The courage to resist can be liberating* (v. 73). He also encourages us to guard against the reactive voices in our heads:

The wise reside in the core, not on the surface; in the fruit, not in the flower. (v. 38)
Seal the openings, close the doors, and life will always be easy. Succumb to the desires of the outer world and you will suffer to the end of your days. (v. 52)
Be as dust: a profound unity. Those who attain this cannot be seduced or rejected, promoted or impeded, honored or disgraced. (v. 56)

Theory of mind is central to understanding interactions among humans. The stories in our heads play games with us, and we are not as rational as we think we are. We don't analyze and solve problems with powerful, unbiased cognition. Our decisions are shaped by our emotions, relationships, and cultures. We use many different mental heuristics to solve complex problems.

Speed is sometimes more important than accuracy. Imagine a scenario in which danger is immediate and the senses are receiving urgent inputs. What was that cracking noise? Is the cliff face collapsing? What's that brown shape moving through the trees? A bear? That rustling in the grass, what's that? What's that smell? Sometimes it is better to ignore some of the input—the beautiful, sunny day with blue skies and the twittering of the song birds—in order to increase processing speed. Mental triage skips some of the fluff to foreground immediate needs.

Another thing we do is create stories in our minds so that we can draw conclusions about how events fit the story. It's an incredible system but imperfect. Sometimes we'd be better off slowing down and taking fewer shortcuts in order to get things right. The elephant-rider mental duality is a simplified way of considering the root cause of hundreds of mental heuristics (shortcuts) including negativity biases, the bandwagon effect, the masked man fallacy, the availability heuristic, the ostrich effect, confirmation biases, the sunk cost fallacy, the IKEA effect, the hot hand fallacy, the halo effect, and many others.[14] And there's one particularly fascinating group of heuristics that has a huge influence on the shaping of human societies: morals.

Ancient texts speak frequently of morals, sometimes wisely but often dogmatically and without wisdom. Oscar Wilde probably had it right when he wrote the line, "Morality is simply the attitude we adopt towards people whom we personally dislike" for Mrs. Cheveley.[15] Isaac Asimov's fictional psychohistorian Salvor Hardin might have been even closer when he pronounced, "Never let your sense of morals prevent you from doing what is right."[16] And yet, morals are held in the highest esteem. The US Republican Party claims to be the party of morals. It's lying to itself, of course, but that it makes the claim at all is indicative of its reverence for morals. Republican party morals, that is, not Oscar Wilde's.

So, what are these things we call morals? They vary, of course, from time to time, place to place, and culture to culture. Victorian gentlemen judged Africans as immoral and felt morally justified in enslaving them. Today's morals condemn those awful Victorian gentlemen. One can only hope that we will make further social progress such that tomorrow's morals will condemn us for refusing to tear down today's systems of enslavement.

Morals form part of the structure of a community. They mix rules and laws with clusters of unspoken norms and expectations to make a matrix of ways of being. We know, somehow, how to act, dress, speak, and behave so that we will conform with the moral landscape of our time and place. It's okay to wear pajamas when you're working from home but not when you show up to the office. Abhorrent now, but there was a time and a place where it was moral to fly a swastika flag and the Confederate battle flag.

Laozi's understanding of morals makes up a large amount of what he represented as De, which I most often translate as "virtue." The difficulty in understanding morals is illustrated in verse 38: *Lacking Dao, we fall back on De. Lacking De, we fall back on kindness. Lacking kindness, we fall back on morality. Lacking morals, we resort to rituals and rules.* This human tendency to subordinate cognition to morals is an important feature of our working minds. Morals are hard to define, but as US Supreme Court justice Potter Stewart said about pornography, we're not sure we can define it, but we know it when we see it.

This might make it seem as though morals can't be defined, that they change entirely with culture, and that there can't be any universal morals. Jonathan Haidt and his colleagues beg to differ. Moral foundations theory is detailed in Haidt's wonderful book *The Righteous Mind*,[17] which defined six moral foundations.

The first moral foundation is care. It is universally considered moral to care for others and to limit harm. Kindness and compassion are considered a moral foundation everywhere:

> *To big or small, to many or few, respond to vice with virtue.* (v. 63)
> *I have three treasures. . . . The first is compassion.* (v. 67)

The second moral foundation is fairness, which attenuates the moral of care. We may generally wish the best for people and care about them, but we don't like it when they cheat. It makes us care a bit less. Humans have a strong sense of justice: "That's not fair!" We respond differently and with greater or lesser degrees of proportionality, but we all see fairness as moral in some ways and to some degree. An important heuristic stemming from our sense of fairness is reciprocity. We tend to give more to people who have given to us. We tend to expect more help from people we have helped. Laozi recognizes this as a weakness. *The wise are ruthless. They treat all people equally* (v. 5).

The third moral foundation is loyalty, and here we think of moral characteristics such as patriotism and self-sacrifice. Not everybody is convinced about the virtues of patriotism, and we choose different targets for our actions of self-sacrifice, but the concept is universal because everybody is drawn toward group loyalty in some way and to some degree. The *Daodejing* warns against false loyalty: *When the family falls into conflict we hear talk of dutiful sons. When the country falls into chaos the patriots present themselves* (v. 18). The *Daodejing* also cautions leaders that loyalty can be fickle: *The more calls are made for law and order, the more robbers and bandits will abound* (v. 57). The power of loyalty is evident in eights rowing boats.

The fourth moral foundation is respect for authority, and the differences among people become more obvious. People with an anarchic spirit are frustrated by those they see as mindless sheeple—who see those tatty anarchists as selfish. Hierarchies are a part of our moral landscape. Some people, in all positions within the hierarchy, are more comfortable with hierarchy than others.

Meanwhile, hierarchies perpetrate real and symbolic violence. Sociologists have observed how people in dominant positions in a hierarchy tend to stand erect and speak with confidence (and in the language of their choice), while people in subjugated positions may stoop and mumble.[18] Our location in a hierarchy acts out in our behaviors and affects our health and life expectancy. Our comportment reinforces our place in the hierarchy, and our place in the hierarchy manifests in our lived experiences.

Laozi recognizes that authority presents serious problems, cannot be forced, and should come from respect:

> *Can you love people and guide them without manipulation?... To lead without dominating: this is profound virtue."* (v. 10)
>
> *When the humble leader has done her work the people will say, "Look! We did it all ourselves!"* (v. 17)

But he respects authority above anarchy: *Worst, are the leaders people despise*" (v. 17).

The fifth moral foundation is a sense of purity or sanctity, which has a few different outlets. People have different ideas of bodily purity or sanctity, particularly in sexuality. A sexual preference might be viewed by one person as an expression of beauty and another as a perversion; playful or corrupting, delightful or diseased, loving or degrading, harmless or subversive. It's not black or white. It's fifty shades of . . . my bad. Patriotism and religion also play on sanctity, particularly sanctity of the spirit. Laozi treads a central line through this territory, expressing no disgust but warning against an excessive focus on the *desires* or *cravings*:

> *The five colors blind the eye. The five notes deafen the ear. The five tastes dull the palate.* (v. 12)
>
> *The greatest mistake is desire. The worst misfortune is discontent. The greatest curse is craving.* (v. 46)

The sixth moral foundation is the desire for liberty, or resistance to oppression, that might be viewed in a larger political sense as hatred for oppressors or, in a more local sense, as aversion to bullies. Laozi has no time for oppressors or bullies. He sees them as *leftover food, pointless exertion, things that the world despises* (v. 24) and antithetical to the Dao:

> *The more heavily the government arms itself the more the people will riot.* (v. 57)
>
> *When government is restrained, unobtrusive, the people will be simple, genuine. When government is severe, prying, the people will be needy, cunning.* (v. 58)

The people are unruly. Their leaders interfere with their lives. That is why they are unruly. (v. 75)

We navigate these six dimensions of morality, using them as mental shortcuts to align ourselves with the people around us. We all have all six morals, but each is amplified or reduced as if six moral voices were being blended on a morality graphic equalizer. Fairness to one person might mean the death sentence, which might represent an unforgiveable lack of compassion and care, to another. Loyalty might mean stepping up and going to war for one's country, but it might also mean refusing to fight an unjust war. Purity: carnality or art?

There is enormous value in knowing something about moral foundations theory, especially in the political arena, because it can help us resist alienation and support an ethic of respectful disagreement and honest debate. "How on earth could they possibly believe that?!" is a useless question when spat out rhetorically but a valuable one when asked inquisitively and tackled with honesty. To know other people, to understand why they espouse certain views, and to understand when their opinions are driven by morality or other heuristics rather than cognition are borderline superpowers.

The ways of people are difficult to understand, and part of the problem is that we think it's easier than it actually is, or as Mark Twain said, "It ain't what you don't know that gets you in trouble. It's what you know for sure that just ain't so." We think it's easy because our mind is doing all the thinking and telling us it's easy. The mind lies. It doesn't have everything all under control. It takes shortcuts. It makes huge mistakes. Our mind blocks us from understanding our weaknesses. Morals and other heuristics trick us into a false sense of knowing.

We are unaware of the many mental shortcuts we use in decision-making. We exhibit certainty about things, often very important things, that we barely understand. The groupish behavior of people reveals just how animal-like we really are. A truly intelligent species would probably consider us interesting but predictable and clearly not yet fully conscious. And not at all enlightened.

ON FREE WILL AND JUSTICE

Those who follow the rules blindly earn no respect, and so they roll up their sleeves and act with force. (v. 38)

There is already a great executioner who is skilled like a master carpenter and whoever tries to supplant the master carpenter, and carve their wood, will not escape without injuring their hands. (v. 74)

So, the ways of people are strange and frequently surprising, and isn't it a little bizarre that we continue to be surprised?[19] We keep expecting people to be rational even when, time and time again, they refuse to conform to our expectations. We keep expecting people to do things that we know, when we think about it for more than two seconds, that they won't do. The entire discipline of economics was based on the idea that *Homo economicus* would rationally choose the best value and, acting in rational self-interest, would deliver competition, innovation, and balance. It's obviously too good to be true. It keeps not happening, and we keep being surprised. Why is that?

Another way to approach this is to ask why people make the choices they make. And here we're going to get into some really strange territory, because I'm going to argue that people don't actually choose to do the things they do—at least not in the way we usually think of choosing. In other words, I'm going to argue that there's no such thing as free will.

To question the idea of free will is a little out there for most people. It even seems strange to those who study it. Even those who accept the idea intellectually and advance it seem to find that it *feels* strange.

The idea that there is no such thing as free will is basically the idea that you don't make any decisions or choices independent of prior determinants. You may have felt as though you chose to do something, but other things happened prior to the decisive-seeming thought. Those prior things determined, or at least biased, what you then went on to think. In other words, you don't control your thoughts with your thoughts, so you don't have free will.

Consider movie night. You think you have free will in answering the question "What movie shall we watch tonight, honey?," but you don't. Your freedom of choice is constrained in many ways. Let's say you choose *Butch Cassidy and the Sundance Kid* (again!) rather than *Millennium Actress.* You've loved George Roy Hill's classic since you were a kid, and you've never heard of Satoshi Kon's classic. How could you choose the movie if you've never heard of it? No-brainer. (I love the term no-brainer.) Thousands of other movies you've never heard of were also not in your brain.

Consider the following scenario. You and your partner have been invited to dinner at the house of another couple. A third couple, also invited, start making lewd jokes about gay people. Do you intervene and ask them to stop speaking disrespectfully? You are free to either speak up or let it pass. Your morals are not the question here so much as your free will to act on them. You imagined this scenario in a certain way depending on many prior determinants.

Okay, let's change the scenario. Let's say you imagined straight couples. Now imagine them as gay. Let's say you imagined a dinner party in a farmhouse in rural Indiana. Now imagine it in a basement apartment in the Bronx, a yachty suburb in Miami, a yurt in Mongolia, or an informal settlement in India. Had you been in these different settings you may have reacted very differently while still feeling you had done so with free will.

Consider a different scenario. You are serving on a jury. A man is accused of murder. The main evidence against him comes from two eyewitness accounts. Both eyewitnesses had a clear sight of the murder and are confident that they saw him kill the victim. Do you vote guilty or not guilty? You are free to choose.

Again, let's flip the scenario. First, change the racial heritage of the accused and then that of the victim and then that of the jury. Did any combinations make you think differently, say a white jury judging a white accused based on the testimony of white witnesses against a Black victim? Now, move the scenario to a different culture, say Russia, Saudi Arabia, or South Sudan. Do you still have the same reaction to the evidence?

We could change lots of other things in our scenarios. Make the jurors fearful, angry, or hungry, and they are likely to make a harsher judgment. Lots of things can affect how we "choose" to behave.

We think we have freedom to choose what to do because we think we have freedom to think what to think, but we actually have very little control over what we think. What thought will you think next? Well, it's not your choice. Thoughts arise out of consciousness based on prior determinants, and those prior determinants were influenced by what came before. And what came before was experience, culture, epigenetics, culture, and genetics all the way back to the experiences of your ancestors, both human and prehuman, that shaped your genome. Do you choose to react to the sight of a snake? No, your brain reacts to snakes because brains evolved to react to snakes millions of years ago.

If you're considering the challenge to free will for the first time, you should probably be objecting strenuously by now. It feels like you are in control of your own mind, and the idea that you are not, at least not in the way you think, is unsettling. It's easier to ignore the idea and move on. But don't. Let's try a different tack.

Consider brain damage. Things can go wrong with the brain. (Honestly, the brain is so intricate it's amazing anything ever goes right with it.) In the famous case of Phineas Gage, what went wrong with his brain was an explosion on a railroad construction site that speared his brain with a metal rod. Remarkably, Phineas survived the accident but suffered significant personality changes. Accounts are often exaggerated, but poor old Phineas appears to have become a bit of an asshole for a while. So, what of his free will? We presume that he didn't choose to become an asshole overnight. He presumably still felt as though he had free will, the ability to make choices, but he was making different choices after the restructuring (understatement!) of his brain. We make our choices using the brain that we have, and we don't get to choose our brain any more than Phineas Gage did. Eventually, Phineas Gage died of complications from epilepsy.

And isn't epilepsy a fascinating case.

Do epileptics choose to set off uncontrolled bursts of activity in their brains causing all kinds of trauma, including violent seizures? No, of course not. That's ridiculous. To imagine epileptic seizures as being under the control of free will would be, well, until recently, it would have been quite common. Epilepsy has been linked to sinful ways for millennia, and thanks to Jesus ridding an epileptic boy who "foameth and gnashesh with his teeth" of unclean spirits in Mark 9: 25–27, Christians were stuck with the idea of epilepsy as a form of demonic possession for centuries. Thousands of epileptic women were burned as witches. It took clear science and modern sensibilities to recognize that epilepsy made people's brains do things against their will. Progress, clear and simple.

Next step: Let's look at a mental illness that has very obvious impacts on thought processes and behavior. Schizophrenia is a disease causing scattered patterns of thought, delusions, paranoia, and hallucinations. People with schizophrenia struggle socially and suffer high rates of violence and suicide. They don't make the same choices that nonschizophrenics make. So, are they making their choices with free will? Sure, with the free will a schizophrenic brain allows rather than with the free will a nonschizophrenic brain allows.

Let's draw an interim conclusion before pressing on to encompass more. Any system of justice worthy of the name should pay attention to our understanding of diseases such as epilepsy and schizophrenia that so obviously change the way the mind works. These people do things that they wouldn't do if they had control of their minds—if they had free will. So, why punish them with things such as jail time? What does that achieve? Treating people makes sense, and separating them from others make sense, but punishment does not. *The wise . . . are trusting of people who are honest and also of those who are dishonest. Thus, they have the virtue of faithfulness* (v. 49).

Okay, next step. Let's look at a couple of consequential but less dramatic mental disorders. The term "attention deficit hyperactivity disorder" (ADHD) was first used in the *Diagnostic and Statistical Manual of Mental Disorders* as recently 1987, and the term "autism spectrum disorder" (ASD) as recently as 2013, only a dozen years ago, but ADHD is now diagnosed in 15 percent and ASD in 3 percent of US college students.[20]

"Kids these days!" I know, right? But no, kids haven't changed as much as our understanding of their minds. Kids with ADHD and ASD are not dilatory malcontents or willful troublemakers. They are kids who struggle with emotional and behavioral regulation. And although the struggle is largely in their brains, it cannot be controlled by force of will. Kids with ADHD and ASD will not magically develop more willpower just by setting deadlines or creating sticky note reminders.

So, another interim conclusion. Any system of education worthy of the name should pay attention to our understanding of disorders such as ADHD and ASD that so obviously narrow the horizons of free will in a classroom setting. Why are we teaching and assessing students the way we do? Why are we trying to make kids sit still in boring lectures? Why are we giving any of our students all these pointless quizzes, tests, and exams? Are we actually trying to help them learn, or is the purpose of the education system to sort and grade kids as if they were eggs or apples?

Okay, last step: the so-called neurotypical, bless their hearts. What is it, really, this thing we call free will? In any given circumstance, our freedom to think a certain way is constrained by our genetics and our culture; narrowed by our environment and our educational background; constricted by hunger, dehydration, or tiredness; influenced by day of the week, the time of year; and hugely biased by the last thing we saw, heard, or smelled. If you're hearing this for the first time your mind is probably rebelling against it, but it's devilishly difficult to investigate your mind honestly with your mind. Your mind is not yours in quite the way you think it is. That's okay, but it's better to know it. *The crowds have an abundance, a surfeit. Me? I have nothing; I am confused, a fool. Most people seem bright; I seem dull. . . . I am not like other people. I am nourished by the great mother* (v. 20).

The argument against free will is a lot. My mind rebels against it. But while it's extremely difficult to develop a feeling of no free will, it's easy enough to make sense of it intellectually, and the notion is extremely important, I think, in understanding why we struggle to solve complex problems. Our minds present complex problems to us in simplified and biased ways. Our minds also distract us from the pain of grappling with stressful problems if they think that will better serve our selfish genes.

If we join the idea of no free will to the concept of no self that we discussed in Chapter 5, we begin to see why we are struggling to manage our modern crises. We are not who we think we are. Collectively, we are a much less capable species than we believe, and we are much less in control of our minds than we think. We are, indeed, not who we think we are either individually or collectively. Laozi had some inkling of this:

> *The brightest path appears dark[;] . . . the clearest things are opaque.* (v. 41)
> *Tempering desire you see the depths. Embracing desire you see the surfaces. . . . This unity is the deep mystery, the mystery of mysteries, and the gateway to spiritual awakening.* (v. 1)
> *To know your ignorance is good. To be ignorant of your ignorance is a sickness.* (v. 71)

LETTING GO

> *Though the gates of heaven may open and close can you abide like a bird with her nestlings? Though your mind may penetrate the secrets of the cosmos can you continue to practice nonaction?* (v. 10)

We do have the capacity to solve our modern crises—kind of, in theory—but we will fail the test. Multiple tests, actually. We have the technology and the intelligence but lack the temperament. The first test is the letting go that could allow the environment to recover. The second test is the letting go that could stop the unnecessary misery that people cause to others. The only test we can pass is the third one: the letting go of our selves.

It's not in the nature of people to work as a global community toward sustainability. It is necessary to convince many wealthy and powerful countries, corporations, and people to release the environment from their grip and to work together in common cause, but it will not be possible. Something akin to this level of cooperation has proven possible in wartime when large groups of people have been convinced to do violence against other groups of people. In wartime levels of commitment and motivation can be extremely high, and both community togetherness and self-sacrifice are key features. It has been suggested that we frame climate change as the enemy in order to leverage the us-versus-them mentality into an us-versus-climate mentality, but the problem is too nuanced and the enemy is too abstract.

And if we were to come together in common cause, what cause would we adopt? Would we actually turn our collective efforts toward saving the environment, or would "saving the environment" really mean saving ourselves? I'm afraid it's much more likely that the common cause would be ours, not the environment's.

And these war analogies reveal our tendency to solve problems by control. We see climate change as a problem that has gotten out of control and therefore one over which control must be restored. The level of control needed is much greater than any control that humanity has hitherto mustered, so we need a massive effort—a moonshot effort (stop!)—to bring people together in common cause to focus the effort and wrestle the biggest enemy ever. These are the ways of people. It is in our nature to squabble with each other, and it is in our nature to control and dominate. It is not in our nature to let go.

We need to resist the urge to tighten our grip on the environment. We need to loosen our grip. We need to let go. The *Daodejing* passes two key concepts down to us through the millennia. They have always been vital teachings, although few ever seem to have learned from them, and they remain as vital today as they were when they were first uttered. The first is *wei wuwei*: do not-doing, embrace inaction, cede control. *Do without doing. Act without acting* (v. 63). The second is Dao: the Way, the Path. The Dao of humanity should be to embrace nature, follow its guidance; be natural. The Dao of nature, the Eternal Dao, shows us the Way but is indifferent to us. *Nature is ruthless. It has no special love for any creature. . . . The space between heaven and earth is a bellows. Empty and yet inexhaustible* (v. 5).

There is no fixing the environmental mess we're in, and the more we struggle the deeper the hole we will dig. The action required is inaction: stop digging.

People rebel at the idea of ceding control, understandably so. It sounds like giving up. Wait, what, your plan to fix this mess is to do nothing? Yep, that's right, although it's not a plan, just a statement of principal. Slow down. Do less.

The next test is whether or not we can cede control over each other. The *Daodejing* passes down a number of valuable teachings and two central concepts to help us with this. The first concept is De: virtue:

> *It is virtue to attend to your own obligations. It is not virtue to insist others do the same.* (v. 79)
> *Can you love people and guide them without manipulation?* (v. 10)

The virtues of De are all about slowing down and releasing control. They promote humility, equanimity, and compassion. *The wise cleave to the one as their foundation. Not conceited, they shine. Not emphatic, they are reliable. Not boastful, their renown endures* (v. 22). These messages are offered explicitly to leaders:

> *To raise without possessing. To nourish without spoiling. To guide without controlling.* (v. 51)
> *So the wise, to stand above, must speak from below; to lead, must follow. . . . The wise do not resist and thus are not resisted.* (v. 66)

The second concept is yin and yang, the opposing yet complementary poles between which we should seek balance. The path we should shape is the never-ending sinuous path that meanders between yin and yang. People tend to strike with the gauntlet of yang rather than stroking with the kid gloves of yin and will tend to benefit from steering back toward yin, but the overarching rules should be to cede control, to let go. Exerting too much control over either yin or yang bends the path out of shape.

This message does not weigh the same for everybody, of course, because power and control are not shared equally. Some people exert excessive control over the lives of others, and some people have precious little control over their own lives.

We live in a colonized world. The countries with the most equitable, socially minded, and democratic governments, which see themselves as the beacons of hope for civilized society, are also, by grim irony, the global colonizers. They became rich and civilized by conquest and dispossession, deriving wealth and power and then maintaining it through military and economic control. The wealthy, both wealthy people and wealthy countries, could transform societies overnight by ceding control, but that's not going to happen. The colonizers see themselves (ourselves) as the righteous saviors of the world: the best hope for freedom and democracy. No, things are not perfect, we say, but surely our power and control are needed to hold this mess together. We could loosen our chokehold over the flow of global resources and take our feet off the necks of the global poor, we suppose, but what disasters might lurk? The fear is that the great and glorious "we" might end up like the unwashed and inglorious "they."

The world is trapped in a vast cognitive dissonance rationalization; a sort of rich man's burden.[21] It's terrible-terrible, but what's to be done? What's to be done is to cede control. Let go. But we won't.

How do I know? I know (and you know) because you and I are among the wealthy and powerful, and we're not willing to let go. Maybe we're not part of the disgusting 0.1%, you and I, but if you're reading this book you're probably pretty comfortably positioned on the pyramid of privilege. I'm picturing you reading under an electric light in a chair in a house. Are you willing to give that up? Why should you when there are others who have so much more?

People don't cede control unless they think their contributions will gain traction and bring significant change. People do seek community and status within it and will make enormous sacrifices for the greater good. What's needed is commitment to a shaping of the path with patience, persistence, and equanimity. Transformation may not be possible, but incremental change is always happening, and you do get to choose in which direction you would prefer to shape those changes.

There's no hope for a dramatic transformation in human nature, and that's probably a good thing. Rousing people into drastic actions is not wise. Govern in accordance with the Dao and the evil spirits will be left asleep. *They are always there, but the wise can step quietly around them* (v. 60). Utopias descend into dystopias. Community building and the development of effective social systems are never sudden, urgent, and immediate needs; they are always-needs. It will be helpful to let go of our ideologies and settle into the long, patient work of shaping the path.

And as we settle in to shape the path, even as it may seem hopeless and even as it may keep being torn up or eroded away and need reshaping again and again, we can remember Laozi's favorite vehicle of metaphor: water. *Nothing can match it. . . . Soft gets the better of hard. Gentle gets the better of rough* (v. 78). Or as James Carse might say, true power comes not from winning finite games but from continuing honest play in the infinite game.[22]

We need to let go of the environment because trying to control the environment tends to make matters worse, and we need to let go of others because controlling others creates misery. To achieve any of this, we need to let go of ourselves: our selves. And so, to paraphrase T. S. Eliot, we reach the end of our little exploration and find ourselves back at the beginning. We never cease from exploring, and at the end of our journey we return to where we started and know ourselves for the first time:

> *The motion of the Path is circular.... Everything is born of being.* (v. 40)
> *A flower grows, blooms, returns to the root.* (v. 16)

Letting go isn't easy, at least not the kind of letting go we're imagining here. It's a bit like letting yourself go out the door of a plane. The parachute has been carefully packed, the pull line has been firmly attached, and the plane is above the airfield. All you have to do is step out of the door, let yourself go, and yet: not easy. To let go, you have to take that step. The mad clamor of the plane, the wind rushing by, the turbulence, the shaking, the shouting, the anxiety and then the dizzying drop, the gut-wrenching you had feared, but then the parachute catches you. The view. The silence.[23]

The *Daodejing* encodes various concepts that draw us toward a deeper understanding of the impermanence of physical things, the oneness and connectedness of everything, and our own place in the grand scheme of things: the Dao. The *Daodejing* also encodes various pieces of specific advice on self-investigation with regard to not only humility and simplicity but also advocating stillness, meditation, mindfulness, and selflessness:

> *Be simple, like undyed silk; like the uncarved block. The self recedes. Desires soften.* (v. 19)
> *The wise put themselves last and yet advance, keep to the outside and yet remain centered, and through selflessness, find themselves.* (v. 7)

There may not be much that you can do to combat climate change and biodiversity loss or create a just society, but you can at least care for yourself. *Cultivate yourself to develop genuine virtue. Cultivate the village to support enduring virtue. Cultivate the world to sustain universal virtue.... In myself I see the self.* (v. 54). The human characteristics advocated by the *Daodejing* are centered on simplicity and letting go. In meditation, learn to let go of trains of destructive thought. In leading an ethical life, let go of cravings and desires. In dealing with others, let go of the desire to control and dominate. Engage with the world deeply but maintain a childlike trust, a simplicity, and release the ego: let go of the self.

Very few people seem to have taken the time or put in the effort to understand how to change their own minds. Rumi understood this: "Yesterday I was clever so I wanted to change the world. Today I am wise so I want to change myself." Laozi also understood this:

The person who tends to their self can be trusted to lead people and care for the world. (v. 13)

To know others is to be wise. To know yourself is to be enlightened. (v. 33)

What will you do with your fleeting moment of consciousness? Be happy and be kind, is all. This is De. You are a speck on a mote in a whirlpool in the middle of an ongoing explosion. This is Dao.

THE *DAODEJING* OF LAOZI

1

The path that can be trodden is not the Eternal Path
The name that can be spoken is not the eternal name

Nameless it is the origins of the universe
Named it is the mother of the ten thousand things

Tempering desire you see the depths
Embracing desire you see the surfaces
  Different perspectives but of the same source

This unity is the deep mystery
  the mystery of mysteries
  and the gateway to spiritual awakening

2

Admiring the most beautiful creates ugliness
Praising the greatest good creates evil

Existence and nonexistence arise together
Difficult and easy become each other
Long and short shape each other
High and low incline toward each other

Sound and tone harmonize each other
Before and after follow each other

Therefore the wise
  manage without controlling
  teach without telling
  tend to everything without favoritism
  raise without possessing
and claim no reward

Because they claim no reward
their rewards never diminish

3
Diminishing celebrity limits striving
Moderating wealth limits theft
Restraining desire limits yearning

Therefore the wise govern by
  emptying hearts and filling bellies
  weakening ideology and strengthening bones
  showing people how to live simply satisfied
  preempting challenges from the treacherous

Practicing not-doing to maintain balance

4
The Dao is an empty vessel
  that cannot be drained
It is bottomless
  and the forebear of all

It can blunt the sharp
  untangle the knotted
  soften the glaring

It is like settled dust
  like a deep pool

I do not know whose child it is
It seems like the ancestor of god

5
Nature is ruthless
It has no special love for any creature
The wise are ruthless
They treat all people equally

The space between heaven and earth
is a bellows
Empty and yet inexhaustible
The more it is pumped
the more it produces

Words are not inexhaustible
Say less and remain centered

6
The valley spirit never dies
Call her the mysterious female
Hers is the gateway
that birthed heaven and earth

She endures forever an endless thread
Tireless and abundant

7
Heaven and earth are eternal
Since they do not cling to life
they cannot be claimed by death

The wise put themselves last
and yet advance
keep to the outside
and yet remain centered
and through selflessness

find themselves

8

The highest good is like water
Water benefits everything without fuss
It settles in the lowest places
This is how it shows us the Path

Live in connection with the earth
Love generously
Speak the truth
Govern peacefully and in search of order
Work expertly
Act in time

Avoid conflict and contention
and there will be no regrets

9

Overfill a bowl and it will spill
Oversharpen a blade and its edge will brittle
Hoard wealth and your home will be a target for thieves
Amass prestige and you invite downfall and disgrace

Do good work and then step back
This is the Way of heaven

10

Can you unify the elements of your soul
    and keep them from dividing?
Can you focus your vital breath
    until you are as supple as a newborn?
Can you polish your inner mirror
    until its reflection is pure?
Can you love people and guide them
    without manipulation?

Though the gates of heaven may open and close
    can you abide like a bird with her nestlings?
Though your mind may penetrate the secrets of the cosmos
    can you continue to practice nonaction?

To give birth and nurture
To bear without possessing
To act without claiming
To lead without dominating
This is profound virtue

11
Thirty spokes join at the hub
but the axle turns in its empty space

Clay is shaped to make a bowl
but its hollow is what you use

Doors and windows are cut to make a house
creating the voids that allow you to enter and live

What is present makes a thing valuable
What is absent makes it work

12
The five colors blind the eye
The five notes deafen the ear
The fives tastes dull the palate

Aggressions   chasing hunting   derange the mind
Ambitions   power riches   lead one astray

The wise tend to the belly not the eyes

They reject that
They accept this

13
Be equally wary of honor and disgrace

Regard mental anguish as physical pain

Why do we say
Be equally wary of honor and disgrace?

Honor can demoralize
We are apprehensive about gaining it
We fear the disgrace of losing it

Why do we say
Regard mental anguish as physical pain?
The mind devises its own suffering
but without a physical self
how can it be conscious of suffering?

The person who tends to their self
can be trusted to lead people
and care for the world

14

Look for it it can't be seen
Listen for it it can't be heard
Reach for it it can't be touched
These three mysteries merge as one

In rising it does not brighten
In setting it does not darken
An unbroken thread of nameless things
from now back to the chaos
before the first

Call it the formless form
the imageless image
the unthought thought

Face it and you see no beginning
Follow it and you see no end

Hold tight to the Ancient Way
in order to master the present
To know the ancient beginnings
is the essence of the Dao

15

The ancient masters were subtle
    Mysterious   penetrating   profound
    too profound to understand
but perhaps we can describe them

Cautious as if crossing a frozen river
Vigilant as if sensing enemies on all four sides
Courteous like polite house guests
Yielding like melting ice
Sincere and uncomplicated like an uncarved block
Receptive like a valley
    Opaque   inscrutable   like muddy water

Who by nothing but stillness
    can render muddy water clear?
Who by persistent gentleness
    can quicken the moribund?

Those who follow the Path guard against excess
and are beyond the concerns
of old age and decrepitude

16

Attain complete emptiness
Maintain absolute stillness

All living things arise in unison
    and their arising is a return
A flower grows
    blooms
    returns to the root

Returning to the root is peaceful
    a return to one's original nature
    to the immutable
Knowing this is true wisdom
Not knowing this is disastrous

To know what endures is to be
enlightened   majestic   heavenly
in accordance with the Eternal Path

Following the Path leads to immortality
Though the self is ephemeral
there is no fear

17
Great leaders are barely known
Next are the leaders people admire
Next are the leaders people fear
Worst are the leaders people despise

If you give no trust
you will receive no trust

When the humble leader has done her work
the people will say
"Look! We did it all ourselves!"

18
When the great Path is deserted
humanity and morality take its place

When cleverness and intellect dominate
hypocrisy soon follows

When the family falls into conflict
we hear talk of dutiful sons

When the country falls into chaos
the patriots present themselves

19
Reject holiness   forgo cleverness
The people will profit a hundredfold

Reject benevolence   forgo righteousness
The people will rediscover authentic kindness

Reject craftiness   forgo profit
There will be no thieves

These are three valuable rules
but more important is the foundation

Be simple
    like undyed silk   like the uncarved block

The self recedes
Desires soften

20

How different is a formal *yes* from an informal *yeah*?
How different is good from evil?

Should we fear what others fear?
It seems we always have—but what foolishness!

The crowds are thriving and happy
    as if at the Tailao festival
    as if basking on the summer terrace

Me? I am quiet and calm
    like a newborn babe still too young to giggle
And so very tired   and with nowhere to go

The crowds have an abundance   a surfeit
Me? I have nothing   I am confused   A fool

Most people seem bright   I seem dull
They seem to have purpose   I don't know . . .
    I drift about like a desolate ocean
    I blow around like a feckless wind

They seem skilled   useful
Me? I am clumsy

I am not like other people
I am nourished by the great mother

21
Great virtue only comes from following the Path
The Path is indistinct and vague

Indistinct and vague   but at its center   shape
Indistinct and vague   but at its center   substance
Obscure   veiled   but within it   spirit
The spirit is true   and within it   trust

Known since ancient times
It is never forgotten
The ancestor of everything

How do I know it is the great ancestor?
By this

22
Yield to become complete
Be twisted to be straight
Be emptied to be full
Be broken to be whole
Have little to gain much
Have too much and be restless

The wise cleave to the one
as their foundation

Not conceited   they shine
Not emphatic   they are reliable
Not boastful   their renown endures
and since they do not compete
they cannot be challenged

Why did the ancestors say
Yield to become complete?
Were these just empty words?
Indeed not!
To be complete is to return

23

Nature is not a blabbermouth
    A storm doesn't go on all morning
    A cloudburst doesn't gush all day
What makes the wind and the rain?
Heaven and earth
    So if heaven and earth aren't long-winded
    surely people don't need to be

Engage with the Path to be one with the Path
Engage with virtue to be one with virtue
Engage with loss to be one with loss

Be one with the Path to master the Path
Be one with virtue to master virtue
Be one with loss to master loss

If you don't show trust
you won't find trust

24

He who tiptoes will be unsteady
He who strides will not walk far
The opinionated are not bright
The self-righteous are unaware
Braggarts achieve little of value
Boasters are eventually exposed

To the Dao such people are
    leftover food
    pointless exertion
Things that the world despises

So why imitate them?
Followers of the Path do not indulge

25

Something came to end the chaos
before the formation of heaven and earth
Silent
Empty
Standing alone unchanged
Everywhere
Always
Call it the mother of everything under heaven

Great means always flowing
Always flowing leads to reaching far
Reaching far results in returning to the root

Thus Dao is great
Heaven is great
The world is great
The king can be great

There are four greats and the king can be one of them

People emulate the earth
earth emulates heaven
and heaven emulates the Dao
The Dao simply is

26

Steadiness is the master of frivolity
Stillness is the ruler of impatience

The wise stay with the baggage wagons
when they travel
They may see magnificent sights
but remain satisfied with the simple
like a swallow in a nest

Why would a powerful ruler
    a commander of ten thousand chariots
rush about like a fool?

By frivolity   mastery is lost
By impatience   the ruler is deposed

27

A skilled tracker leaves no trace
A skilled speaker leaves no doubt
A skilled bookkeeper needs no gadgets

A well made door needs no padlock
    and yet cannot be forced
A well made binding needs no rope
    and yet cannot be loosened

The wise help everybody ignoring none
    saving everything
    wasting nothing
an inclusiveness that makes them luminous

Good people serve as teacher to those
    who need to learn
    who in turn
serve to help the teacher grow

Anyone who disrespects a teacher
    or undervalues a student
    may seem clever
but is on the wrong road

This is one valuable teaching of the Dao

28

Know the masculine
but cleave to the feminine
Be the mountain stream of the world
Being the mountain stream

your virtue is secure
and you return to infancy

Know the light
but cleave to the dark
Be an example to the world
Being an example
your virtue will not fail
and you return to boundlessness

Know your honor
but cleave to your humility
Be the river valley of the world
Being the river valley
your virtue will be inexhaustible
and you become like the uncarved block

The uncarved block can be worked
and shaped into useful things
The wise are turned into leaders
without any carving

29

Conquer the world and change it?
It can't be done
The world is sacred
it can't be controlled
Try to defeat it
you will lose it

The way of nature is
to lead but also to follow
to be calm and yet sometimes agitated
to be strong but not the strongest
to feel safe and then suddenly frightened

The wise limit wastefulness and pride
and temper the desire to control

30

Controlling by force of arms
is in opposition to the Dao
It invites retribution

Where armies bivouac thorn bushes grow
Where armies clash harvests fail

The wise get results and then withdraw
They don't presume to take by force
They get results without bragging or boasting
    without arrogance
Results only as a last resort
Results without intimidation

We grow strong and then grow old
but we are not the Path
    on the Path   at best   a piece
and what is not the Path must die

31

Weapons no matter how beautiful
are the tools of violence
All men should detest them
Followers of the Dao should forswear them

In peacetime a gentleman favors his left
In war he wears weapons on his right

Weapons are the tools of violence
not the tools of a gentleman
They should only be used as a last resort
and with humility

In victory be solemn
To glorify victory is to glorify killing
If you glorify killing you can never be whole

The left side is fortunate
and the right side is stricken
The officer stands to the left of his commander
    in battles   and at funerals

When people have been killed
hear their pitiful cries of sorrow
Treat victory as a funeral

32

The Dao is eternally nameless
The uncarved block   Minuscule
and yet beyond the scope of heaven and earth

If leaders could only abide by it
everything would pay homage to them
    heaven and earth would rejoice
    sweet dew would fall
    citizens
    without needing to be coerced
    would live in harmony

But we split the block
and give the pieces names
    to control
    to govern
When the names multiply it's time to stop
If you know when to stop you are safe

The Dao   to the world
    is as the stream to the valley
    is as the river to the ocean

33

To know others is to be wise
To know yourself is to be enlightened
To master others takes force
To master yourself takes strength

To be content is to be rich
Be persistent   develop willpower
hold your place   remain steady
and you will endure

To die remembered   undefeated
is close enough to immortality

34
The great Way is wide   in flood
    flowing left   flowing right
Everything depends on it for life
It gives freely   sparing nothing
It clothes and nourishes everything
but makes no claim on anything

It has no needs   no desires
Call it small
Everything returns to it   unbidden
Call it great

The wise do not claim to be greater than anything
which is why they can become great

35
Hold onto the great image
and let the world come to you
It will come quietly and peacefully

Fine music and exotic food
are passing pleasures
They attract passersby

The Path boasts no great speeches
no exotic flavors
no dramatic vistas
no grand music

but you can never have too much of it

36

To draw something in
    first stretch it out
To make something weak
    first allow it to grow strong
For a thing to be ruined
    it must first be raised
For a thing to be seized
    it must first be given

This is the secret insight
    how the soft and weak
    defeat the hard and strong

The big fish that rises up from the deeps
    can be hooked
The country that brandishes all its weapons
    can be overthrown

37

The Path maintains eternal nonaction
and yet leaves nothing undone

If leaders could abide by its example
everything would transform naturally

If desires were to arise
they would be calmed
The nameless uncarved block tempers desire

With desire managed all is quiet
The world settles into peace

38

True virtue is higher than virtue
    unassuming
    and therefore virtuous
Fake virtue is simply for display
    and therefore not virtuous at all

The most virtuous observe nonaction
    and are unselfish
The less virtuous make sure they are seen
    to act
The kind act generously
The righteous act ostentatiously
Those who follow the rules blindly
    earn no respect
    and so they roll up their sleeves
and act with force

Lacking Dao we fall back on De
Lacking De we fall back on kindness
Lacking kindness we resort to morality
Lacking morals we resort to rituals and rules

Rituals may have the appearance of loyalty
    and honesty
    but they reside at the edge of chaos
Blind obedience to the rules
    is the fountainhead of stupid

The wise reside in the core
    not on the surface
    in the fruit   not the flower

They reject that
and accept this

39

These ancient things attained wholeness

The sky   which became clear
The earth   which became placid
The spirits   which became divine
The valley   which was filled
The ten thousand things   which were brought to life
The kings of old   who were virtuous

If the sky loses its clarity   it might shatter
If the earth loses its tranquility   it might splinter
If the spirits lose their divinity   they might dissipate
If the valley is not replenished   it will empty and dry up
If the ten thousand things are not nurtured   they might be annihilated
If the ruler is not virtuous   he will fall

Noble has its origins in the common
The foundation of high is low

This is why rulers claim to be orphans   widows   beggars
They know the lowly are the root of the exalted

Don't desire to be precious like jade
Be tough like common stone

40
The motion of the Path is circular
The method of the Path is yielding

Everything is born of being
except being
which is born of nothing

41
When the best student hears of the Path
she studies in order to follow it
When the average student hears of the Path
her understanding comes and goes
When the weakest student hears of the Path
she laughs out loud
    but then   without laughter
    it wouldn't be the true Path

So it is said
The brightest Path appears dark
Advancing along the Path seems like retreating
The level Path is rugged
The most elevated virtue is a valley

The clearest things are opaque
The most abundant virtue feels insufficient
The staunchest virtue seems unsteady
The purest thing seems tainted

The great square has no corners
The perfect tool is unfinished
The finest music is hushed
The greatest image is blurred

The Path is hidden and nameless
yet only the Path gives and completes

42
Dao birthed one
One birthed two
The two birthed a third
The three birthed the ten thousand things

The ten thousand things carry
    Yin on their backs and enfold
    Yang in their arms
They blend with their Qi to attain harmony

++++

People loathe being abandoned   alone   unworthy
which is perhaps why kings take these as titles

Gain can come from losing
Loss can be the result of gaining

So here is a simple rule
The violent die violent deaths
This is a good basis for teaching

43
The softest things in the world
    override the hardest

The formless
    infiltrate the impenetrable

Thus we understand the influence
    of doing not-doing
    of teaching without telling

Few possess this influence

44

Which matters more
    your name or your body?
Which is more precious
    your body or your wealth?
Which is more painful
    loss or gain?

Great desire can be costly
Hoarded wealth can be lost

Know when you have enough
    there's no disgrace in that
Know when to stop
    there's no danger in that

The key to lifelong contentment

45

The great whole seems incomplete
    but can be used forever
The completely full seems empty
    but can never be drained

The straightest seem curved
Great skill appears clumsy
The most eloquent seem to mumble

Movement overcomes cold
Stillness overcomes heat
Calmness keeps the world in order

46

When the world is on the Path
fine stallions leave their manure in the fields
When the world loses its Way
mares are bred for warhorses

The greatest mistake is desire
The worst misfortune is discontent
The greatest curse is craving

When you are content with enough
There is always enough

47

Know the world
    without leaving your front door
Know heaven's Path
    without looking out of the window

The further you go the less you know

The wise know without going out
They see without looking
They don't act   and yet they complete

48

Those who study daily
    gain knowledge daily
Those who practice Dao daily
    relinquish knowledge daily
    dwindling until they master not-doing

Not-doing
    to ensure that nothing is left undone

Gain the world by not-doing
Try to control the world
    and it will evade you

49
The wise have no preconceived ideas
so they embrace the needs of the people

They treat good people well
and they treat bad people well
Thus they have the virtue of goodness

They are trusting of people who are honest
and also of those who are dishonest
Thus they have the virtue of faithfulness

The wise engage with the world
and remain simple at heart
Thus the people turn their eyes to them
and their childhood is restored

50
Between birth and death
  three in ten pursue life
  three in ten pursue death
  three in ten rush toward death
by pursuing their desires

Only the tenth
  can walk on the hills
  without meeting wild buffalo or tiger
  can enter a battle
  without weapons or armor

The buffalo finds no place to jab its horn
The tiger finds no place to sink its claws
The soldier finds no place to thrust his knife

Why?
The tenth one
  does not present a place for death

51

Dao gives birth to them
De raises them
Matter forms them
Energy animates them

and each of the ten thousand things
respects Dao and honors De

Their respect for Dao
and honor for De
are not by command
but by virtue of their very being

Because Dao gives them life
And De raises them
    nurtures them
    teaches them
    shelters and heals them
    protects and comforts them

To raise without possessing
To nourish without spoiling
To guide without controlling
This is the Primal De

52

In the beginning was the mother of the world
Knowing her you can know her children
    and the children can return you to the mother
    free of sorrow

Seal the openings   close the doors
and life will always be easy
Succumb to the desires of the outer world
and you will suffer to the end of your days

To see the small is enlightenment
To remain tender is strength

Use its light
    to return to clarity
    avoid misery
    and learn constancy

53

It only takes the least scrap of sense
to stay on the broad Path
but I fear wandering off

The broad Path is flat and straight
but people are fond of detours

The palace is full of splendor
    while the fields are choked with weeds
    and the granaries are left bare
They dress in extravagant clothes
    sporting fine swords at their side
    gorging on exotic food and drink
    accumulating wealth in abundance

This boastfulness and vanity is robbery
by people who have most certainly left the Path

54

What is well rooted is not easily pulled
What is firmly attached is not easily separated
Your descendants will honor their ancestors for generations

Cultivate yourself to develop genuine virtue
Cultivate your family to foster a wealth of virtue
Cultivate the village to support enduring virtue
Cultivate the country to promote abundant virtue
Cultivate the world to sustain universal virtue

Therefore
In myself I see the self
In my family I see what family means
In my village I see all villages

In my country I understand what countries are
In the world I see everything under heaven

55

To fully embody virtue
be like a newborn
Venomous insects   scorpions   snakes
will not bite or sting him
Wild animals will not claw him
Birds of prey will not swoop down on him

His bones are weak
his muscles are tender
and yet his grip is tight

He has yet to experience sex
and yet he gets firm erections
His vitality is great!

He screams and cries all day
without getting hoarse
His harmony is true!

To know this harmony is to know the eternal
To know the eternal is to be enlightened

Overfilling life is foolish
Letting the mind control the Qi is perilous

It causes exhaustion   a turning from the Path
What turns from the Path soon ends

56

Those who know don't speak
Those who speak don't know

Subdue your senses   Constrain your desires
Blunt your sharpness   Unravel your knots
Soften your glare

Be as dust
A profound unity

Those who attain this cannot be
    seduced or rejected
    promoted or impeded
    honored or disgraced

Therefore they are the most highly revered

57

Be straightforward in ruling a nation
Be unpredictable in war
Use not-doing in dealing with the natural world

I know this because
the more prohibitions and laws are enacted
    the poorer the people become
The more heavily the government arms itself
    the more the people will riot
As people become more ingenious and crafty
    the stranger they behave
The more calls are made for law and order
    the more robbers and bandits abound

So the wise say
Practice not-doing
    and the people will thrive independently
Invite quietness
    and the people will calm by themselves
Don't micromanage
    and the people will prosper freely
Be restrained
    and the people will enjoy
a simple and happy life

58

When government is restrained   unobtrusive
the people will be simple   genuine

When government is severe   prying
the people will be needy   cunning

Happiness teeters above misery
Misery lurks beneath happiness
Who knows which is in the future?

Without guidance
the upright revert to evil
and confusion and anarchy reign

So the wise are
sharp without being cutting
pointed without piercing
assertive without bullying
and brilliant without dazzling

59

In governing show moderation
    like a farmer storing grain
    like living off the land
Live sparingly and flexibly
This is what it is to accumulate virtue

With abundant virtue
    everything can be overcome
    anything can be achieved
and you are fit to rule
Rule like the mother
and you will rule long

Have deep roots and a solid base
This is the Path of longevity and clarity

60

Governing a big country
is like cooking a small fish

Govern in accordance with the Dao
and the evil spirits will be left asleep
They are always there
but the wise can step quietly around them

If evil has no reason to flourish
the wise have no reason to intervene

61

A great nation is the delta
at the end of the valley
the lowest point
where the river merges with the sea

Consider the female
Quieter than the male
she takes the lower position
and yet surmounts him

If a small country yields to a great one
it will be annexed
If a small country conquers a large one
it will eventually be absorbed

Some who yield conquer
Some who yield are conquered
A great nation needs more people
A small nation needs to serve

Both can have their way
It is fitting to yield and merge

62

Dao is the refuge of all things
Treasure for the noble
Protection for the wicked

Beautiful words earn admiration
Good deeds win respect

but those lacking beautiful words
    and good deeds
why would the Dao abandon them?

So at the coronation of the emperor
or the investiture of the three ministers
where a gift of fine jade might be made
    or a team of four horses

Kneel instead
humbly
and offer to teach
the Way   the Dao

The ancients valued the Dao highly
They said
Seek   and you will find
Offend   and you will be forgiven

Thus is the Dao a gift of the world

63

Do without doing
Act without acting
Find flavor in the bland

To big or small
to many or few
respond to vice with virtue

Tackle the difficult in its simplest form
Tackle big problems while they are small
Difficult problems arise from simple ones
Big problems arise from small ones
So the wise
    do not struggle with big problems
    and yet they solve them

Frivolous promises negate trust
Halfhearted work creates complications
So the wise
    by treating the easy as hard
    find everything easy

64

That which is settled is easily maintained
That which still develops is easily managed
The brittle is easily broken
The small is easily scattered

Act before problems develop
Govern well before disorder emerges

The massive tree first grows as a sapling
The tall tower is built from a pile of bricks
The journey of a thousand miles begins
    with a single step

Those who act cause harm
Those who snatch fumble
So the wise
    leave things alone to avoid causing harm
    and don't snatch at things to avoid dropping them
(The unwise often fail near the end
Take care at endings as much as in beginnings)

The wise do not desire desire
    nor treasure treasures
They learn to unlearn
    so they can restore to people
    what they have overlooked

Thus they return everything to its true nature
    and dare not act

65

The ancients were devoted followers of the Path
They were cautious when teaching the people
Knowledge can encourage craftiness
and crafty people can be difficult to govern

Likewise it is deceitful to use trickery to govern
Governing without trickery is a great blessing

To see this is to see a deeper pattern
a deeper pattern that leads to profound virtue
profound virtue that reaches far back
into the place to which everything returns
where everything is guided
toward order and unity

66

The seas and great rivers are the kings
of the hundred valleys and ravines
They rule by lying below
Water flows down to them
giving the valley shape

So the wise   to stand above
must speak from below
to lead   must follow

So the wise can be placed over people
without being a burden
can be ahead of people
without causing an obstruction
can be praised
without becoming tiresome

The wise do not resist
and thus are not resisted

67

Everyone says my Dao is great
but it is simply mine unique
and therefore for this great

I have three treasures
that I hold and protect

The first is compassion
The second is moderation
The third is humility

The compassionate can be courageous
The frugal can be generous
The humble can be great leaders

but to be courageous without compassion
to trade moderation for extravagance
to forsake humility in order to win
This is death

Compassion in battle brings victory
Compassion in defense builds strength
Heaven protects with compassion

68

A good commander doesn't rush ahead
A good warrior doesn't lose his temper
A good leader overcomes without confrontation

The best rulers put themselves below the people
This is the virtue of noncontention
the source of power of strong leaders
in harmony with heaven's Way

69

The master of war says
"I dare not strike first
but prefer to defend

I dare not advance an inch
but prefer to retreat a foot"

This is to advance without advancing
reach out without striking
confront without attacking
hold your ground without weapons

No mistake is worse
than underestimating your enemy
Underestimating your enemy
can cost you everything

When well-matched armies clash
the side that yields will win

70

My words are easily understood
    easily followed
and yet none seem to understand them
    none seem to follow them

My words have an origin
    my deeds have a sovereign
If people don't know them
    how can they know me?
The few who do understand
    are precious to me

The wise are sages
    dressed in sack-cloth
concealing jade at their hearts

71

To know your ignorance is good
To be ignorant of your ignorance is a sickness

To be sick of sickness is healthy

The wise see sickness for what it is
and so they are healthy

72
If the people weary of authority
a great force will be unleashed

Don't constrict their lives
Don't limit their livelihoods
Don't show them contempt
and they will not weary of you

The wise love themselves without vanity
know themselves without arrogance

They let go of that
and choose this

73
Rash courage can be fatal
The courage to resist can be liberating

Similar things   Very different outcomes

When heaven provokes failure
who knows the reason?

Heaven's Path
doesn't strive   and yet ably wins
doesn't speak   but answers fully
doesn't call   and yet responds
doesn't rush   but plans calmly

Heaven's net is vast
    wide-meshed
but it misses nothing

74

If people don't fear death
why threaten death as a deterrent?

If people did fear death
we could seize the ones who acted strangely
and kill them

But who will do this?

There is already a great executioner
who is skilled like a master carpenter
and whoever tries to supplant the master carpenter
and carve their wood
will not escape without injuring their hands

75

The people are hungry
Their leaders tax them too hard
This is why they are hungry

The people are unruly
Their leaders interfere in their lives
This is why the people are unruly

The people take death lightly
They pursue life too heavily
This is why they take death lightly

Those who strive less
respect life more

76

People are born supple   tender
They die rigid   stiff
Living things   grass   trees
grow pliant   sinuous
They die brittle   shriveled

So hard and stiff belong to death
and tender and gentle belong to life

Thus is the unyielding army shattered
and the unbending tree splintered

The strong and big are inferior
The soft and weak are superior

77

The Way of heaven is like a stretched bow
    Its higher tip is bent down
    Its lower tip is bent up
    It takes from what has too much
    and gives to what has too little
The Way of heaven
    empties what is too full
    and fills what is too empty

The way of people is not so
    It takes from those who already have little
    and gives to those who already have much

Who has plenty and yet offers it to the world?
Only one who possesses the Dao

So the wise
    act without laying claim
    and accomplish without claiming credit
They do not flaunt their worth

78

Nothing is softer or gentler than water
and yet nothing is more potent
for attacking the hard and rough
Nothing can match it

Soft gets the better of hard
Gentle gets the better of rough

Everybody knows this
and yet none practices it

So the wise say
Bear the nation's humiliations
to become worthy of its fertile soil
and abundant harvests
Bear the nation's misfortunes
to become a lord of the world

True words seem false

79

When bitter rivals make peace
some grievances are likely to linger
How to manage this?

The wise keep their part of the deal
but don't insist on all their rights

It is virtue to attend to your own obligations
It is not virtue to insist others do the same

The Way of heaven does not play favorites
but it does favor goodness

80

Imagine a small country with few citizens

It is well equipped with tools
but few of them are used
The people take death seriously
and do not roam
There are boats and carts
but they are seldom ridden
They have armor and weapons
but feel no need to display them
They have even returned to using knotted cords
in place of writing

Their food is nutritious
Their clothes are comfortable
Their customs are cheerful

Other nations are very close
    Dogs can be heard barking
    Roosters can be heard crowing

But imagine these people
They can grow old
and die
without feeling any need to explore

81

Truthful words are not pretty
Pretty words are not true

Good people are not argumentative
Contentious people are not good

Wise people are not learned
Learned people are not wise

The wise do not hoard
    but by serving others receive more
    and by giving to others gain more

The Way of heaven
    is to help without harming
The Way of the wise
    is to serve without competing

NOTES

PROLOGUE: WISE ANCIENTS?

1. Roy Scranton, *Learning to Die in the Anthropocene: Reflections on the End of a Civilization* (City Lights Books, 2015).
2. I'm going to use the term "human nature" from time to time. Let's get some of the caveats out of the way. Better terms might be "humans' nature," "human natures," and "humans' natures." And which humans? All humans? Humans with whom we are familiar from a Western scientific perspective? Settler-colonists from the capitalist patriarchy? The term is freighted, and all those interpretations apply. I'll try to clarify if it's not reasonable to assume that I mean all people.
3. Kamesh R. Aiyer "Dharma in the Mahabharata as a Response to Ecological Crises: A Speculation," *The Trumpeter* 2, no. 2:18–40.

1. THE WAYS OF NATURE

1. James Lovelock, *The Revenge of Gaia: Why the Earth Is Fighting Back and How We Can Still Save Humanity* (Penguin, 2007).
2. Elizabeth Kolbert, *The Sixth Extinction: An Unnatural History* (Henry Holt, 2014).
3. The term "Anthropocene" was made popular by Elizabeth Kolbert's *The Sixth Extinction*. The term "Homogenocene" originates with Chares Mann, who proposed it in his magnificent books about the Americas before and after Christopher Columbus. See Charles C. Mann, *1491: New Revelations of the Americas Before Columbus* (Alfred Knopf, 2005); and Charles C. Mann, *1493: Uncovering the New World Columbus Created* (Alfred Knopf, 2011). The concept of the Capitalocene seems to come from Jason Moore's argument that it's not just humans in general who have wrought a new age but also those humans engaged in unfettered capitalism. Jason W. Moore. *Capitalism in the Web of Life: Ecology and the Accumulation of Capital* (Verso, 2015).
4. Steve Hallett, *The Efficiency Trap: Finding a Better Way to Achieve a Sustainable Energy Future* (Prometheus Books, 2013).
5. William Stanley Jevons, *The Coal Question: An Inquiry Concerning the Progress of the Nation and the Exhaustion of our Coal Mines* (MacMillan, 1865).
6. Peter F. Drucker, "What Executives Should Remember," *Harvard Review* 84, no. 2 (February 2006): 144–53, 166.

7. Stephanie Dalley, *Myths from Mesopotamia: Creation, the Flood, Gilgamesh, and Others* (Oxford University Press, 1989).
8. I will use the phrase "the Buddha said" or similar phrasing despite the fact that none of the Buddhist texts can be attributed to Buddha Siddhartha Gotama with complete confidence. Such confidence would presume faithful oral transmission for centuries, faithful transcription into writing, and then faithful translation into new languages. As far as we know, no Buddhist text was written by Siddhartha Gotama or any of his contemporaries.
9. Chief Seattle (ca. 1780/1786–1866) was a relatively contemporary figure.
10. Aldo Leopold, *A Sand County Almanac* (Oxford University Press, 1949).
11. Adam Smith, *An Inquiry into the Nature and Causes of the Wealth of Nations* (Strahan & Cadell, 1776).
12. Lynn Margulis and Dorion Sagan, *What Is Life?* (University of California Press, 2000).
13. Moore, *Capitalism in the Web of Life.* Moore's book was followed by a collaboration with Raj Patel, the author of *Stuffed and Starved: The Hidden Battle for the World Food System* (Melville House, 2007) to produce the eminently readable Raj Patel and Jason W. Moore, *A History of the World in Seven Cheap Things: A Guide to Capitalism, Nature, and the Future of the Planet* (Verso, 2018).
14. Steve Hallett and John Wright, *Life Without Oil: Why We Must Shift to a New Energy Future* (Prometheus Books, 2011), 78.
15. Moore, *Capitalism in the Web of Life*, 172.
16. Arne Naess, "The Shallow and the Deep, Long-Range Ecology Movement: A Summary,*Inquiry*16,nos.1–4(1973):95–100,https://doi.org/10.1080/00201747308601682.
17. I laughed when I saw the title because "Welcome to Earth" is a great line of Will Smith's from *Independence Day* when he punches an alien in the face. Darren Aronofsky, dir., *Welcome to Earth* (Protozoa Pictures-Nutopia-Westwood Studios, 2021).
18. Camille T. Dungy, "Trophic Cascade," in *Trophic Cascade* (Wesleyan University Press, 2017), 16.
19. This directly from Alan Watts, heard on Sam Harris's meditation app *Waking Up*. See Alan Watts, *The Nature of Consciousness* (audio recording), The Alan Watts Electronic University, 1969.

2. EMERGENCE

1. Nick Lane, *Life Ascending: The Ten Great Inventions of Evolution* (Norton, 2009).
2. A few primers. Stephen Hawking is thoroughly readable and largely understandable. See Stephen Hawking, *A Brief History of Time* (Bantam Books, 1988); and Stephen Hawking, *The Universe in a Nutshell* (Bantam Books, 2001). Also valuable is the *Cosmos*

series, both in its original Carl Sagan version (*Cosmos: A Personal Voyage*, directed by Adrian Malone, PBS, 1980) and its revamped Neil Degrasse Tyson version (*Cosmos: A Spacetime Odyssey*, directed by Brannon Braga, Bill Poe, and Ann Druyan, Cosmos Studios et al., 2014).

3. Forgive the simplification. Include RNA and whatever other parts of the genomic machinery you wish.
4. Richard Dawkins, *The Selfish Gene* (Oxford University Press, Oxford, 1976).
5. Again, molecular biology friends, we're sticking with the central doctrine and keeping it simple.
6. Generally called "Alfred, Lord Tennyson," because he was Baron Tennyson, but let's just ditch the aristocratic nonsense, shall we?
7. Stephen Jay Gould, *The Richness of Life: The Essential Stephen Jay Gould*, ed. Steven Rose (Norton, 2006).
8. Stephen Jay Gould, "Kropotkin Was No Crackpot," *Natural History* 97, no. 7 (1988): 12–21. The article references Petr Kropotkin's *Mutual Aid: A Factor of Evolution* (McClure, Philips & Co., 1902).
9. "The days of our years are threescore years and ten; and if by reason of strength they be fourscore years, yet is their strength labor and sorrow; for it is soon cut off and we fly away" (Psalm 90:10). Much can be done to increase human lifespan, notably a healthy diet, regular exercise, and (most importantly) timely medical interventions. Despite all our efforts, however, the length of a fully healthy and active life has been extended by only a few years, and our maximum lifespan has stubbornly refused to extend beyond 115 or 120.
10. People have relevance beyond reproductive age if they can offer education and wisdom to the community, sometimes known as the grandmother hypothesis.
11. Whales have two pectoral flippers, but they retain vestigial hind limb structures.
12. The California sea slug, *Aplysia californica*, is hardly humanlike to the eye and yet shares 70 percent of its genes with us, and the biochemical machinery of its nervous system is basically the same as ours. Robert Sapolsky discusses this in his fabulous book *Determined: A Science of Life without Free Will* (Penguin, 2023). The sea slug data is best summarized in Eric Kandel's Nobel Prize speech, available in written form: Eric Kandel, "The Molecular Biology of Memory Storage: A Dialogue between Genes and Synapses," *Science* 294 (2001): 1030.
13. David Chalmers, "Facing Up to the Problem of Consciousness," *Journal of Consciousness Studies* 2 (1995): 200–19.
14. Max S. Bennett, "Five Breakthroughs: A First Approximation of Brain Evolution from Early Bilaterians to Humans," *Frontiers in Neuroanatomy* 15 (2021): 693346.
15. Anil Seth, *Being You: A New Science of Consciousness* (Penguin, 2021).
16. S. Tero et al., "Rules for Biologically Inspired Adaptive Network Design," *Science* 327 (2020): 439.

17. Daniel Quinn, *Ishmael* (Bantam Books, 1992).
18. The Dalai Lama, *Illuminating the Path to Enlightenment* (Thubten Dhargye Ling, 2002).
19. The concept of the meme comes from Richard Dawkins, *The Selfish Gene* (Oxford University Press, 1976). The extended phenotype is from the book of the same name: Richard Dawkins, *The Extended Phenotype: The Long Reach of the Gene* (Oxford University Press, 1982).
20. The species (actually a species-complex) was described by Alfred Russel Wallace, the great colleague-competitor of Charles Darwin, in 1859, the year Darwin published *The Origin of Species*. So, Wallace was out in the tropical forests busily studying zombie fungi while Darwin was busily scooping him. Also [spoiler alert!], I'm told the zombie fungus is the inspiration for the epidemic in the video game that became the TV series *The Last of Us*.
21. Although also illustrative. The word "meme" has mutated, has been selected in a new environment, and is being reproduced on a massive scale. The selfish meme meme has become a very successful meme.
22. Cute scene with Emma Thompson and Lulu Popplewell. *Love Actually*, directed by Richard Curtis (StudioCanal, Working Title Films, DNA Films, 2003).
23. Arguable. Many extant archaea and bacteria appear unchanged over hundreds of millions of years, but appearance is subjective. Is the apparent sameness of their structure and function the result of stasis or of dynamic change in mutable niches?
24. This idea appears throughout the Buddhist canon, e.g. the Samayatta Nikaya (12.61) and Kimsuka Sutta (35.204).
25. My new favorite animal, the sarcastic fringehead (*Neoclinus blanchardi*), is a small saltwater fish with territorial behavior and a very big mouth.
26. Nicholas Gutierrez, "What's Next for the Gene-Edited Children from CRISPR Trial in China?," New Scientist, June 29, 2022, https://www.newscientist.com/article/mg25533930-700-whats-next-for-the-gene-edited-children-from-crispr-trial-in-china/.
27. Sarah Zhang, "A Biohacker Regrets Publicly Injecting Himself with CRISPR," *The Atlantic*, February 20, 2018.
28. Generative Pre-trained Transformer 4.
29. M. A. Lebedev et al., "Cortical Ensemble Adaptation to Represent Velocity of an Artificial Actuator Controlled by a Brain-Machine Interface," *Journal of Neuroscience* 25 (2005): 4681–93.
30. Steven Kotler, "Vision Quest," Wired, September 1, 2002, www.wired.com/2002/09/vision/.
31. This guy again. He was a pretty interesting tech guy with great ideas for a while, and then he became a worrying and slightly laughable oddity, but as I edit this page in March 2025, he has become a much bigger problem. And it's a lot less funny.

32. Ray Kurzweil, *The Singularity Is Near: When Humans Transcend Biology* (Penguin, 2005). See also the follow-up, Ray Kurzweil, *The Singularity Is Nearer: When We Merge with AI* (Viking, 2024).
33. David Chadwick, *Crooked Cucumber: The Life and Zen Teaching of Shunryu Suzuki* (Broadway Books, 1999), 209–10.
34. Kurt Vonnegut, *Slaughterhouse Five* (Random House, 1969).
35. Vonnegut, *Slaughterhouse Five*, 27.
36. "Trinity Site History," n.d., https://home.army.mil/wsmr/contact/public-affairs-office/trinity-site-open-house/trinity-site-history.

3. THE WAYS OF PEOPLE

1. Isaac Asimov, *Foundation* (Bantam, 1951); and Frank Herbert, *Dune* (Chilton Books, 1965). The *Dune* series added *Dune Messiah, Children of Dune, God Emperor of Dune, Heretics of Dune* and *Chapterhouse: Dune*, and then after Frank Herbert's death dozens of additional books were added by his son, Brian Herbert, and by Kevin J. Anderson. See also George Orwell, *1984* (Secker & Warburg, 1949); Cormac McCarthy, *The Road* (Alfred Knopf, 2006); Aldous Huxley, *Brave New World* (Chatto & Windus, 1935); David Mitchell, *Cloud Atlas* (Sceptre, 2004); and the film *The Matrix*, written and directed by the Wachowskis (Warner Bros., 1999)
2. Robert Costanza, "Four Visions of the Century Ahead: Will It Be Star Trek, Ecotopia, Big Government, or Mad Max?," *The Futurist*, February 1999.
3. Peter Frase, *Four Futures: Life after Capitalism* (Verson, 2016).
4. Kim Stanley Robinson, *Three Californias: The Wild Shore, The Gold Coast, and Pacific Edge* (Tor Essentials, 2020).
5. Jared Diamond, *Guns, Germs, and Steel: The Fates of Human Societies* (Norton, 1997); and Jared Diamond, *Collapse: How Societies Choose to Fail or Succeed* (Viking, 2005).
6. David Graeber, *Possibilities: Essays on Hierarchy, Rebellion and Desire* (AK Press, 2007); and David Graeber and David Wengrow, *The Dawn of Everything: A New History of Humanity* (Farrar, Strauss & Giroux, 2021).
7. Perhaps it's time we started defaulting to calling Indigenous Americans simply American. It's intellectually lazy to use the term "American" when we're really thinking of white Americans (i.e., European Americans.) We've accustomed ourselves to the terms "African American" and "Black American" after all, so especially in this historical era, Kandiaronk was an American and the invaders were Europeans (mostly French and British).
8. Graeber and Wengrow, *The Dawn of Everything*, 55.
9. Robin Wall Kimmerer, *Braiding Sweetgrass: Indigenous Wisdom, Scientific Knowledge, and the Teachings of Plants* (Milkweed Editions, 2013).

10. Tyson Yunkaporta, *Sand Talk: How Indigenous Thinking Can Save the World* (HarperCollins, 2020).
11. M. Kat Anderson, *Tending the Wild: Native American Knowledge and the Management of California's Natural Resources* (University of California Press, 2005).
12. Thomas Hobbes, *Leviathan—or—The Matter, Forme, and Power of a Commonwealth Ecclesiasticall and Civil* (London, 1651).
13. John Locke, *Two Treatises of Government* (Andrew Millar, 1689).
14. Jean-Jacques Rousseau, *Du Contrat Social—ou—Principes du Droit Politique* (Amsterdam, 1762).
15. Steven Pinker, *The Better Angels of Our Nature: Why Violence Has Declined* (Penguin, 2011); and *Enlightenment Now: The Case for Reason, Science, Humanism, and Progress* (Penguin, 2019).
16. R. M. Callaway et al., Novel Weapons: Invasive Plant Suppresses Fungal Mutualists in America but Not in Its Native Europe, *Ecology* 89 (2008): 1043–55; and Kristina A. Stinson et al., "Invasive Plant Suppresses the Growth of Native Tree Seedlings by Disrupting Belowground Mutualisms," *Public Library of Science (Biology)* 4 (2006): e140.
17. Jared Diamond, *Guns, Germs & Steel: The Fates of Human Societies* (Random House, 2011).
18. Maybe. Do humans have free will? More on this in Chapter 6. Messy stuff.
19. Sun-Tzu, *The Art of War*, trans. Lionel Giles (Luzac & Co, 1910); Thucydides, *The Peloponnesian War*, trans. Rex Warner (Penguin, 1954); Niccolo Machiavelli, *The Art of War*, trans. Neal Wood (1521; Da Capo, 2001); Jack S. Levy and William R. Thompson, *Causes of War* (Wiley Blackwell, 2010); Greg Cashman and Leonard C. Robinson, *An Introduction to the Causes of War: Patterns of Interstate Conflict from World War I to Iraq* (Rowman & Littlefield, 2007); and Geoffrey Blainey, *The Causes of War*, 3rd ed. (Free Press, 1973).
20. Garrett Hardin, "The Tragedy of the Commons," *Science* 162, no. 3859 (1968): 1243–48.
21. Hardin, "The Tragedy of the Commons," 1244.
22. Raj Patel, *The Value of Nothing: How to Reshape Market Society and Redefine Democracy* (Picador, 2010).
23. Alexandr Solzhenitsyn, *The Gulag Archipelago, 1918–1956*, trans. Thomas Whitney (Editions du Seuil, 1974), 357.
24. Francis Fukuyama, *The End of History and the Last Man* (Simon & Schuster, 1992).
25. Although this quote has been used widely and attributed to Dahle and is consistent with the message he delivered in a number of speeches, there doesn't seem to be a record of him using this exact phrase.
26. Mark Fisher, *Capitalist Realism: Is There No Alternative?* (Zero Books, 2009), 1.

27. David Foster Wallace, *This Is Water: Some Thoughts, Delivered on a Significant Occasion, about Living a Compassionate Life* (Little, Brown, 2009), 3–8. This is a transcription of Wallace's commencement speech at Kenyon College in 2005 that has become a contemplative classic.

4. SHAPE THE PATH

1. The organization 350.org was so named to highlight the perils of allowing the concentration of CO_2 in the atmosphere to surpass 350 ppm. The concentration is 425 ppm at the time of writing.
2. Statement by John Lewis on March 1, 2020, while speaking from the Edmund Pettus Bridge in Selma, Alabama during a commemoration of Bloody Sunday in 1965.
3. Vaclav Havel's *The Power of the Powerless* is available in various forms, including free downloads from numerous websites. A Samizdat was an informal dissident publication copied secretly and spread in the Soviet Bloc.
4. David Mitchell, *Cloud Atlas* (Sceptre, 2004), 529.
5. William Sloane Coffin, *Credo* (Westminster John Knox, 2004), 127.
6. Haha. Not anymore, thank DOGE.
7. Better called the Great Famine, the Great Hunger, or the Gorta Mór and not caused primarily by late blight of potatoes (*Phytophthora infestans*) but by the casual cruelties of British imperial capitalism.
8. In the United States, you don't mess with Christmas because the Christian nationalists will admonish you to keep the Christ in Christmas. So, why don't the pagans admonish us to keep the sun in solstice? But I digress.
9. Marvin Harris, *Cows, Pigs, Wars, and Witches: The Riddles of Culture* (Vintage, 1974).
10. Joseph Campbell, *Myths to Live By* (Penguin Compass, 1972), 90.
11. Don't stop on the road in a car! It's single track. The locals will be pissed.
12. Note that a good way to establish a hedgerow is to build a rickety wooden fence, plant a hedgerow along it, and then allow the fence to decay away while maintaining the maturing hedgerow that has replaced it.
13. James Howard Kunstler, *The Long Emergency: Surviving the End of Oil, Climate Change, and Other Converging Catastrophes of the Twenty-First Century* (Grove Press, 2005).
14. Wai Fung Lam and Elinor Ostrom, "Analyzing the Dynamic Complexity of Development Interventions: Lessons from an Irrigation Experiment in Nepal," *Policy Sciences* 43. no. 1 (2010): 1–25.
15. I've been fortunate to have traveled to some cool places. I've been to China with my friend David Umulis and students from Purdue University five or six times.

16. David R, Montgomery, *Dirt: The Erosion of Civilizations* (University of California Press, 2007); and Jared Diamond, *Collapse: How Societies Choose to Fail or Succeed* (Viking Press, 2005).
17. An additional sidenote about the Longji terraces and other rice terraces systems like them. I worry that as they become tourist hotspots rather than community farming centers, the impetus for maintaining them will become artificial. If their management is redesigned for efficiency, then I think that the resilience that was adapted as required will fail.
18. E. F. Schumacher. *Small Is Beautiful: Economics as If People Mattered* (Blond & Briggs, 1973). And a huge shout-out to Andrew Flach's upcoming book from University of Arizona Press, *Feeding the World as If People Mattered.*
19. Will Storr, *The Status Game: On Human Life and How to Play It* (HarperCollins, 2021).
20. Storr, *The Status Game*, 13–14.
21. Robin Wall Kimmerer, *Braiding Sweetgrass: Indigenous Wisdom, Scientific Knowledge, and the Teachings of Plants* (Milkweed Editions, 2013).
22. Wade Davis and Jean Paul Gagnon, "Democracies in the Ethnosphere: An Anthropologist's Lived Experience of Indigenous Democratic Cultures," *Democratic Theory* 8 (2021): 118–38.
23. M. Kat Anderson, *Tending the Wild: Native American Knowledge and the Management of California's Natural Resources* (University of California Press, 2005).
24. Thomas Freidman, *The World Is Flat: A Brief History of the Twenty-First Century* (Farrar, Strauss and Giroux, 2005).
25. Robert Pirsig, *Zen and the Art of Motorcycle Maintenance: An Inquiry into Values* (William Morrow, 1974), 353.
26. Aldo Leopold, *A Sand County Almanac* (Oxford University Press, 1949), 211.
27. James P. Carse, *Finite and Infinite Games: A Vision of Life as Play and Possibility* (Simon & Schuster, 1986), 3, 149.

5. THE WAYS OF THE MIND

1. From William Shakespeare's *Hamlet.*
2. This is basically the concept of the "triune brain" from Paul MacLean, *The Triune Brain in Evolution: Role in Paleocerebral Functions* (Plenum, 1990), but we must be careful. The idea of reptile-to-mammal-to-human as a direct evolutionary path is misleading. See, for example, Joseph Cesario, David J. Johnson, and Heather L. Eisthen, "Your Brain Is Not an Onion with a Tiny Reptile inside," *Current Directions in Psychological Science* 29, no. 3 (2020): 255–60. Reptiles are just as evolved as humans. That they don't eat with chopsticks is not evidence that their brains stopped evolving once the mammals

branched off. A better model of brain evolution is the "Five Breakthroughs" model of Max Bennett: brains evolving the capacities of steering, reinforcing, simulating, mentalizing, and speaking. Max S. Bennett, "Five Breakthroughs: A First Approximation of Brain Evolution from Early Bilaterians to Humans," *Frontiers in Neuroanatomy* 15 (2021): 693346, https://doi.org/10.3389/fnana.2021.693346. See also Chapter 6 in this volume.

3. Donald Hebb, *The Organization of Behavior: A Neuropsychological Theory* (Wiley, 1949).
4. Jonathan Haidt is one of the most important thinkers in America today. See Jonathan Haidt, *The Happiness Hypothesis: Finding Modern Truth in Ancient Wisdom* (Basic Books, 2006); Jonathan Haidt, *The Righteous Mind: Why Good People are Divided by Politics and Religion* (Vintage Books, 2012); and Jonathan Haidt and Greg Lukianoff, *The Coddling of the American Mind: How Good Intentions and Bad Ideas Are Setting Up a Generation for Failure* (Penguin, 2019). In addition to Haidt's books, there are great TED talks and articles, including "Why the Past 10 Years of American Life Have Been Uniquely Stupid," *The Atlantic*, April 11, 2022.
5. The quote is from Anil Seth's TED Talk "How Your Brain Invents Your 'Self,'" https://www.ted.com/talks/anil_seth_how_your_brain_invents_your_self, which summarizes some of the material covered in his wonderful book, *Being You: A New Science of Consciousness* (Penguin, 2021).
6. Haidt, *The Happiness Hypothesis*, 40.
7. The concept is from Donald Hebb, *The Organization of Behavior: A Neuropsychological Theory* (Wiley & Sons, 1949), 62, and was turned into this memorable mnemonic by Carla Shatz, "The Developing Brain," *Scientific American* 267 (1992): 60–67, https://10.1038/scientificamerican0992-60.
8. Functional magnetic resonance imaging is a key tool used in neuroscience. It measures oxygen concentrations to reveal areas of brain activity (aerobic respiration) in real time.
9. Rinske A. Gotink, Rozanna Meijboom, Meike W. Vernooij, Marion Smits, and M. G. Myriam Hunink, "Eight-Week Mindfulness Based Stress Reduction Induces Brain Changes Similar to Traditional Long-term Meditation Practice: A Systematic Review, *Brain & Cognition* 108 (2016): 32–41; and Yi-Yuan Tang, Rongxiang Tang, and Michael I. Posner, "Mindfulness Meditation Improves Emotion Regulation and Reduces Drug Abuse," *Drug and Alcohol Dependence* 163 (2016): S13–S18.
10. Jon Kabat-Zinn, Leslie Lipworth, and Robert Burney, "The Clinical Use of Mindfulness Meditation for the Self-regulation of Chronic Pain," *Journal of Behavioral Medicine* 8 (1985): 163–90, https://doi.org/10.1007/BF00845519; John D. Teasdale, Zindel V. Segal, J. Mark G. Williams, Valerie A. Ridgeway, Judith M. Soulsby, and Mark A. Lau, "Prevention of Relapse/Recurrence in Major Depression by Mindfulness-Based Cognitive Therapy," *Journal of Consulting & Clinical Psychology* 68 (2000): 615–23;

John Kabat-Zinn, *Full Catastrophe Living: Using the Wisdom of Your Body and Mind to Face Stress, Pain, and Illness* (Bantam Books, 2013); and Yi-Yuan Tang, Changhao Jiang, and Rongxiang Tang, "How Mind-Body Practice Works—Integration or Separation?," *Frontiers in Psychology* 8 (2017): 866, doi: 10.3389/fpsyg.2017.00866.

11. Alan Watts, *There Is Never Anything but the Present & Other Inspiring Words of Wisdom*, compiled by Joan Watts and Anne Watts (Pantheon Books, 2021).
12. The Sallatha Sutta, SN 36:6.
13. Daniel Kahneman, *Thinking, Fast and Slow* (Farrar, Strauss & Giroux, 2011).
14. Haidt, *The Happiness Hypothesis*; Haidt, *The Righteous Mind*; and Haidt and Lukianoff, *The Coddling of the American Mind.*
15. Lukianoff and Haidt, *The Coddling of the American Mind*, 29, 22, 237.
16. Marcus Aurelius, *The Meditations of Marcus Aurelius Antoninus*, trans. A. S. L. Farquarson (Oxford University Press, 1944), Book VI, verse 29; Book X, verse 9; Book VIII, verse 47.
17. Aurelius, *The Meditations of Marcus Aurelius Antoninus*, Book 7, verse 56.
18. This looks like a Bible quote, but it's actually from the Book of Common Prayer: "We therefore commit this body to the ground, earth to earth, ashes to ashes, dust to dust; in sure and certain hope of the Resurrection to eternal life."
19. Marcus E. Raichle, Ann Mary MacLeod, Abraham Z. Snyder, and Gordon L. Shulman, "A Default Mode of Brain Function," *PNAS* 98, no. 2 (2011): 676–82.
20. Dan Harris, *10% Happier: How I Tamed the Voice in My Head, Reduced Stress without Losing My Edge, and Found Self-Help That Actually Works—A True Story* (Dey Street Books, 2014), 96.
21. I have followed Sam Harris for a long time. I have very much admired his work as one of the "Four Horsemen" of "New Atheism," particularly his on-stage debates and his book *The End of Faith: Religion, Terror, and the Future of Reason* (Norton, 2005). Shelley, my beloved, often listens to Sam's *Making Sense* podcast, which does a decent job of unraveling some of our political angst. Most valuable to me have been the book *Waking Up: A Guide to Spirituality without Religion* (Simon & Schuster, 2014) and the meditation app of the same name. This particular quote is from the *Waking Up* app. I wrote it down during a walk through my local park. Apologies: I don't remember which episode it was from.
22. Abraham Lincoln, "Address before the Wisconsin State Agricultural Society," Milwaukee, Wisconsin, September 30, 1859, https://www.abrahamlincolnonline.org/lincoln/speeches/fair.htm.
23. Okay, so we're not entirely without clues. We get a sense of some people, Tenzin Gyatso, for example, as being highly practiced in meditation and reaping many of the rewards of awakenings. We get a sense of others, Donald Trump, for example, as being unpracticed, cravings-riddled, desires-addled, and pathetically unaware, but our evidence comes indirectly from analyzing their behavior, not directly from knowing their minds.

6. MEETINGS OF THE MINDS

1. I'm discounting the social insects—bees, ants, wasps, and termites—incredible though they are, because their colonies are really just single organisms with detached parts, multiple asexual, cloned workers with a single reproducing queen. Yes, I know, I'll be expecting a strongly worded letter from E. O. Wilson acolytes. I'm also discounting dogs, dolphins, and chimpanzees, none of which is social at our level, and the cephalopods, cool though they are.
2. Stanley Milgram, *Obedience to Authority: An Experimental View* (Harper Collins, 1974).
3. Philip Zimbardo, *The Lucifer Effect: Understanding How Good People Turn Evil* (Random House, 2007).
4. Alexsandr Solzhenitsyn, *The Gulag Archipelago, 1918–1956*, trans. Thomas Whitney (Editions du Seuil, 1974).
5. And so much more. Human behavior is influenced by so many things. It might be that the only thing that can't be proven to influence human behavior is free will.
6. From William Shakespeare's *Hamlet*, "There is nothing either good or bad but thinking makes it so."
7. Solomon Asch, "Effects of Group Pressure on the Modification and Distortion of Judgments," in *Groups, Leadership and Men*, ed. H. Guetzkow (Carnegie Press, 1951).
8. Solomon Asch, "Opinions and Social Pressure," *Scientific American* 193: 33–35.
9. Hannah Arendt, *Eichmann in Jerusalem: A Report on the Banality of Evil* (Viking, 1963).
10. Will Storr, *The Status Game: On Human Life and How to Play It* (HarperCollins, 2022), 20. See also Chapter 4 in this volume.
11. Storr, *The Status Game*, 1, 22.
12. Thanks, Eddie.
13. Tim O'Brien, *The Things They Carried* (Mariner Books, 2009), 57.
14. For a humorous and comprehensive guide to mental heuristics, see "Buster's Notes," www.busterbenson.com.
15. Spoken by Mrs. Cheveley to Lady Chiltern in Act II of the play. Oscar Wilde, *An Ideal Husband* (L. Smithers, 1899).
16. Isaac Asimov, *Foundation* (Bantam, 1951), epigraph to Part 4, Chapter 1.
17. Jonathan Haidt, *The Righteous Mind: Why Good People Are Divided by Politics and Religion* (Vintage Books, 2012).
18. A good example of this is observed in hierarchies of Mestizo and Indigenous Mexican farmworkers on a strawberry farm in Washington's Skagit Valley: Seth Homes, *Fresh Fruit, Broken Bodies: Migrant Farmworkers in the United States* (University of California Press, 2013).

19. Much of this section draws on two spectacular books by Robert Sapolksy: *Behave: The Biology of Humans at our Best and Worst* (Penguin, 2017) and *Determined: Life without Free Will* (Penguin 2023).
20. "Undergraduate Student Reference Group: Executive Summary," American College Health Association, Spring 2025, https://www.acha.org/wp-content/uploads/NCHA-IIIb_SPRING_2025_UNDERGRADUATE_REFERENCE_GROUP_INSTITUTIONAL_EXECUTIVE_SUMMARY.pdf.
21. Play on words from Rudyard Kipling's cringeworthy poem "The White Man's Burden."
22. James P. Carse, *Finite and Infinite Games: A Vision of Life as Play and Possibility* (Simon & Schuster, 1986).
23. And then, in my case, the broken leg.

INDEX

ABOUT THE AUTHOR

Steve Hallett is a professor of horticulture at Purdue University and teaches classes on sustainability, environmental science, and food justice. He is the co-founder of the Purdue University Student Farm and the Sustainable Food and Farming Systems degree program. Hallett is an award-winning teacher listed in Purdue's Book of Great Teachers and a member of its Teaching Academy. He is the author of *Life Without Oil, The Efficiency Trap, A Life for a Life*, and *Laozi's "Daodejing": A New Translation With Environmnetalist Commentary.*

www.ingramcontent.com/pod-product-compliance
Lightning Source LLC
Chambersburg PA
CBHW052005270326
41929CB00015B/2796

* 9 7 8 1 6 2 6 7 1 2 9 5 9 *